KING ARTHUR'S LAUREATE

King *Arthur* and his valiant Knights of the Round *Table*.

Sir Triftram.	*Sir* Launcelot.	*Sir* Galahad.	*Sir* Perciuall.
Sir Gauwin.	*Sir* Ector.	*Sir* Bors.	*Sir* Lionell.	*Sir* Griflet.
Sir Gaheris.	*Sir* Tor.	*Sir* Acolon.	*Sir* Ewaine.	*Sir* Marhaus.
Sir Pelleas.	*Sir* Sagris.	*Sir* Turquine.	*Sir* Kay.	*Sir* Gareth.

Sir Beaumans.	*Sir* Berfunt.	*Sir* Palamide.	*Sir* Beleobus.
Sir Ballamore.	*Sir* Galohalt.	*Sir* Lamarecke.	*Sir* Floll.
Sir Superabilis.	*Sir* Paginet.	*Sir* Belvoure.	

Woodcut from 1816 edition of Malory's *Morte Darthur*.

KING ARTHUR'S
LAUREATE

A Study of Tennyson's
Idylls of the King

J. Philip Eggers

New York
NEW YORK UNIVERSITY PRESS

1971

Copyright © 1971 by New York University
Library of Congress Catalog Card Number: 79-142373
ISBN: 8147-2150-8
Manufactured in the United States of America

For Beth and David

Acknowledgments

I am happy to express my special gratitude to Professor John D. Rosenberg of Columbia University, who first stimulated my ambition to write a dissertation on Tennyson's *Idylls* and who has offered invaluable advice and criticism through all stages of my work. His lectures on Victorian literature have inspired and influenced me greatly, especially his insights into the *Idylls,* which have anticipated much of the recent published controversy on the poem. I am grateful, too, to Professor Carl Woodring of Columbia, who also read my dissertation and whose immense knowledge of the nineteenth century helped me maintain a higher level of accuracy than would otherwise have been possible. Advice and guidance of various kinds were given by Professors Louis Cornell, W. T. H. Jackson, L. P. G. Peckham, and the late Elliot V. K. Dobbie, all of Columbia. Among the Tennyson scholars with whom I have corresponded and conversed, I wish to mention above all Sir Charles Tennyson, whose continuing and irreplaceable service to the heritage of his grandfather sets a high standard for all scholars and critics of the poet. Helpful commentary has been given me by Professor J. M. Gray, who is doing important work on the sources of the *Idylls,* and by Professor Philip L. Elliot of Furman University. I wish to thank Mr. R. F. Smith and Mrs. N. Cambell of the Tennyson Society for introducing me to the Tennyson Research Centre at Lincoln. Thanks are due as well to the editors of New York University Press, who helped make my presentation more readable and concise, and to the editors of *Victorian Poetry* for allowing me to use material that first appeared in their journal, including "The Weeding of the Garden: Tennyson's Geraint Idylls in *The Mabinogion*" (Vol. IV, No. 1, pp. 45-51). Finally, the greatest source of encouragement and inspiration has been my wife; to her and our son this book is dedicated.

Contents

Introduction

Camelot in recent years has become a synonym for utopian ventures. Perhaps because of the modern reluctance to believe in visions of a perfect society, Arthurian romance has taken on an air of charming unreality; and the Victorian revival of the story of the Round Table accordingly has to recover not only from whatever pejorative feelings that we may still hold concerning Victorianism but also from the devaluation we have given it as a result of our considering it as the outgrowth of utopian dreaming. It is particularly rewarding to undertake a close study of *Idylls of the King*—an eminently Victorian poem—for we find it to be the work of a highly realistic intelligence: most realistic and most intelligent when we confront the quality and problems of modern society.

The best modern critics of the *Idylls*—J. H. Buckley, E. D. H. Johnson, and F. E. L. Priestley—find the permanent core of the greatness of the poem to be its portrayal of society. It is not likely that the *Idylls* will ever again be dismissed as an ornate exercise or smug tribute to

British imperialism; nor is it necessary to seek in the poem a wholly twentieth-century sensibility. It is, in the finest sense, a Victorian pronouncement, belonging with the admonitory visions and prophecies of Ruskin, Mill, Arnold, Morris, and Pater.

This study is an attempt to capture the social meaning of the poem from various perspectives—its place in literary tradition, its effect upon readers of Tennyson's day, its relation to Arthurian sources, its competition with rival Arthurian poems, its growth as a series of installments, and its structure as a completed work of art.

Few poems reveal so well the truth that a poem is not only a structure of words but an event that occurs in relation to what M. H. Abrams calls the "coordinates of criticism." Yet these coordinates, which include the artist, the audience, and the universe outside the poem, are in continuous flux; just as there is no absolute frame of reference by which to measure events in the physical universe, so too there is no poet who does not develop, no audience that does not change, no tradition that is frozen into immutability. The truth, says Merlin, "is this to me, and that to thee"; the critic who would be true to the meaning of a poem as an event cannot stand in lone judgment or treat it as a specimen in a sealed jar. The *Idylls* in particular (is it one poem, twelve poems, or four installments?) cannot be fully interpreted without reference to its lively existence in many contexts. This book is an attempt to give an interpretation of the *Idylls* that accounts for a number of these contexts as part of the setting in which the poem happened.

Sancho, my friend, you must know that, by the will of Heaven, I was born in this iron age of ours to revive the age of gold or, as it is generally called, the golden age. It is for me that are reserved perils, mighty feats, and valorous exploits. It is I, I say once more, who must revive the order of the Round Table. . . .

Don Quixote

KING ARTHUR'S LAUREATE

1.

No Grander Subject

It required a large amount of poetic license for Aubrey De Vere to write of Tennyson in 1893:

> Great Arthur's legend he alone dared tell;
> Milton and Dryden feared to tread that ground;
> For him alone o'er Camelot's fairy bound
> The "horns of Elf-land" blew their magic spell.[1]

Yet until Tennyson wrote *Idylls of the King*, few subjects had been so often sidestepped by major English poets or so ambitiously but unimpressively attempted by others as the legends of the Round Table. The news that a recent Cambridge student was about to write a long poem on King Arthur might have provoked from the well-read Englishman of 1840 the kind of amused skepticism that would today greet the self-elected author of the Great American Novel. Tennyson faced a jury of experts dubious about the whole undertaking, a public poorly informed on Arthurian matters, and a subject that was prodigious in its possibilities without having a unifying thread to hold its diverse elements together. Chaucer's light treatment of chivalry in *The Wife of Bath's Tale,* and Shakespeare's rare allusions to Merlin's prophecies and Arthurian ballads helped little to encourage serious consideration of the subject. As Sir Walter Scott reminded the readers of *Marmion,* however,

> . . . the mightiest chiefs of British song
> Scorned not such legends to prolong.
> They gleam through Spenser's elphin dream,
> And mix in Milton's heavenly theme;
> And Dryden in immortal strain,
> Had raised the Table Round again,
> But that a ribald king and court
> Bade him toil on to make them sport. . . .[2]

Coleridge joined the camp of skeptics by thundering, "As to Arthur, you could not by any means make a poem on him national to Englishmen. What have we to do with him?"[3] And Wordsworth made it no easier for later poets to dare attempting to bend the bow of the great Arthuriad when in *The Prelude*—published only nine years before the first four *Idylls of the King*—he dismissed his own flirtation with that goal:

> Sometimes the ambitious Power of choice, mistaking
> Proud spring-tide swellings for a regular sea,
> Will settle on some British theme, some old
> Romantic tale by Milton left unsung. . . .
>   (Book I, lines 168-171)

Clearly, the stories of the Round Table continued to hold interest for the best poets, but almost no one expected anyone to write a long serious poem that would unify them. Nevertheless, Tennyson began to think about such a poem in the 1830s, and two quite different schemes occurred to him: a twelve-book epic, for which he wrote a prose draft in 1833, and a musical masque—no doubt suggested by Dryden's operatic masque, *King Arthur*— for which he outlined a plot in five acts some time before 1840.[4] Unlike most of the uncountable minor writers of Arthurian poetry in the nineteenth century, Tennyson was aware that the subject presented special difficulties of at least two kinds: the genre into which such hetero- geneous material could be cast was not easy to find, and the lay public was not ready to seek and appreciate Arthurian literature. He used his three introductory lyrics, "Sir Launcelot and Queen Guinevere," "Sir Gala- had," and "The Lady of Shalott" accordingly, not only to experiment with form but also to educate his readers. Kathleen Tillotson describes the situation succinctly:

> In 1842 Arthurian story was still strange to the ordi- nary reader, and even felt to be unacceptable as a subject for poetry; and this was undoubtedly one rea- son for the first long interval of seventeen years be- tween the serial appearances. Here the spread of time and the deepening of the impression are particularly important. . . . There is no clearer instance of a poet creating the taste by which he was enjoyed; though that taste also eventually recoiled upon him, through his imitators, his rivals, and his sources themselves.[5]

While Tennyson introduces his readers to the subject matter, he also uses the first three lyrics to explore themes that blossom into full drama in the *Idylls*. Tennyson pre- sented his Arthurian vision as the flowering and demise of an ideal society rather than the battles of a single hero. He did so successfully mainly because he struck (to use the often-quoted phrase from *The Princess*) a "strange diagonal" between traditional forms. Although in the *Idylls* Tennyson achieves epic and dramatic effects, they are, except for "The Holy Grail," which is a dramatic monologue, lyrics of such depth, irony, and tragic spirit that they transcend the lyric form. The three early lyrics thus point a way between epic and drama that eludes the strictest demands of either form.[6]

By beginning with the lyric and broadening it into a larger genre, Tennyson carried into the *Idylls* the most genuine passion of his lyrics. He pictures happy days in retrospect in his most intense and characteristic poetry— *In Memoriam*, "Tears, Idle Tears," and "Ulysses." In "Locksley Hall" he reminds us "That a sorrow's crown of sorrow is remembering happier things." In the *Idylls* the lost golden days are both social, when Arthur "made a realm and reigned," and personal, when Lancelot "returned/Among the flowers, in May, with Guinevere." The tragic paradox in the poem resembles that posed by Freud in *Civilization and its Discontents:* two impulses, the personal and the social, the aesthetic and the moral, the pleasure principle and the reality principle, or, for Tennyson, Sense and Soul, strive against each other within all men.

This tension between human instincts and the ideals of civilization is central to Tennyson's early lyrics as well as to the *Idylls*. "The Lady of Shalott" symbolically portrays an aesthetic psyche bound by the curse of her own perfection and destroyed—like Camelot in the *Idylls*— in the clash between rules "no man can keep" and her longing for the imperfect world of desire and Lancelot. She is, as Gerhard Joseph describes her in *Tennysonian*

Love, "caught between two worlds to neither of which she can commit herself." [7] Lancelot himself is torn by divided impulses in a somewhat different manner in the *Idylls.* Sir Galahad, although not portrayed in a social context as he is in "The Holy Grail," achieves his "strength of ten" only by renouncing the "kiss of love." "Sir Launcelot and Queen Guinevere" implies that an opposite abandonment to the kiss of love might cost a man "all his worldly worth." In all of his Arthurian writings Tennyson stresses the conflict between spirit and sense and the harm man can cause society and himself if he indulges in either sensual or spiritual extremes. In the *Idylls* Tennyson portrays this conflict as the mutual destruction of Guinevere's fantasy of a paradise with Lancelot and Arthur's dream of an Order that depends for its continuance upon the perfection of human conduct.

Although the *Idylls* is in part a hypothetical portrait of Victorian England with its high idealism, strict morality, and warring extremisms, Tennyson deliberately baffles any effort by the reader to localize the details of his poem regarding Arthurian sources, historical setting, philosophical school, or religious dogma. Tennyson presented his vision of the Order of the Round Table by drawing from an extremely large number of general materials—Anglo-Saxon social customs, bardic ideals, classical myths, Welsh myths, Victorian ethics, renaissance imagery, and many Arthurian legends.

Tennyson blurs other details as well. Merlin's riddling is an aesthetic principle: We are not told that Pelleas returns as the Red Knight, but surmise it; Old Merlin in the prose draft of "Gareth and Lynette" [8] becomes an unidentified. "ancient man" and "old Seer" in the published idyll. In the same draft Bellicent has a definite reason for sending Gareth to mingle with the kitchen help at Arthur's court: she hopes to learn from gossip that Guinevere has indeed been false with Lancelot, since the queen's adultery, she thinks, will cover the shame of her connection with Lamorack. In the idyll itself Tennyson makes her motive appear to be partly to protect Gareth from combat but largely he leaves it as an enigma.

In the prose draft, too, the tower of Camelot appears and disappears because of "driving showers," but in the idyll the mist alternately obscuring and revealing Camelot seems more supernatural. than meteorological. Malory places Camelot at or near Winchester, but in the *Idylls* its location is hard to ascertain. In the proofs of the Geraint idylls, entitled "Enid," Tennyson wrote that Geraint "fell/At Longport, fighting for the blameless king." [9] Longborth is the location of Geraint's end in the elegy of Llywarch Hen, as Tennyson knew, and it was identified by some scholars as Portsmouth.[10] But in order to avoid localizing the setting or calling attention to the one source, Tennyson concluded the idyll instead with Geraint's death "Against the heathen of the Northern Sea/In battle, fighting for the blameless King." His Geraint is, in fact, at the same time the hero of Llywarch Hen, the protagonist of the Celtic *Geraint ab Erbin,* the Erec of Chrétien de Troyes' *Erec et Enide* (in one manuscript Tennyson, perhaps inadvertently, wrote *Erec* instead of *Geraint* [11]), and a figure of his own transcending all of these.

In an early set of notes on Arthurian legend Tennyson jotted down details far more explicitly than he presented them in the *Idylls.* He noted that Arthur's mother was "Dame Igraine," the "wife of the Duke of Tintagil"; named Sir Kay as Arthur's foster brother; and wrote that Arthur received the Round Table and one hundred knights from the queen's father, and that the Order included one hundred and fifty knights at its height.[12] In "The Coming of Arthur," however, Tennyson keeps Arthur's lineage as a major mystery; he does not give the source of the Round Table itself; and he leaves the size of the Order to the reader's imagination. Tennyson distinguishes his Lancelot from Malory's Launcelot by the spelling (Malory's spelling was the better known, although Scott had used *Lancelot* previously in "The Bridal of Triermain"). This was a conscious alteration, for he used *Launcelot* in the early proofs.[13] In the epilogue Tennyson refers to the rare *Malleor* rather than the familiar English *Malory,* perhaps again to awaken feelings of strangeness, just as he does in changing Nimuë, the rather well-known figure in Celtic lore, to Vivien.[14]

Tennyson made innumerable changes of the kind described above, from the prosaic and recognizable to the distant and mythical. The proofs of "The Last Tournament" for the *Contemporary* show a change from "my share of beauty trebled" to the less-common "dole of beauty trebled" and the everyday "See there" to the biblical "Lo there." [15] In the proofs of 1869 he changed *you's* to *ye's* and made *enough* the more archaic *enow.*[16] In the prose draft of "The Holy Grail" he referred in Arthur's concluding speech to "the Xt," but altered it in the poem to the more elliptical "One/Who rose again." [17] He added Percivale's last line, "So spake the King: I knew not all he meant," to the conclusion, perhaps to recall the frame of the idyll and set off the action more clearly in time. In the prose draft as well, Camelot is important to Arthur because it is "the costliest in the world" of all towers, but in the idyll he treasures it for more symbolic reasons. Arthur's statue in the prose draft stands quite literally "on the top" of the sculptures at Camelot, but in the poem it stretches meaningfully "over all." "Arthur's wain," mentioned in the prose sketch for the Bors episode of the grail quest, becomes the less-prosaic and identifiable "seven clear stars of Arthur's Table Round," which might be Ursa Major, Cassiopeia's Chair, or the Pleiades. In the prose sketch for "The Last Tournament" Tennyson begins with Sir Gawain, Sir Modred, and Sir Gaheris riding into the woods, apparently to meet their adulterous loves.[18] In the poem, he makes the woods a symbol of bestiality more than a place of specific misdoing.

When Tennyson remarked, "There is no grander subject in the world than King Arthur," [19] he meant his own ideal King, "who spent himself in the cause of honour," [20] and not "that gray king" of local legends, "or him/Of Geoffrey's book, or him of Malleor's . . ." (Epilogue, lines 39-42). His unfortunate topical allusion to Prince Albert in the dedication as "my own ideal knight" brought him the ridicule of Swinburne and Sir Leslie Stephen, who perhaps took it too literally; he nevertheless changed the tribute to the Prince Consort as "Scarce other than my king's ideal knight" in 1882, leaving the King a mythical presence free of limiting associations.

Although it may not be possible to explain how a poet arrives at his final masterpiece, we can say at least that Tennyson's work on the *Idylls* shows this one clear tendency—to erase from the stories any unnecessary topicality and to merge them into a large mythical heritage. The chief fault in the manner in which his readers responded to the poem was in fact the tendency they had to search for recognizable elements in the poem and to assume that Tennyson was obligated to reproduce Arthurian sources, English landscape, Victorian behavior and taste, or some other narrowing entity outside the poem.

Although we may be tempted to search for recognizable elements, such an approach leads to certain misunderstandings of the poem. To insist, for example, that Tennyson should not depart from Arthurian tradition is to forget the diversity of the tradition itself. Tom Peete Cross has made the helpful but potentially misleading statement that Tennyson attempted to "ground his Idylls on the most reputable authorities of his day." [21] No one familiar with Tennyson's reading would question the fact that he acquainted himself with a great deal more than the two important sources for the *Idylls*—Malory and the Celtic Geraint story.[22] He undoubtedly made use of romances, chronicles, and scholarly studies when they suited his purposes. It is true as well that he departed widely from "authorities" when to do so would further his artistic idea. The ending of "Gareth and Lynette," for example, asserts his preference for an ending to the story more humanly right than Malory's.

The best example of Tennyson's willingness to defy authorities, sources, and nearly all medieval tradition is his conception of King Arthur's character. It is apparent from an early notebook (watermarked 1833) that he considered making some use of the Arthur of Malory, for he jotted there a genealogy that identified Morgause as "Arthur's sister" and Mordred as her "Son by Arthur." [23] But for the *Idylls* he chose instead the "blameless King" of his own imagining whose only imperfection is his inability to see the imperfections of others. Nevertheless, the Arthurian authority, Sharon Turner, ridiculed such purifying of the king's character as apocryphal. He denounced such statements as Joseph of Exeter's "flos regum Arthurus"—which became the epigraph for the *Idylls*—as "fiction to be despised" and likewise dismissed the statement from the *Brut ab Arthur*—another favorite of

Tennyson's: "God has not made, since Adam was, the man more perfect than Arthur." [24] In renaissance allegory, however, Arthur already had been made a perfect courtier when the humanists, led by Polydore Vergil, began to undermine public credence in King Arthur as an historical figure. A freer, less traditional kind of Arthurian literature developed as a result, the best example of which is *The Faerie Queene.*

The renaissance brought into being conditions that, like Victorian England, made King Arthur and the Round Table attractive as an epic subject—an England at the height of European glory and a revival of classical forms that might induce poets to consider an Arthuriad. Nearly every major poet of the seventeenth century did, but none of them wrote one, possibly for the reason given by Ben Jonson—that "for a Heroick poem—there was no such ground as King Arthur's fiction." [25] That is, traditionally the epic poet was supposed to believe in the story he told. Furthermore, few renaissance poets were willing to commit themselves to the Arthurian epic in the face of the humanists' skepticism. Milton, furthermore, probably had more than one reason for abandoning the aim; one was no doubt his greater belief in the fall of man than in the tragedy of the Round Table. Robert Southey, in the introduction to his edition of Malory, quotes Milton as saying,

As to Arthur, more renowned in songs and romances than in true stories, who he was and whether even any such reigned in Britain, hath been doubted heretofore, and may again with good reason. No less is in doubt who was his father,—and as we doubted of his parentage, so may we also his puissance. Considering all things, there will remain neither place nor circumstance in story which may administer any likelihood of those great acts that are ascribed to him.[26]

While the epic ambition thus rusted unburnished, renaissance writers turned to allegory, symbolism, and fairy mythology for ways of recasting Round Table story as a reflection of their own time.[27] Not sharing either this completely free attitude toward the tradition nor the credulity of the medieval writers, Tennyson again follows a strange diagonal by remaining true to the large outlines of Malory's tragedy but portraying a king not far different from Spenser's courtly abstraction, Prince Arthur, a composite of all virtue. Malory retells as much as possible of the story and Spenser embellishes it with cavalier freedom. Tennyson retells the central myth, but interweaves it with a symbolic social message using medieval stories as foundation stones and architectural fragments around which he builds an ancient, modern, yet strangely timeless edifice—like Camelot itself, with "New things and old co-twisted, as if Time/Were nothing." ("Gareth and Lynette," lines 222-223) The influence of *The Faerie Queene,* as a poem in the Arthurian tradition but not bound by previous plots and characters, has been pointed out in discussions of the *Idylls.* Christopher Ricks has also indicated parallels between passages of the two poems in his edition, *The Poems of Tennyson* (London: Longmans, Green & Co., 1969). Both poets employ the twelve-book patterns and seasonal imagery (Spenser uses the latter in his "Cantos of Mutabilitie") . There are stylistic similarities, such as the use of archaisms and epic similes. Recurrent beast images in Spenser denote unchivalrous behavior, just as bestiality encroaches upon Tennyson's Camelot. Camelot is a Victorian version of the New Jerusalem, and the city of Revelations appears in *The Faerie Queene* (I, x, stanzas 53-61). In Spenser's allegory Prince Arthur's destiny is to marry the Faerie Queene, Gloriana, and become the Faerie King. Tennyson's Arthur, of course, marries Guinevere; but in "Lancelot and Elaine" the people of Camelot, when they see Elaine's body on the barge steered by the silent oarsman, remark:

> Look how she sleeps—the Fairy Queen, so fair!
> Yea, but how pale! what are they? flesh and blood?
> Or come to take the King to Fairyland?
> For some do hold our Arthur cannot die,
> But that he passes into Fairyland.
>
> (lines 1247-1251)

The example of Dryden, whose operatic masque, *King Arthur,* was more easily available to the public for a time than Malory, should also be mentioned. Dryden's king, morally faultless but vulnerable to illusions and deceptions, provides another precedent for Tennyson's conception of the king. At one important moment at least Tennyson seems to have been influenced by Dryden: after the knights in the *Idylls* have pledged themselves to search for the grail, King Arthur warns them:

> Go, since your vows are sacred, being made.
> Yet—for ye know the cries of all my realm
> Pass thro' this hall—how often, O my knights,
> Your places being vacant at my side,
> This chance of noble deeds will come and go
> Unchallenged, while ye follow wandering fires
> Lost in the quagmire!
>
> ("The Holy Grail," lines 314-320)

Dryden's repentant fairy Philidel warns Arthur not to trust "false deluding lights" that will leave him in "Bogs and Marshes." [28] In *The Hind and the Panther* Dryden says, "My manhood, long misled by wandering fires,/Followed false lights. . . ." [29]

The Round Table, for medieval bard and renaissance poet alike, was an emblem of civilization at its height. Tennyson's dying king recalls the "goodliest fellowship of famous knights/Whereof this world holds record." ("The Passing of Arthur," lines 183-184) Tennyson, like many of his Arthurian predecessors, touches on the archetypal response of his reader to the myth of the Golden Age, first mentioned in Hesiod, Ovid, Virgil, and other classical authors. Possibly Tennyson learned some of the facts about the myth from Jacob Bryant's *Analysis of Antient Mythology,* a book which Sir Charles Tennyson says his grandfather knew as a boy at Somersby and which "may have helped him towards the mystical feeling which was to pervade in after life in his conception of Arthurian legend." [30] Bryant quotes from Hesiod a description of a race, created by the immortals, who lived like gods and after their deaths were raised by Jove to be spirits of the air and guardians of mankind, "Who sternly right maintain, and sorely punish wrong"—much like King Arthur and his knights in the *Idylls.* While this golden race survived, Astrea, the spirit of justice, exerted her influence and all mankind was one family under the mild rule of Saturn. Later, however, as Bryant quotes from Aratus, "an unworthy and degenerate race" succeeded them. The silver, brass, and iron ages were invented by the poets, according to Bryant, to describe the decline. Tennyson's Gareth, it seems, belongs in the silver age, when, says Hesiod, "The fostering mother, with an anxious eye,/Cherish'd at home the unwieldy backward boy." In the silver age men had long lives by nature but often were cut off in their prime—as is Geraint. In the brazen age men fell into feuds and died, "each by his brother's hand"; "Balin and Balan" comes to mind. In the iron age men were continually engaged in wars and murders, as Bryant says, "finally cut off by one another's hands, in acts of robbery and violence . . . many for carrying away the wives of their friends and neighbours." [31] These same misdeeds occur in the later *Idylls*—in the internecine nightmare of the last battle and the murdering of Tristram by King Mark, whose wife Tristram has taken. The *Idylls* shows the whole decline from the Golden Age to the Iron Age and typifies the characters of men in each. Even the new knights created to fill the vacant places left in the Order by the grail quest resemble the demigods Jove created to redeem the Iron Age.

A loose connection exists between Arthurian legend and classical mythology. Saturn, the ruler during the Golden Age, was thought to remain with his followers in an isle west of Britain, much like Arthur in Avalon. Tennyson strengthens the parallel by portraying an Arthur whose mild temperament resembles Saturn's. The British believed traditionally that they were descended from the ancient Trojans through the eponymous founder of England—Brut, or Brutus.[32] Troy, according to legend, was built to the music of Apollo's lyre; it was thus a natural linkage for Tennyson to make Camelot a "city built to music." And just as Arthur is supposed by legend to return when Britain needs his help, the Golden Age—according to Virgil's fourth eclogue (the "Pollio," cited by Tennyson in "To Virgil")—is expected to return when mankind reaches its worst behavior. Optimistic patriots like Spenser and Dryden predict that Arthur will return and restore the Golden Age. Tennyson dampens this hopeful metaphor by his extremely tentative references to the *rex futurus* of legend. The main plot of the *Idylls* is tragic, resembling less the Pollio than a passage from the *Aeneid* spoken by the king Evander:

> These woods were once the home of indigenous
>   fauns and nymphs,
> And of men who had sprung from hard-wood
>   oaks, who had no settled
> Way of life, no civilization: ploughing, the
>   forming of
> Communal reserves, and economy were unknown
>   then.
> They lived on the produce of trees and the
>   hard-won fare of the hunter.
> The first thing was that Saturn come hither from
>   Olympus,
> An exile deprived of his kingdom, fleeing the
>   power of Jove.
> He made a united nation of this intractable folk
> Scattered among the hills, gave laws to them,
>   chose the name of
> *Latium*—a word suggesting the safe refuge he
>   found here:
> His reign was the period in legend called the
>   Golden Age,
> So peacefully serene were the lives of his subjects.
>   It lasted
> Till, little by little, the time grew tarnished,
>   an age of baser
> Metal came in, of mad aggression and lust for gain.[33]

In "The Coming of Arthur" the king creates an Order among a barbarous people in a way similar to Saturn's in this passage; his realm, too, reverts to aggression and selfish behavior.

The fall of Camelot results from the clash of two

opposite dreams of the Golden Age. In "Guinevere" the
queen's memory slips back to "the golden days/In which
she saw him first, when Lancelot came" (lines 379-380);
Arthur appears and blames her for spoiling "the golden
days before thy sin" (line 497). The ruins of two para-
dises confront each other. But in "The Passing of Arthur"
the king as a mythical hero transcends his failure, just as
Saturn departs from his fallen kingdom in Italy. Arthur
passes to Avilion, "Where falls not hail, or rain, or any
snow,/Nor ever wind blows loudly" (lines 429-430). Again
Tennyson follows a mythical example: Homer describes
the Elysian Fields as "the land where living is made easiest for mankind, where no snow falls, no strong winds
blow and there is never any rain. . . ." [34] Avalon is traditionally west of Britain, but since Tennyson associates
the West in his poetry with quiescence, dreaming, and
art, he has Arthur vanish into the rising sun, as if making
a pilgrimage to the East, which Tennyson associates with
a new order of life and action.[35]

Tennyson's knowledge of the Welsh bards shows up
in the *Idylls* as well. Wearing one color, white for the
Druids, signified ethical values such as truth and purity
to the bards.[36] In "The Last Tournament" Tennyson
accordingly implies the shedding of truth and purity by
the fact that the women "cast the simple white" and
"glittered . . ./Variously gay" (lines 226, 232). Perhaps
Tennyson even took from the bards his central image of
Arthur as the white light which splinters into the colors
of the spectrum as the Order declines. The bardic ways
of life and beliefs probably influenced his conception of
the Round Table: a bard, like an Arthurian knight, must
"above all things be a good man." The bards believed that
if men were evil they would fall into a reversal (as they
do in a figurative sense in the *Idylls*) of their "former

progression through brutal animation." The bardic slo-
gan, "The Truth Against the World," [37] was a favorite
of Tennyson's; it sums up the ideal by which his King
Arthur lives.

Tennyson is indebted as well to the medieval chronicles for his picture of Arthur as a great king and his
reign as a high point of civilization. Geoffrey of Monmouth writes that Britain under Arthur's rule

> had arrived at such a pitch of grandeur, that in abun-
> dance of riches, luxury of ornaments, and politeness
> of inhabitants, it far surpassed all other kingdoms.
> The knights in it that were famous for chivalry, wore
> their clothes and arms all of the same colour and
> fashion: and the women also no less celebrated for
> their wit, wore all the same kind of apparel; and
> esteemed none worthy of their love, but such as had
> given proof of their valour in three several battles.
> Thus was the valour of the men an encouragement for
> the women's chastity, and the love of the women a
> spur to the soldier's bravery.[38]

In "The Coming of Arthur" Tennyson describes the
moment of Arthur's wedding as just such a high point
of chivalry:

>   . . . the King
> That morn was married, while in stainless white,
> The fair beginners of a nobler time,
> And glorying in their vows and him, his knights
> Stood round him, and rejoicing in his joy.
> Far shone the fields of May through open door,
> The sacred altar blossomed white with May,
> The Sun of May descended on their King,

> They gazed on all earth's beauty in their
>   Queen. . . .
>
> (lines 454-462)

Although the chronicles do not portray King Arthur extensively as a person, their references to him suggest a
leader of Saturn's mildness but of superhuman prowess
in battle. Nennius first mentions the twelve battles (al-
luded to in "The Coming of Arthur" but not to be
found in Malory, Tennyson's major source); at the battle
of Badon Hill, Arthur, according to Nennius, killed nine
hundred forty of his enemies. Wace and Layamon carry
Geoffrey's portrait of Arthur's reign to extreme proportions, making Arthur an emperor sought by all European
nobility.[39] Tennyson does not accept this historical exag-
geration, and in his epilogue he distinguishes his king
from Geoffrey's; nevertheless the hero of the Idylls shares
some personal characteristics attributed to King Arthur in
the chronicles.

Tennyson makes Arthur's greatness most evident
when the king appears in triumph in the beginning and
when he passes in transcendent glory at the end. Otherwise he focusses on the Order itself as a mirror of Victorian society. King Arthur and his ideals provide a
framework against which Tennyson judges his own milieu;
his judgment is more adverse than complimentary. Hallam Tennyson wrote that his father hoped to combat "the
cynical indifference, the intellectual selfishness, the sloth
of will, the utilitarian materialism of a transition age." [40]
Tennyson portrays attitudes, behavior, philosophies, and
character traits typical of Victorian Englishmen in his de-
pictions of the Knights of the Round Table. Arthur's
idealism reflects the need for a sustaining purpose in the
Victorian era but also the sometimes foolish utopian hopes

of the Victorians. Arthur's Order proves far less sound than he imagines. In his prose sketch of 1833 Tennyson described Camelot as the most beautiful mount in the world, "But all underneath it was hollow, . . . and there ran a prophecy that the mountain and the city on some wild morning would topple into the abyss and be no more." [41] Such an explicit warning of doom no doubt proved too heavy-handed for use in the *Idylls,* but the ghost of Gawain in "The Passing of Arthur" shrills an echo of this early prophecy: "Hollow, hollow all delight!" (line 33) Tennyson believed that his own society, like Arthur's Order, was deeply in trouble; and the *Idylls* was his greatest attempt to understand its problems. In 1886 he remarked,

> When I see society vicious and the poor starving in great cities, I feel that is a mighty wave of evil passing over the world, but that there will be yet some new and strange development which I shall not live to see. . . . You must not be surprised at anything that comes to pass in the next fifty years. All ages are ages of transition, but this is an awful moment of transition. . . . I tried in my "Idylls" to teach men the need of the ideal. . . .[42]

When he said that there was no grander subject in the world than King Arthur, Tennyson meant an idea as well as a legend: man's continuing effort to create a better society.

Notes

1. Aubrey De Vere, "Alfred Tennyson," *Medieval Records and Sonnets* (London: Macmillan, 1893), 258.
2. Sir Walter Scott, *Marmion, Complete Poetical Works* (Cambridge, 1900), 90.
3. S. T. Coleridge, *"Table Talk,"* in T. M. Raysor, ed., *Miscellaneous Criticism of Samuel Taylor Coleridge* (London, 1936), 429.
4. Both are quoted in Hallam Tennyson's introduction to the *Idylls* in the Eversley edition and reprinted by Christopher Ricks in his edition, *The Poems of Tennyson* (London: Longmans, 1969), 1460-1461.
5. Kathleen Tillotson, "Tennyson's Serial Poem," *Mid-Victorian Studies by Geoffrey and Kathleen Tillotson* (London: University of London, The Athlone Press, 1965), 82.
6. Tennyson objected to the use of the term *epic* in reference to the *Idylls* in a letter to Sir George Grove, December 2, 1872. C. L. Grove, *Life and Letters of Sir George Grove* (1903), 197-198. This letter is cited in Tillotson, 99n.
7. Gerhard Joseph, *Tennysonian Love: the Strange Diagonal* (Minneapolis: University of Minnesota Press, 1969), 49-50.
8. Harvard Notebook 40.
9. Page proofs of "Enid and Nimue," 1857, in the Tennyson Research Centre, Lincoln.
10. William Owen, trans., *The Heroic Elegies of Llywarch Hen* (London: Printed for J. Owen, Piccadilly, and E. Williams, Strand, 1792). Arthur Hugh Clough sent Tennyson a copy of this book in 1856. See P. G. Scott, "Tennyson's Celtic Reading," *Tennyson Research Bulletin*, No. 2 (November 1968), paper 2.
11. Harvard Notebook 35.
12. Harvard Notebook 16.
13. In the 1859 proofs located at Lincoln a handwritten note asks, "Is the word Launcelot or Lancelot?" Tennyson then changed it to the spelling he had used in "The Lady of Shalott," which was not based on Malory.
14. Harvard Notebook 16 also has *Nineve* among Tennyson's jottings.
15. Page proofs of "The Last Tournament," Lincoln.
16. Page proofs of 1869 idylls, Lincoln.

17. Harvard Notebook 38. This also contains the prose sketch for the Bors episode mentioned below, but does not include Bors in the original plan.
18. Harvard Notebook 40. This also includes a manuscript of "Gareth and Lynette," partly prose and partly verse.
19. Reported by James T. Knowles, *Nineteenth Century*, xxxiii (1893), 182.
20. Tennyson, see Ricks, *Poems of Tennyson*, 1469.
21. Tom Peete Cross, "Alfred Tennyson as a Celticist," *Modern Philology*, XVIII (1920-1921), 156. P. G. Scott confirms part of Cross's argument in his paper, "Tennyson's Celtic Reading," *Tennyson Research Bulletin*, No. 2 (November 1968), paper 2.
22. Walther Wüllenweber did an early study of fourteen possible sources for the first idyll in his Marburg dissertation, *Über Tennysons Königsidylle "The Coming of Arthur" und Ihre Quellen* (1889), yet it is doubtful that he exhausted the possibilities.
23. Harvard Notebook 16.
24. Sharon Turner, *History of the Anglo-Saxons,* fifth edition (London: Longman, Rees, Orme, Brown, & Green, 1828), vol. I, 286n, 299.
25. R. Florence Brinkley, *Arthurian Legend in the Seventeenth Century* (Baltimore, 1932), 23-24.
26. Southey, ed., *The Byrth, Lyf, and Actes of Kyng Arthur* (2 vols.; London, 1817), vii. See also Brinkley, 140.
27. See Charles Bowie Millican, *Spenser and the Table Round* (Cambridge, Mass., 1932), 6.
28. Dryden, *King Arthur*, Montagu Sommers, editor, *The Dramatic Works of John Dryden* (London, 1931), Vol. VI, 231-289.
29. Dryden, *The Hind and the Panther*, James Kinsley, editor, *The Poems of John Dryden* (Oxford, 1958), Vol. I, 472.
30. Sir Charles Tennyson, *Alfred Tennyson* (New York: Macmillan, 1949), 32-33.
31. Bryant, *Analysis of Antient Mythology*, Third Edition (London: 1807), Vol. IV, 210-217. Arthur Lovejoy gives the most complete account of the myth in the ancient world in *Primitivism and Related Ideas in Antiquity* (Baltimore: The Johns Hopkins Press, 1935).
32. See Robert Hanning, *The Vision of History in Early Britain* (New York: Columbia University Press, 1966), 104-106, 157-159.
33. *The Aeneid*, translated by C. Day Lewis (Garden City: Doubleday, 1954), 188-9.
34. *The Odyssey*, translated by E. V. Rieu (Baltimore, Penguin, 1960), Book IV, p. 79.

35. See G. Robert Stange's discussion of "The Hesperides" in "Tennyson's Garden of Art," from John Killham, ed., *Critical Essays on the Poetry of Tennyson* (New York: Barnes and Noble, 1960), 104.

36. William Owen, trans., *The Heroic Elegies of Llywarch Hen* (London, 1792), xxxix.

37. *Heroic Elegies*, xxvi, xxix, xxxvi. J. M. Gray suggests that the secret of Arthur's origin is a sort of *cyvrinach*, or secret kept within the bardic order. Gray, *Man and Myth in Victorian England: Tennyson's "The Coming of Arthur"* (Lincoln: The Tennyson Society, 1969), 12.

38. "Geoffrey's British History," *Six Old English Chronicles*, translated by J. A. Giles (London: Henry G. Bohn, 1848), 244-245. This volume is contained in Tennyson's library at Lincoln and was probably the source of his familiarity with Geoffrey, Gildas, and Nennius.

39. The extent of Tennyson's borrowings from the chronicles is still to be completely determined. See J. M. Gray, "Tennyson and Nennius," "Tennyson and Geoffrey of Monmouth," and "Tennyson and Layamon," *Notes and Queries,* CCXI (September 1966, 341-342; CCXII (February 1967), 52-53; and CCXIII (May 1968), 176-178.

40. Hallam Tennyson, *Memoir,* II, 128.

41. *Memoir*, II, 12.

42. Quoted in Sir Charles Tennyson, *Alfred Tennyson*, 491.

2.

The Major Sources

Weeding the Garden

Few poems offer such possibilities for source study as the *Idylls,* but I shall consider here only the manner in which Tennyson arrived at his portrait of a society in decline by reshaping his two chief sources—Malory and the Celtic "Geraint the Son of Erbin." These two are indisputably important; their quantitative influence upon the plots of the idylls is greater than that of all other sources combined.

Nevertheless, a reader who was not aware of Arthurian sources would never guess the diversity of materials upon which the *Idylls* are based—or even that the Geraint idylls stem from a different origin than the rest. Tennyson developed his own style, meaning, and structure of images while he assembled plots from Arthurian sources. In reshaping the Geraint story he creates a social meaning where none had existed before. In forming idylls from the heterogeneous tales of the *Morte Darthur* he changes a comment on society already present to point more insistently at the symptoms of social decline in Victorian England. He borrows narrative and even language without change if the original happens to serve his artistic purpose; if not, he freely adds, omits, or alters to suit his plan.

The Geraint idylls fit meaningfully between the golden days of "Gareth and Lynette" and the seriously decaying social climate of "Balin and Balan." To convey the interim state of the realm, Tennyson employs the image of the garden threatened by the overgrowth of weeds. He derives the two poems from Lady Charlotte Guest's translation of the *Mabinogion* and to a much lesser extent from Chrétien de Troyes' *Erec et Enide*.[1] They portray Arthur's struggle to maintain his ideal Order; at the end he seems to be successful, but the images of nature in the poems leave us uncertain whether or not he really has been.

Tennyson wrote the two idylls in 1856 as one poem entitled "Enid." He first printed this work the following year with "Vivien" (now "Merlin and Vivien") in six private copies.[2] The title of the volume, *Enid and Nimuë: or, the True and the False,* makes it apparent that from the outset Tennyson intended to give a thematic unity to the spontaneous and charming but confusing "Geraint the Son of Erbin," presenting Enid as the noble foil to the sensual *femme fatale,* Vivien. The original story is to be classed in the loosest sense as part of the *Mabinogion* proper, since it is based, unlike most of the others, upon a French source.[3] The courtliness of the original brings the story somewhat nearer to Malory than the purely Welsh stories. In plot and character, however, it shares the diffuseness of the *Mabino-*

gion in general. Tennyson adheres closely to the narrative but reshapes it subtly into an aesthetic whole.

Tennyson's garden imagery gives the key to his social idea. Just as in *Paradise Lost* before the fall Adam and Eve had the one task of keeping the garden trim, King Arthur faces the task of removing the wicked influences from the garden of his kingdom. Ultimately Tennyson is questioning the adequacy of the ethical idea concluding *Candide,* for cultivating our garden is only an immediate responsibility that can prove shortsighted. Even Enid's provincial directness does not penetrate the growing evil in the Order, and Geraint's unreasonable suspicion hits nearer the larger truth than her perspicuous and loyal interpretation of events around her.

Tennyson's creation of organized meanings out of his episodic source is itself a kind of weeding process. He pares it of its overflowing detail, omitting a number of events and much description in order to focus more intently upon the characters and the moral state of the realm. His omissions, however, are less important than his alerations and additions. The essential plot remains nearly the same, comprising two parts, later separated into the two Geraint idylls: the first ("The Marriage of Geraint") recounts the tournament in which Geraint defeats Edyrn, the son of Nudd, an enemy of Enid's family, and returns to Arthur's court with Enid and marries her. The second ("Geraint and Enid") is the adventure three years later (one in Tennyson) in which Geraint, suspecting his wife of disloyalty, sets out with her ahead of him into the wilderness, where, through a series of encounters with caitiff knights, he regains his trust in her.

The reasons for Geraint's suspicions and for his domineering character are not made clear in the Celtic version of the story, especially in a figure who is given to moments of passive uxoriousness. Tennyson gives Geraint, however, a more dominant role within the plot and, more importantly, a symbolic meaning within the *Idylls*. As a result, his actions, which seem arbitrary in the original story, further the meaning of the entire poem. Geraint is the knight who takes true for false by reaching conclusions on the basis of outward appearances. Unlike his counterpart in the source tale, he takes the initiative in all escapades. The hero of the original version leaves the court of Arthur at Caerleon after his father requests him to defend his lands on the Severn against bandits; Tennyson's Geraint goes to Arthur himself for permission to leave the court. Throughout the two idylls, Geraint's actions, although of less superhuman grandeur than those of his prototype, carry a symbolic importance. In his transformation from suspicion, vanity, delusions of omnipotence, and blindness to inner reality, to a state of faith in which he would rather die than doubt, Geraint functions as the central male figure around whom the others arrange themselves: each experiences a parallel regeneration through being humbled or is slain at the moment of his greatest arrogance.

Edeyrn (Tennyson renames him Edyrn), son of Nudd, in the original is the morally neutral enemy of Enid's father whom Geraint must defeat in tournament before taking Enid as his bride. Tennyson alters the details of the story of the tournament against Edyrn, whom he makes a villain and whose repentance after his defeat stands as a triumph for the values of the Round Table. Edeyrn in the *Mabinogion* is the popular ruler of the town of Cardiff which he has wrested from the control of Enid's father, Earl Ynywl (whom Tennyson renames Yniol). He lives in the town while the elderly earl dwells

in a decaying palace outside the city. Tennyson paints
a different picture in "The Marriage of Geraint." He
reduces Edyrn's home from a fortress and castle to merely
a fortress. Edyrn does not live within the city, but remains
in alien defiance at the opposite side of the valley from
the aged earl. The town itself is filled with "brawling"
like the clamor of rooks. As does the *Mabinogion,* Tennyson depicts the citizens busy preparing arms for the tournament, but the spirit of their activity has been changed
from one of cheerful anticipation to that of surly absorp-
tion in their labor. The grimness of Tennyson's town be-
tokens the state of fear in which it is held by Edyrn, whom
Yniol labels a "hedgerow thief" for his usurpation of
the earldom. Edeyrn in the Celtic version has a claim
to the earldom equal, perhaps superior, to that of Ynywl
because he has seized it from the latter in revenge for
not receiving an inheritance owed him by his uncle Ynywl.
Tennyson's Edyrn, in contrast, has unjustifiably gained the
rulership of the town by arousing the townspeople against
Yniol through slander, because Yniol has refused him his
daughter's hand. Thus Edyrn becomes in Tennyson both
a morally culpable enemy and an unsought rival of Geraint for Enid's hand. After his defeat and reform, however, he admits that he instituted the deadly tournament
of the sparrow hawk not for the sake of winning Enid
so much as to humiliate other suitors who might battle
in her behalf. Both villain and hypocrite, a foil to Enid's
trusting purity, Edyrn is a parallel to Geraint, who, before
gaining faith, takes true for false.[4]

Edyrn in Tennyson's poem undergoes a dramatic
reform and Geraint a deeping of awareness. Neither of
these is a significant part of the *Mabinogion.* Just as
Edryn, who believed himself unconquerable, can reveal
to Geraint, "By overthrowing me you threw me higher,"

and just as Geraint himself must nearly die to attain a faith stronger than death, so, too, the unregenerate knights must die if they cannot be reformed. Earl Doorm and Earl Limours, who correspond to Earl Limours and Earl Dwynn, respectively, in the *Mabinogion* (Tennyson reverses the names),[5] seem about to succeed in betraying Enid by tempting her with superficial glamor. The threat they pose is put down by their deaths. They serve as the parallel to Geraint's love of surface when, at the beginning of "The Marriage of Geraint," Geraint bedecks Enid in "crimson and in purples and in gems."

Guinevere herself introduces the theme of the Geraint idylls when, in "The Coming of Arthur," she overlooks the king because he rides a simple knight among his knights. Tending to judge by appearance, she fails to recognize his greatness underneath his simple apparel. The collapse of the Round Table is partly the result of the flaw that threatens Geraint's marriage—the confusion of reality and appearance.

Ultimately the most important male figure in the Geraint idylls is King Arthur. He also has Geraint's tendency to rely upon appearance, though in the *Idylls* he suffers blind faith rather than blind doubt, and no happy awakening is possible for him. Arthur voices the touchstone assertion of the Geraint idylls when he says, near the end of "Geraint and Enid,"

> The world will not believe a man repents:
> And this wise world of ours is mainly right.
> Full seldom doth a man repent, or use
> Both grace and will to pick the vicious quitch
> Of blood and custom wholly out of him,
> And make all clean, and plant himself afresh.

Edyrn has done it, weeding all his heart
As I will weed this land before I go.

(lines 899-906)

With almost perfect wisdom Arthur realizes the rarity
but not the impossibility of the social relationships he
aims to make prevail, yet he has a childlike blindness
toward the immediate situation. He believes that his
outlying lands are well protected, when, according to
Geraint's report, they are not. Arthur believes his eyes
have been opened by Geraint's request to return to his
own princedom. When Geraint offers his request, Arthur
hesitates. In the *Mabinogion* he does so because he is
reluctant to part with such an attractive couple as Geraint
and Enid, though the lands on the Severn do need protecting. But in Tennyson's story the king feels a sudden
pang of conscience. He wonders if he may be allowing
parts of the land to stagnate through his failure to see
its real condition, "By having look'd too much thro' alien
eyes,/And wrought too long with delegated hands." Arthur
seems to gain insight into the state of his realm (although
it is not necessarily true that it has become evil yet) and
into the difficulty of maintaining his utopian society.

Arthur also fails to recognize the important truth
of Guinevere's love for Lancelot, which began even before
the marriage of the king and queen. Nor does Arthur
know of the rumor spreading that the queen is already
disloyal to him. The shadow of Guinevere's rumored
guilt falls with double foreboding across the landscape of
the Geraint idylls because it comes at the time when
Arthur thinks he has just saved himself from carelessness.
Of all the purblind race Arthur is most blind because
his moral perfection resists plain immoral fact. Geraint's

request to return to his beleaguered lands on the Severn gives Arthur what he believes to be new sight, although it may only have blinded him further, and the king does not see Geraint's real motive behind the request. In the *Mabinogion* Geraint reveals his true motive: he must help cleanse the land. But in "The Marriage of Geraint," Tennyson, with the ironic touch of the master, has Geraint use the request only as a pretext for taking Enid away from the taint she suffers through her intimacy with Guinevere, whose guilt is being (perhaps falsely, at this point) bruited about. The situation is complicated by a double irony, for not only is Arthur's new assurance of insight undermined by a more critical oversight, but Geraint's new-found trust is marred by a suspicion of the queen which, like his renounced suspicions of Enid, may conceivably be ill founded. Truth seems almost impossible to attain, and even we, as readers, do not possess it. The only avoidable error is complacency.

Tennyson departed widely from the *Mabinogion* when he framed his moral conception of Geraint and Arthur. Geraint in the Celtic version is obstinate, uxorious, and excessively suspicious, just as he is in the *Idylls;* Arthur is simply his moral superior. For Tennyson Arthur's superiority is still a fact, but in the larger moral idea of the *Idylls* that same purity makes him incapable of seeing what lesser men arrive at through common inquisitiveness. Arthur's perfection is a strength raising him above the realm itself but a weakness more damaging than Geraint's more obvious failings in that it disables him from correcting the real shortcomings of those in his Order. Geraint must test reality to find out the truth about his wife; Arthur, who never really doubts Guinevere, has the truth thrust upon him too late. Tennyson again reveals a sensitivity to the pathetic ironies of reality

when he borrows from the *Mabinogion* the mistake made
by Geraint when he sees Enid crying at the beginning
of the story. She is actually true in love and true to
honor; she loves him through all the vicissitudes of the
story and is true to his code of honor when he becomes
uxorious. She weeps because he is neglecting his responsibilities as a knight; he impulsively concludes that she
weeps for the opposite reason of dreaming about another
knight. Opposite to Enid's loyalty, Guinevere's laxness
parallels Geraint's. The queen and Geraint meet, significantly, while Arthur is hunting the stag (an event derived
from the Celtic source), both "forgetful of the hunt" and
too late to participate in it. The queen forgot because
she has (as Enid has not) been dreaming of her favorite
knight; Geraint forgot because of his idle jealousy. The
queen, who should be the bearer of higher moral principles than the provincial Enid, is or will be guilty of the
sins Geraint suspects in his wife. Arthur, who should
possess keener insight than his younger subordinate, trusts
his queen as if she were Enid.

Enid, even more than Geraint, gains dramatic reality
in Tennyson. She exists for the reader in a way that she
does not in the *Mabinogion*. Her character in outline
is the same: she is the combination of Cinderella, the
obscure girl of great beauty who suddenly shines and
marries the prince, and Griselda, Boccaccio's patient, long-
enduring wife of a severe husband. But there the resemblance ends. Tennyson reveals her inner life as well as
her outer meaning in the story. We worry with her when
she is troubled over the threat of Limours—when she
knows he is planning her abduction in the morning, and
yet she cannot speak to Geraint because he has commanded
her to silence. In the original episode of Earl Dwynn,
Enid simply breaks silence and tells him of the planned

abduction; but Tennyson interpolates a fearful dream in which she feels herself slipping down horrible precipices and clutching at a rootless thorn. Similarly, her fears over her inadequacy, insignificant in the source tale, are made tormenting because they heighten the theme of reality (her sense of honor) and appearance (the old dress Geraint forces her to wear). She dreams of herself as an ugly fish in the pond at Arthur's court which the children point at and ask to be taken out to die. The dream is not a prophecy of Enid's fate, for her story ends happily, but rather a sign of danger indicating that persons of honor will be victimized later in the story.

Tennyson depicts Enid by drawing off much of the comic detail and pleasant fullness of the original. Enid's moral truth is conveyed by a small cluster of images running counter to the destructive forces in nature. She sings, not like the rooks in the town, but with a bird's "sweet voice." Her nature is that of a garden: her happiness as they ride away from Doorm's castle is better than the first roses blowing in paradise, her gladness is lasting, ironically, like the "mist in Eden," not transitory like a summer shower.[6] But she lives, like Elaine, in fantasy, not knowing the rumors about the queen.

The imagery that pervades the Geraint idylls is unsettling to the reader. Whereas "Geraint the Son of Erbin" leads the reader robustly through romance episodes, "The Marriage of Geraint" and "Geraint and Enid" leave the reader subtly troubled, even after Geraint gains faith, Edyrn is reformed, and Arthur has cleansed the realm of corrupt officers and wicked knights. The reader is aware of the rumor concerning Guinevere, "the world's loud whisper breaking into storm." But the troubling effect derives as well from the landscape of the poem, which disrupts confident feeling the plot would otherwise give us.

There is a kind of irony or tension between what is going on in the action of the poem and what happens in the reader's consciousness as the result of the omnipresent images of slipping, falling, losing, darting, flashing, and rippling. Nature is everywhere elusive and uncertain, like weather about to break into storm. The faithless friends of Earl Limours desert him like fish darting in a stream; Geraint smiles like a stormy sunlight; and Enid fears Edyrn even after his reform because in a hollow land where old fires have broken, new ones may break out. Man's nature has a "vicious quitch" that can send out roots and choke the good plants in the garden. Geraint's enemies fall like a great piece of promontory sliding from the cliff to the beach. In a lawless realm people care no more for a woman like Enid weeping over her fallen knight than for a summer shower. Everywhere nature seems to undermine, snatch away, threaten, and destroy the things man values. Geraint's order for Enid to wear her faded dress falls on her like flaws on summer corn; Earl Doorm's men's souls have been drawn down like withered leaves pulled into the earth by worms. Limours rises to speak to Enid like a man who tries a bridge that he fears may collapse. Arthur's court is no longer a golden world. King Arthur hopes to maintain the state of paradise in his realm; he says he will weed the land before he goes. But he too lives in fantasy: while he is ridding his realm of its vicious quitch, he fails to see its loveliest flower being plucked while his back was turned.

Malory and the Social Tragedy

The ethic of weeding our gardens is not the most important ideal of the *Idylls,* for Arthur's reliance upon that principle seems in the light of the tragedy he is to encounter to be like putting a ship in order while letting it blindly drift toward disaster. Even the ideal behind the king's wise advice to the grail knights after their return—that the king must tend his fields and not follow wandering fires—ignores the fact that the realm seems lost beyond recovery; tilling the fields would, to borrow Morris' language, be useless toil rather than useful work. More important to Tennyson than laboring in the moment is the difficult work of finding directions and ideals. The warning against taking true for false and false for true concerns the large danger of a whole society pursuing destructive goals. Working industriously on immediate tasks—following the Victorian ethic of work— would in such a context do little to prevent a social calamity.

Malory's greatness as a tragedian differs from Tennyson's, and the difference is reflected in their styles. Malory's prose—direct, pellucid, moving—suits well the story of an Order brought to its end by fate and conflicting desires. What could equal the simplicity of Galahad's last prayer:

"Lord, I thank thee, for now I see that
which hath been my desire many a day;
now blessed Lord would I no longer live,
if it might please thee good Lord." [7]

Eugene Vinaver finds this passage one of the most deeply religious moments in any version of the grail quest.[8] Malory's Galahad follows his desire to see the grail, much as all of the knights live by impulse and a charming freedom from hard ethical choices. Tennyson does not give most of the knights in the *Idylls* this sort of innocence; in fact he stresses their ethical perplexities. In "The Holy Grail" Tennyson has Sir Percivale describe Galahad's disappearance:

> A thousand piers ran into the great Sea.
> And Galahad fled along them bridge by bridge,
> And every bridge as quickly as he crost
> Sprang into fire and vanish'd, tho' I yearn'd
> To follow; and thrice above him all the heavens
> Open'd and blazed with thunder such as seem'd
> Shoutings of all the sons of God. And first
> At once I saw him far on the great Sea,
> In silver-shining armor starry-clear;
> And o'er his head the Holy Vessel hung
> Clothed in white samite or a luminous cloud.
>
> (lines 503-513)

The description is as religious as Malory's passage but in the manner of a Victorian recessional; it has the brilliant silver notes of a cathedral organ's state trumpets. The difference is more than one of period styles. Malory's Galahad in the twelfth book of the *Morte Darthur* simply dies, and the angels bear his soul to heaven. Tennyson instead conceives of Galahad's disappearance as an apotheosis parallel to Arthur's passing at the conclusion of the *Idylls*. Arthur and Galahad are set apart by their ethical perfection from the corruption of the Round Table and are received by celestial hosts in an Order befitting their characters. Everyone is included in Malory's version of the tragedy; all are imperfect, but Tennyson sees the possibility of a hero's transcending human failure. For Malory there is one world—human society; for Tennyson two spheres of being conflict with each other—the ideal, or the world of spirit, and the social, or the world of the senses.

Launcelot is Malory's hero, whose failure to live the life of purity the author—himself a knight who had spent time in prison—no doubt felt to be his own fate and mankind's. Tennyson's hero is the king himself, whose quixotic perfection he felt to be a needed example for modern man.[9] Malory's Launcelot epitomizes the simultaneous strength and weakness of the chivalric code: he fails in love, in religion, and in chivalry because of his relationship with Guinevere.[10] The ideals of chivalry are tested against his humanity; the absence of chivalric perfection seems to increase the humanity of the whole order of knights. Tennyson's morally impeccable king has no parallel in Malory's; the blameless king epitomizes not the Order but the consciences or spiritual ideals of the Round Table—their mystery as to origin, their sublimity, and their vulnerability to antisocial forces.

Malory's vision is humanistic; Tennyson, living in a society in which humanism is only one of many contending philosophies, sees the complexities caused by diverse intellectual positions and yet upholds the transcending moral responsibility of which Arthur's code is symbolic. Deviations from the code in the *Idylls* are not just the result of natural weaknesses of human beings, as in Malory, but the self-assertions of men who feel that their rights have been impinged upon and their ideas contradicted. Arthur blames Guinevere for her betrayal; he calls Bedivere traitor-hearted; and he finally sees that "all whereon I lean'd in wife and friend/Is traitor to my peace. . . ." ("The Passing of Arthur," lines 24-25). Guinevere, Vivien, Balin, Tristram, and the Red Knight (Pelleas) all blame Arthur for the strictness or hypocrisy of his vows and consider him a fool.

Malory's king is a human member of a society in which the chivalric code has grown organically; Arthur brings together the Order of the Round Table but is not the founder of a whole way of life, as he is in the *Idylls*. In "Gareth and Lynette" Tennyson adds to Malory's story of Beaumains a passage describing the change Arthur has brought to his society. Lynette says that the four evil knights guarding Lyonors are

> . . . of the foolish fashion, O Sir King,
> The fashion of that old knight-errantry
> Who ride abroad, and do but what they will;
> Courteous or bestial from the moment, such
> As have nor law nor king. . . .
>
> (lines 613-617)

Arthur has created a code of values at a time before which barbarism had existed. Throughout the *Idylls* a self-conscious tone of Victorian social concern sets the story apart from Malory; the separation widens into Tennyson's repudiation of the *Morte Darthur* as "Touched by the adulterous finger of a time/That hovered between war and wantonness" (Epilogue, lines 43-44) in its portrait of the king. Tennyson seems to imply that Malory portrays the style of old knight-errantry condemned in "Gareth and Lynette."

In a period when the French Revolution was still

almost a living memory and one reform bill was to be followed by another, Tennyson not surprisingly portrays King Arthur as a leader who creates, not inherits, the order of chivalry, and whose failure is a warning to those who would take for granted the delicate equilibrium necessary to keep sudden social gains from becoming setbacks. Malory has King Arthur preside over a tradition of chivalry in which he and his knights strive to live by ideals inherited from the past. Camelot, according to Malory, is merely Winchester, but it is a major symbol for Tennyson. The two significant descriptions of Camelot occur in "Gareth and Lynette" and "The Holy Grail"; neither is based upon Malory. Both descriptions suggest the paradox of Victorian time—the simultaneous feeling of rapid change and gradually evolving tradition. Tennyson does not eliminate the past from his Camelot: it is "a city of shadowy palaces/And stately, rich in emblem and the work/Of ancient kings who did their days in stone. . . ." ("Gareth and Lynette," lines 296-298). Merlin's hand has, by its touch, "made it spire to heaven" (line 302). Although Tennyson explained this as "Symbolizing the divine" (see Ricks, 1492n.), Victorian readers no doubt caught the allusion to the Tower of Babel: "Let us build us a city and a tower, whose top may reach unto heaven" (Genesis 11:4). Pelleas later groans, "Black nest of rats, . . . ye build too high" ("Pelleas and Ettarre," line 544), and Arthur himself fears that the tower may fall ("The Holy Grail," line 341). Camelot is in fact a symbol of man's civilization. For Tennyson the action of the poem represented figuratively "a whole cycle of generations." [11] Tennyson is portraying the tragic truth of history underlying short-term gains made with spectacular success in his own society.

The zones of Camelot in "The Holy Grail" also
betoken the advance of civilization:

And four great zones of sculpture, set betwixt
With a mystic symbol, gird the hall;
And in the lowest beasts are slaying men,
And in the second men are slaying beasts,
And on the third are warriors, perfect men,
And on the fourth are men with growing wings.

(lines 233-238)

The evolutionary overtones of the images are evident
enough; it is not, however, clear whether the movement
upward from beast to man to angel is to be immediate
or gradual. In a sense King Arthur brings about a momentary telescoping of the evolutionary process. Tennyson,
like Huxley, is too acute to follow the line of crude social
Darwinism that argues in favor of a society patterned on
the survival of the fittest and a gradual emergence of a
superior human species.

Tennyson also suggests that utopian plans for the
sudden transformation of institutions, with the pattern of
the French Revolution in mind, seemed unlikely to offer
the realization of Camelot's ideals. The *Idylls* does not
indicate man's easiest route to social perfection, but it
does show how men might revert to barbarism. King
Arthur's endeavors are not the way to utopia but prove
only that "one good custom" alone might "corrupt the
world." His King Arthur is capable of facing social change
with equanimity, but the descent into cynicism and betrayal by the knights and ladies, Tennyson believes, cannot be justified by the casting off of an outworn belief.

Because Tennyson portrays a social tragedy rather than an individual one, King Arthur is not a tragic hero in quite the same sense that Oedipus is, for the blindness he suffers is part of the larger blindness of a limited society. Slanderers like Vivien are no less myopic in their moral judgment; she sees wickedness in everything, even where there is none. Being only part of the larger tragic entity, Arthur cannot undergo a purification through suffering. He cannot be purified, being pure; he cannot gain humility, being humble; and he cannot gain humanity, being perfect in a scale of values beyond the human. Tennyson heightens the social tragedy inherent in Malory by viewing the fall of the Order as a widening separation between the King and his followers. The real tragedy is the fall of the Order. Arthur and Guinevere are left looking forward to meeting in heaven and finding perfect love there, but the Round Table "Reels back into the beast, and is no more." ("The Passing of Arthur," line 26) Tennyson consciously refers to the "coming" and "passing" of the king, whereas Malory portrays his actual birth and death, to distinguish Arthur from the evanescent humanity of his Order (except Galahad, who also vanishes into light).

Malory sees the king as a poignant human figure, but Tennyson makes him a Christ figure. Arthur's failure in the *Idylls* is Tennyson's way of warning his society against rejecting its own spiritual conscience. Reflected in the knights' desertion of Arthur one can see the Victorians abandoning the Christian basis of their ethical tradition. To make the analogy more explicit, Tennyson draws a close parallel between Arthur and Christ, just as he shows similarities between the knights and his Victorian contemporaries. Like Christ, King Arthur brings to society a new ideal, founded upon absolute vows and a vision of perfect human relationships. He succeeds in living according to the vows himself but in the end falls victim to an extreme violation of his code—so extreme that he momentarily utters words of despair: Arthur echoes Christ, "My God, thou has forgotten me in my death!" ("The Passing of Arthur," line 27). But he forgives even the worst transgression, for he knows that his soul belongs to another realm: "Nay—God my Christ— I pass but shall not die" ("The Passing of Arthur," line 28). By thus placing the king in a symbolic role beyond tragedy, Tennyson sharpens the effect of the social tragedy. King Arthur, as the Order declines, becomes less and less a part of its society, whereas Malory's king remains an active participant in the plot.

Tennyson surrounds Arthur's origin in mystery, but Malory gives an unequivocal, down-to-earth account:

> So after the death of the duke, king Uther lay with Igraine more than three hours after his death, and begat on her Arthur the same night.[12]

Such particularity would be destructive to Tennyson's purpose of suggesting that ideals themselves are attributed by men to different origins—nature, God, social tradition, etc. The separation of the king from the knighthood marks the dying of the Order; since there can be no Round Table without the ideal represented by the king, the *Idylls* ends abruptly with his disappearance, the Order having ceased to exist. Malory relates the events that take place after Arthur's death. For Tennyson the king is the informing spirit and supporting energy of the Order; for Malory he is the leader of great knights, of whom Launcelot, who lives six years as a monk after the king's death, is the greatest.

In portraying the Round Table rather than the king, Tennyson reverses his method of changing Malory's story. Malory leaves the origin of the table uncertain, but Tennyson describes its creation. Malory emphasizes the separate adventures of the knights; for him the Round Table serves as a convenient setting. The stories themselves derive from various sources and are not arranged in a clear structure.[13] Tennyson, however, brings his stories together in an intricate curve analogous to the Round Table itself, as an "image of the mighty world." Parallels between the beginning and ending of the story, along with seasonal imagery suggesting the condition of the realm at the time each story occurs, convey the impression of historical cycles. The tragic hero for Tennyson is not Arthur, or even Lancelot, as for Malory, but the Order itself, to whose larger story the separate legends are subordinated.

Both Malory and Tennyson depict the failure of an ideal society—or rather the failure of a real society to attain utopia. But Malory's world is "golden" in a different sense from Tennyson's. For Malory the Order is primarily a "fellowship"; its greatness derives from communal spirit as much as heroic action. The king laments the dissolution of this comradery:

> ". . . and therefore wit you well that my heart was never so heavy as it is now; and much more greater sorrow for my good knights' loss, than for the loss of my queen; for queens I might have enough, but such a fellowship of good knights shall never be together in no company." [14]

"Golden," in mythical language, denotes love and friendship. In the *Morte Darthur* the Order remains golden to the end, for despite the human failures and split loyalties, the knights still feel the emotional bond that has made their Order glorious. The fall of chivalry in the *Idylls,* however, is due to a loss of purity and slackening of moral resolve—a failure to maintain Victorian standards.

There are not many instances of fellowship in the *Idylls,* except for the ironic closeness of Arthur and Lancelot in "The Coming of Arthur" and "Gareth and Lynette," which is undermined by the growing relationship between Lancelot and the queen. Otherwise, Balin and Balan stand fast together against Arthur; the Red Knight and his followers revel together in the mock Round Table in the North. The spiritual fellowship the knights achieved at the moment of Arthur's coronation disintegrates into spiritual discord by the time of the "The Holy Grail," in which each knight seems to have his separate and isolated experience. When Sir Bors tries to communicate with Lancelot on the grail quest, Lancelot vanishes wildly with madness in his eyes. Tennyson's world of Camelot is golden, as far as fellowship is concerned, only for a brief moment, if at all.

Tennyson works quite freely, rearranging, adding, dropping, and retelling events in the eight idylls of the Round Table series that he derived from Malory. He makes of Malory's individual romances a single social tragedy, one story told through many episodes, with the Round Table as its tragic protagonist. He ranges from a near retelling of Malory's Pelleas story to almost complete invention in "Guinevere." Sometimes he reduces a famous legend—like the Tristram story—from its prominence in Arthurian tradition to the level of parallel example. It is a subordination necessary to the larger scheme. He reduces the grail quest, the other most popular legend of the century, to a foolish mistake. He makes Lancelot, Malory's hero, a good man, troubled and human, but less important in the story than King Arthur, to whom Tennyson gives enormous importance. Tennyson also makes some characters into bad men. Malory portrays King Mark as rather admirable; Tennyson makes him villainous. He creates entirely new characters, such as Vivien (if not the story of Merlin's imprisonment). The nearest corresponding character Malory wrote of would be Morgan le Fay. Tennyson also changes the fates of some characters: Pelleas, who in Malory rejects Ettarde and marries Nimuë, the Lady of the Lake, under the influence of her love potion, is left by Tennyson in lovesick despair and returns in the next idyll as the Red Knight (who is mentioned in Malory's Gareth story instead). Tennyson changes the essential characteristics of some figures. Malory portrayed Sir Dagonet as the clownish object of ridicule. Tennyson makes him the center of intelligence in "The Last Tournament."

Some of the changes were based on the many other Arthurian works Tennyson knew, but it is a mistake to regard the *Idylls* as a pastiche of fragments from many sources. Many were the result of coincidental similarities, some conscious, some half-conscious, some forgotten. Tennyson's reshaping of Malory's tragedy, nevertheless, can be attributed in large part to conscious craftsmanship.

Tennyson of course sometimes follows Malory very closely, and is often at his best in such passages. Malory's account of Arthur's end is a memorable passage in the *Morte Darthur:*

"Now put me in the barge," said the king. And so he did so softly, and there received him three queens with great mourning; and so these three queens sat them down, and in one of their laps king Arthur laid his head. And then that queen said, "Ah! dear brother, why have ye tarried so long from me? Alas, this wound on your head hath taken overmuch cold." And so they rowed from the land; and sir Bedivere beheld all those ladies go from him. Then sir Bedivere cried, "Ah! my lord Arthur, what shall become of me now ye go from me, and leave me here alone among mine enemies?"—"Comfort thyself," said king Arthur, "and do as well as thou mayest; for in me is no trust for to trust in; for I will into the vale of Avilion, for to heal me of my grievous wound; and, if thou never hear more of me, pray for my soul." But evermore the queens and the ladies wept and shrieked, that it was pitiful for to hear them: and, as soon as sir Bedivere had lost the sight of the barge, he wept and wailed, and so took the forest, and so he went all the night; and, in the morning, he was aware, between two hills, of a chapel and a hermitage.[15]

Tennyson, although he interpolates short passages to bring out the uncertainty of Arthur's destiny and to include in the picture a vision of social change, gives nearly the same account:

> Then murmur'd Arthur, "Place me in the barge."
> So to the barge they came. There those three queens
> Put forth their hands, and took the King, and wept.

But she that rose the tallest of them all
And fairest laid his head upon her lap, ...
Then loudly cried the bold Sir Bedivere:
Ah! my Lord Arthur, whither shall I go?
Where shall I hide my forehead and my eyes?
And slowly answer'd Arthur from the barge:
"The old order changeth, yielding place to new,
And God fulfills himself in many ways,
Lest one good custom should corrupt the world.
Comfort thyself; what comfort is in me?
I have lived my life, and that which I have done
May He within himself make pure! but thou,
If thou shouldst never see my face again,
Pray for my soul. More things are wrought by
    prayer
Than this world dreams of. . . .
But now farewell. I am going a long way
With those thou seest—if indeed I go—
To the island-valley of Avilion; . . .
Where I will heal me of my grievous wound."

. . .
Long stood Sir Bedivere
Revolving many memories, till the hull
Look'd one black dot against the verge of dawn,
And on the mere the wailing died away.

("The Passing of Arthur," lines 373-440)

Malory glorifies a past heroic age to the denigration
of the fallen present; for him the love of Launcelot and
the queen is an example of virtuous devotion that renders
honor to God:

But nowadays, men cannot love, may not endure
by reason; for where they be soon accorded, and

hastily heat soon cooleth; right so fareth love now-a-days, soon hot, soon cold. This is no stability, but the old love was not so. Men and women could love together seven years, and no licorous lusts were between them; and there was truth and faithfulness. And so in likewise was love used in king Arthur's days. . . .[16]

For Malory, that is, the story of the Round Table is primarily (although not entirely) an example for readers of his day to admire and emulate. For Tennyson, the relationship of Lancelot and Guinevere is an example of misconduct, and he makes the story more a warning than a pattern for imitation. The difference is one of central focus, if not of tragic conception. As Caxton, the first publisher of the *Morte Darthur,* says in his preface, through Malory "noble men may see and read the noble acts of chivalry, the gentle and virtuous deeds that some knights used in those days. . . ." [17] Tennyson's reader, in days of grave social crises, is to see and avoid "the darkness of that battle in the west/Where all of high and holy dies away."

Notes

1. The early part of this chapter is adapted from my article in *Victorian Poetry,* IV (Winter 1966), 45-51. See also Herbert G. Wright's extensive comparison of the Geraint idylls and the Celtic story—"Tennyson in Wales," *Essays and Studies,* XIV (1929), 71-103. I do not entirely agree with Wright's view of the images in the poems as perfectly harmonious with the action; I find rather that they tend subtly to counter the effect of the plot. See also Tom Peete Cross, "Alfred Tennyson as a Celticist," *Modern Philology,* XVIII (1921), 485-492, and P. G.

Scott, "Tennyson's Celtic Reading," *Tennyson Research Bulletin*, No. 2 (November 1968), paper 2. Hugh H. Wilson's "Alfred Tennyson: Unscholarly Arthurian," Victorian Newsletter, no. 32 (Fall 1967), 5-11, presents an interesting but not entirely provable case.

2. Richard Jones, *The Growth of the Idylls of the King* (Philadelphia, 1895), 44-45. Ricks mentions a private printing of the work as "Enid, an Idyll" in 1857 at Cranford Manor, along with the Geraint story of Lady Guest's collection. *Poems of Tennyson,* 1525.

3. See Thomas Parry, *A History of Welsh Literature* (Oxford, 1955), 87.

4. See Lady Charlotte Guest, translator, *The Mabinogion* (London, 1902), 273-274.

5. See J. M. Gray, "Source and Symbol in 'Geraint and Enid,' " *Victorian Poetry,* IV (Spring, 1966), 131-132.

6. Chrétien de Troyes in his *Erec et Enide* describes a garden sheltered by air through a magic spell. There the seasons do not affect the flowers, the ripe fruits, and all the singing birds under heaven. Nothing can be taken from this garden without danger. Tennyson may have borrowed the garden image from Chrétien; Geraint's sheltering Enid from the guilt of the queen is a way of protecting her prelapsarian innocence the way the spell protects Chrétien's garden.—Chrétien de Troyes, *Arthurian Romances,* trans. W. W. Comfort, Everyman Library (New York, 1965), 75.

7. *The History of the Renowned Prince Arthur* (2 vols.; London: Walker and Edwards, 1816), Vol. II, 331. Hallam Tennyson says that his father used this edition for the *Idylls.*—*Memoir,* I, 156.

8. See J. A. W. Bennett, *Essays on Malory* (Oxford, 1963), 32.

9. On Malory's prison record and the relation of Malory's life to the ethic of the *Morte Darthur,* see Vinaver in *Essays on Malory,* 30-31. Joanna Richardson argues that Tennyson almost certainly lived by the ideals of the king in the *Idylls. The Preeminent Victorian* (London, 1962), 280.

10. See Charles Moorman, *The Book of Kyng Arthur* (Lexington: University of Kentucky, 1965), 6-37, on Launcelot's role.

11. *Memoir,* II, 127.

12. *The History of the Renowned Prince Arthur* (London, 1816), I, 4.

13. The disunity of Malory's work is even more evident today than it was in Tennyson's time.—See Eugene Vinaver's introduction

to his edition, which he significantly entitles *The Works of Sir Thomas Malory* (Oxford, 1947), Vol. I.

14. *The History of the Renowned Prince Arthur,* II, 432.
15. *The History of the Renowned Prince Arthur,* II, 473-474.
16. *The History of the Renowned Prince Arthur,* II, 386.
17. *Ibid.,* I, xv.

3.

The Gauntlet
of Criticism
I: Form and Meaning

An Arthurian poem can always be interpreted against the background of Round Table myth, but the *Idylls* exists as well in a second world, the Victorian milieu. Victorians did not consider the *Idylls* as merely a poem, but an event, a cultural phenomenon. It was read, memorized, and lived. It helped to define the mentality that we call Victorian, and yet it was highly critical of Victorian society. The age saw in the *Idylls* an exalted reflection of itself as the second coming of the Round Table. Most critics would accept the use of supposedly outdated Arthurian material only for that reason—to see the present as if from a distance, to dignify Victorian society through myth. *The British Quarterly* triumphantly lauded Tennyson for eschewing the traditional epic, which "suits only those nations who turn to a dim age of vanished heroes for their golden time." Tennyson, the reviewer argues, writes for "the living present," his "faith in a reigning Emmanuel" marking him as a spokesman for the Victorian age.[1]

Tennyson did indeed avoid the literary pitfalls of the Arthuriad. The character of King Arthur is too symbolic and too often in the background for him to serve as an epic hero, nor do Lancelot and Guinevere exist quite vividly enough to compare to the reality of Dido or Achilles. As an epic, the *Idylls of the King* would seem unearthly, disconnected, old-fashioned; as a new genre combining lyric, dramatic, and narrative properties, it remains fresh, modern and compelling. Tennyson, while portraying aspects of Victorian society, expressed his deep quarrel with many of its tendencies. He had only recently unleashed some of the strongest hatred of his career against the false golden age in *Maud*. The suicidal narrator of the poem insists sarcastically that

> . . . these are the days of advance, the works
>   of the men of mind,
> When who but a fool would have faith in a
>   tradesman's ware or his word?
> Is it peace or war? Civil war, as I think, and that
>   of a kind
> The viler, as underhand, not openly bearing the
>   sword.
>   (lines 25-28)

In the *Idylls* Tennyson portrays an age of mixed quality through the paradox of the modest hero, the king who does not wear his crown or pursue the grail, who distrusts excesses of all kinds and who speaks tentatively about his destiny—and yet who rages against his enemies

with the fire of God in battle. Tennyson idealizes traditional reverence along with modern self-awareness, the
spirit of ancient heroism with a liberal Protestant theology.

Tennyson reflects his age in such a way as to understand it and to see its shortcomings and not to pretend
that it merits the optimism of many contemporary think-
ers. He sees his age as an artistic and moral monstrosity
and warns that its conflicting extremes could result in anarchy. The *Idylls* contains the antithetical nature of the
era itself, reflecting heroism and anti-heroism, pastoral
beauty and struggle for survival of the fittest, romantic
love and cynical self-indulgence. Tennyson's view of the
Arthurian Golden World is interfused with the spirit of
ironic contrast, with opposite views of the truth making it
impossible to follow, even to define, a single ideal. The
music to which the Idylls is built is atonal: a stately
blank verse sweeps over a landscape peopled by a flippant
queen, a cynical Tristram, a priggish king, a stupid
Elaine, a childish grail quest; but turn the kaleidescope
and the king is exalted, the queen beautiful in her
humanity, Elaine pure and tragic, Tristram a man op-
pressed by rigid vows, the grail quest a sublime error.
The two visions reveal the discordant character of the
Victorian age itself, caught between old and new, trust
and disbelief, authority and radicalism, progress and
misery, peace and inner tension, respectability and pruri-
ence, spiritual enthusiasm and the cash nexus.

A great deal of light is shed upon the relation of
the *Idylls* to the age by the responses of literary reviewers
to the different volumes as they appeared. As is mentioned
above, the *Idylls* was well received by the public, yet
the reviewers were baffled, dismayed, reserved, and occasionally shocked. Each reviewer had his notion of what

the *Idylls* should stand for and why it was Tennyson's masterpiece, but all agreed that Tennyson was intending his masterpiece to mirror the new Golden Age.

In "Aurora Leigh" Elizabeth Barrett Browning expressed the exact sentiments the reviewers had for the *Idylls*. She writes,

> All actual heroes are essential men,
> And all men possible heroes: every age,
> Heroic in proportion, double-faced,
> Looks backward and before, expects a morn
> And claims an epos. Ay but every age
> Appears to souls who live in't (ask Carlyle)
> Most unheroic. Ours, for instance, ours:
> The thinkers scout it, and the poets abound
> Who scorn to touch it with a finger-tip:
> A pewter age,—mixed metal, silver-washed;
> An age of scum, spooned off the richer past,
> An age of patches for old gaberdines,
> An age of mere transition, meaning nought
> Except that what succeeds must shame it quite
> If God please. That's wrong thinking, to my
>   mind,
> And wrong thoughts make poor poems. Every
>   age,
> Through being held too close, is ill-discerned
> By those who have not lived past it.
>
> Nay, if there's room for poets in the world
> A little overgrown (I think there is),
> Their sole work is to represent the age,
> Their age, not Charlemagne's,—this live, throbbing
>   age,
> That brawls, cheats, maddens, calculates, aspires,
> And spends more passion, more heroic heat,

Betwixt the mirrors of its drawing rooms,
Than Roland with his knights at Roncesvalles.
To flinch from modern varnish, coat or flounce,
Cry out for togas and the picturesque,
Is fatal,—foolish too. King Arthur's self
Was commonplace to Lady Guenever;
And Camelot to minstrels seemed as flat
As Fleet Street to our poets. Never flinch,
But still, unscrupulously epic, catch
Upon the burning lava of a song
The full-veined, heaving, double-breasted Age: . . .[2]

The *Idylls* could be all things to all reviewers, not because it was totally misunderstood but because it was not understood enough. Few of the things said about it in the reviews were wrong; nearly all were only partially correct. The tendency was to oversimplify and prejudge, often to ignore and sometimes to distort. Few reviewers saw that the work was a warning against the dangerous tendencies of the age. Only Swinburne seems to have understood the modern relevance of the *Idylls;* but he does so on aesthetic and dramatic principles and not in terms of social philosophy. Swinburne's objection to what he considers the petty moralism of the *Idylls* is the most entertaining part of his case against Tennyson but does not adequately consider the social meaning of the *Idylls*. The Victorian reviewers tended to focus on the ideas, values, and even scenery that they recognized as their own reflected by the *Idylls* and not to follow the complicated thought processes within the work. They were more intent upon tagging and labeling separate aspects of the *Idylls* than upon discovering what was happening within the seemingly idyllic setting of the poems.

At first, the critics debated whether or not the *Idylls*

pictured a glorious society through epic narrative or through the more stylized manner of the idyll. Somewhat later they began looking for allegories, especially those who were intent upon seeing the *Idylls* as a Sunday poem with didactic intent. Still later critics looked upon Tennyson's rich imagery as a kind of art-for-art's sake. Finally, all reviewers, from 1859 to the end of the century, involved themselves with analyzing characters as moral examples, usually with little concern for their function within the story.

The Question of Genre

Tennyson avoided the shortcomings of the Arthurian epic as well as the paean to the modern age by adopting a genre that Marshall McLuhan identifies as the epyllion.[3] It is, as McLuhan points out, a smaller form than the classical epic, and it relates more directly to the author's own milieu. (It is familiar to the modern reader because it has been used by Pound, Yeats, and Eliot.) The epyllion, or little epic, is a perfect form for juxtaposing past and present, ideal and real. The epyllion shares with the dramatic monologue a tenuous relation to the older and larger form from which it derives, and like the dramatic monologue it captures a moment within the larger action instead of portraying an extended story. The *Idylls* is a series of epyllia, revealing moments from the history of the Round Table told through flashbacks.

The critics of the time were not aware of the methods Tennyson used. It was left to an American, Edmund Clarence Stedman, to conclude that the *Idylls of the King* resembled not so much the formal idylls of Theocritus

but the "semi-epic" poems of his later career—"The Dio-
scuri," "The Infant Heracles," and "Heracles the Lion-
Slayer." [4] Many British critics of the *Idylls* tended to
consider the *Idylls* as being in the classical form and of
the epic tradition. Thus, the *Quarterly*, the *Times*, the
Edinburgh, and several others hailed the appearance of
the great British epic.[5] The reviewer for the *London
Quarterly*, in contrast, became bored with a work that
would not fit neo-classical categories and groaned over the
"so-called 'Idylls' of the Laureate,—perhaps as little
idyllic as any poems not in the least epic or dramatic can
be." [6] He was typical of a group that assumed Tennyson
was trying to compose an epic but believed that he could
not do it. The *Spectator,* on July 23, 1859, did praise
Tennyson for having "judiciously evaded" the problem
of giving epic unity to the romances "by foregoing the
attempt to construct an epos out of materials not naturally conformable to such a mode of treatment." *The
Saturday Review,* however, on July 16, asserted that a
modern epic is not possible. *Fraser's Magazine* in September argued against the idea proposed by the *Spectator,*
saying that the material is suited to epic treatment but
that Tennyson's forte is lyricism. A critic in the *National
Review* for October, 1859, disclaimed any conformity of
the *Idylls* to the epic tradition. *The Quarterly,* which
ran Gladstone's eulogy to the new epic in 1859, changed
its position in April, 1869, when the next volume of *Idylls*
appeared, and stated that Tennyson's modern peace-
loving temperament made him unable to compose an epic.
Arthur's farewell speech, the writer insists, sounds as if
the king had been attending Matthew Arnold's lectures
on the grand style. The modernity of the *Idylls* was sometimes attacked (as opposed to Mrs. Browning's appeal for
a modern epic) as unfitting to the epic form. *Blackwood's*

in November 1859 agreed that Tennyson did well to avoid the epic plan because only sublimely great poets could succeed in fulfilling it. Another critic for *Literary World* in the December 17, 1869 issue attacked the *Idylls* for *not* being relevant to modern life and called the *Idylls* a "fairy tale." The *Dublin University Magazine* for January 1869 saw a "tacit disclaimer of epic finish and sublimity" in the terms "idylls" itself. H. D. Traill, writing in *Nineteenth Century,* for December 1892, argued that the *Idylls* was a "morality-play of the human virtues and vices" with "none of the characteristics by which alone the epic *as such* can hope to live. . . ."

In summary, critics were unable to classify the *Idylls* clearly according to familiar categories. They produced a welter of opposing views as a result.

Symbolism in Motion

Just as his genre defies easy classification, Tennyson avoids the rigid, one-for-one correspondences of Bunyan and Spenser in his allegory, or what he called the "parabolic drift" in the Idylls. "I hate to be tied down to say, 'This means that,'" Tennyson protested, "because the thought within the image is much more than any one interpretation." [7] Tennyson's friends, James T. Knowles and Henry Alford, made known the "undertone of symbolism" in the *Idylls*. Knowles wrote a letter to *Spectator,* published January 1, 1870, giving perhaps the first commentary on symbolism in the work. Hallam recorded in the *Memoir,* "Mr. Knowles writes to me: 'He encouraged me to write a short paper, in the form of a letter to the *Spectator,* on the inner meaning of the whole poem, which I did, simply upon the lines he himself indicated. He often said, however, that an allegory should never be pressed too far." Henry Alford, the Dean of Canterbury, and a college friend of Hallam and Tennyson, wrote an article in the *Contemporary* for January, 1870 that gained wide recognition and influenced the later reviews.

Both Knowles and Alford, despite Tennyson's claiming no strict correspondence in his use of allegory, regard the king as a symbol for the self or soul and interpret the collapse of the Round Table as the shattering of the soul's dream of perfection by the conquest of the senses. Knowles goes as far as to see in Arthur's knights the strength of the body, in Merlin the power of intellect, in the Lady of the Lake the church, and in the three queens the three heavenly virtues. But when asked if the three queens "were" faith, hope, and charity, Tennyson replied, "They mean that, and they do not. They are three of the noblest of women. They are also those three Graces, but they are much more." [8] Knowles and Alford also stress the symbolic significance of actions in the poems —the conflict between spirit and flesh, the birth and death of the self, the "crowning of the soul" as the establishing of the ideal in man's life.

When Tennyson in his own words hinted at symbolic meanings, he tended to suggest a broad interpretation that includes but transcends Christian dogma. He described the whole story as "the dream of man coming into practical life and ruined by one sin. Birth is a mystery and death is a mystery, and in the midst lies the tableland of life, and its struggles and performances. It is not the history of one man or of one generation but of a whole cycle of generations." [9] Tennyson used his symbolism to give social meaning to the *Idylls* and not just to serve as a metaphor for the individual self. He was concerned more with historical processes, political idealisms, and social change. The central purpose of the symbolism is to broaden the meaning rather than to restrict it, to place the new Golden Age, with its smugness and dogmatisms, within the context of universals. Thus he sees the British empire of the nineteenth century in the light of centuries and millennia, with their fallen empires and ghostly dreams, and not merely against the background of recent progress. Whereas Spenser employs strict allegory in *The Faerie Queene* to magnify the Christian virtues and incorporates Arthurian legend into his poem to stress the religious consequences of sin, Tennyson employs a subtle background of symbolism to lend a sense of recurrence to the social errors he depicts.

J. H. Buckley defines Tennyson's parabolic drift as a "symbolism," with Arthur not so much equated to the Soul as being one who "bears the banner of the Soul." [10] His actions may be symbolic, but his character cannot be reduced to an abstraction. Otherwise, we should be faced with the absurdity of the Soul eliciting vows from the knights (calling on the strength of the body), marrying Guinevere (who, as Sense, would be still more anomalous, since she shows jealousy, anger, and final repentance), founding the Round Table (the tableland of life is hardly created by the soul), fighting the heathen, being betrayed by wife and friend, fighting the last battle against Modred, and returning his sword to the lake. The Soul could figuratively fight a last battle, but could it go to heaven after having been betrayed by Sense? Could Sense and Soul join in heaven? The *Idylls* would break down under the burden of allegorical explication.

The parabolic drift perhaps suggests that each of the idylls is a Victorian parable. Arthur and Guinevere, whose prototypes are Adam and Eve, might represent Victorian idealism and Victorian love of appearances.

"Merlin and Vivien," a Sampson and Delilah story, might give a warning against the power of instinct over intellect —a subject that was of great concern to Darwin. The grail quest, reminiscent of the worship of the golden calf, condemns the excesses of nineteenth-century religion; and the last battle, clearly a parallel to the biblical account of the end of the world, is a vision of modern society's evils carried to unlimited extremes.

The *Edinburgh* in April, 1886 argued that Tennyson teaches "living lessons by the universality of the humanity he portrays," without veiling his characters "in the dim transparency of the Spenserian allegory." True as this comment might be, it ignored the particular relevance of the stories to the Victorian reader and his society: Tristram's naturalistic philosophy, Guinevere's reliance upon sensationalism, Arthur's blind utopian optimism, Vivien's lewdness (which, as we have learned, was also a powerful undercurrent in Victorian life), Elaine's hopeless altruism, Geraint's belief in masculine domination, and the faith-healing mentality of the knights on the grail quest. Perhaps the symbolic meaning of the *Idylls* was hidden to contemporary reviewers by its very obviousness. Taking their own society's temper as a norm, they failed to experience the peculiarly "Victorian" quality of the *Idylls*.

Again, as in the controversy over the genre of the *Idylls*, an American, viewing the Victorian milieu from without, gave one of the most balanced interpretations of how Tennyson intended to use his allegory. Conde B. Pallen cautions against the temptation to "look for an allegory in every passage, a symbol in every line, a mystery in every syllable, a hidden meaning in every image." [11] Pallen stresses that the social events rather than static details are the vehicle of symbolism; the marriage of Arthur and Guinevere, for instance, suggests the union of spirit and flesh, and the grail quest warns against straying from social aims into private mysticisms. Pallen gives an interesting interpretation of the changing from the old order to the new as Arthur's passing from life in the world to "a new order beyond space and time."

Twentieth-century critics have generally assumed the parabolic drift to be a subtler matter than the more enthusiastic allegory-hunters of Tennyson's time thought it to be. Paull F. Baum takes a complex view of the symbolism.[12] S. C. Burchell finds a "certain shiftiness" in Tennyson's statements about allegory but believes that the Idylls succeeds in making an outcry against modern life.[13] Tennyson in the *Idylls* makes an outcry against Victorian England much as T. S. Eliot does against twentieth-century England in *The Waste Land*. Burchell touches on the essential link between Tennyson and Eliot when he call the *Idylls* "the biography of a wasted civilization."[14] Waste for Eliot is symbolized in the actual waste products of civilization; Tennyson reminds us of the waste of human resources through the innumerable instances in the *Idylls* of throwing away (Guinevere casts away the infinitely precious diamonds; the grail quest is a throwing away of the opportunities of the Round Table) and hoarding, which is the reverse form of waste (Pellam's castle presents hoarding of spiritual value; Geraint possessively clutches Enid's love; and Arthur through his "one will" holds together the Round Table as a rigid state of being, which is a pathology in the world of becoming).

In summary, Tennyson's allegory reminds us of what is gone. A function of the whole movement of the *Idylls*, and not a system of iconography, the symbolism is a "drift" or direction of meaning—a kind of symbolism in motion, eluding definition and blurred to the fixed stare of Christian allegorists, literary realists, and scientific historians.

Exquisite Cabinet Pictures

As the world of Camelot darkens into cynicism and betrayal, it never becomes less beautiful. Its November sadness and winter mists are possibly even lovelier than the golden radiance of "Gareth and Lynette." It is a generic quality of Arthurian romance that it conveys particularly well a writer's vision of the perfect world; the texture of life portrayed in the legends is woven with the rich threads of faith, love, adventure, and hope. The contrast between an imaginary Camelot and the real world is, to the extent of the difference, a criticism of the writer's society. Beauty in the *Idylls*, however, cuts two ways: it is, like Pugin's *Contrasts,* a reminder of the increasing uglification of the English landscape caused by industrialism; it is also a warning that beauty, except in the Golden Age, which does not exist, is not to be equated to goodness. Guinevere is the fairest of all flesh on earth, and Arthur, thinking that he can make the world live by the ways of the Golden Age, trusts her without question, as he trusts Lancelot, the most splendid knight of the world, "to the death." They betray him, but Dagonet, the ugly mock-knight of the Table Round, is loyal to the king beyond all sanity.

The favorite phrase the Victorian reviewers used to describe the visual effects of the *Idylls* was "cabinet pictures." [15] The reviewers noted the resemblance between the landscape of Camelot and the English landscape, but they did not see that Tennyson was pointing out the deterioration of its beautiful appearance and the deteriorating moral condition as a warning against the decay of beauty as well as ideals in their own civilization. Again, Tennyson points up the value of what is being lost instead of merely glorifying what is presently enjoyed. His images carry a kind of ironic force, undermining rather than supporting the beautiful illusion to which King Arthur clings. One senses in the reviewers who happily pointed out the mirror image of their own lovely countryside in the *Idylls* the same kind of blindness to what is really happening that King Arthur suffers as his realm slips from his grasp.

Everywhere beauty is deceitful. April's beauty leads Guinevere into the illusory belief that Lancelot is a better man than Arthur; her beauty leads Lancelot to betray honor, and later in turn to pursue the beautiful grail and its false promise of salvation; Lancelot's knightly beauty deceives Elaine, who dies in the fantasy that he is perfect. Yet the churl in "The Last Tournament," "his visage ribb'd/From ear to ear with dogwhip weals, his nose/Bridge-broken, one eye out, and one hand off" (lines 57-59), his ugliness marring the beautiful fall landscape, is honest and tells Arthur the ugly truth about the Red Knight. King Arthur puts down the ugliness of the barbaric world threatening Camelot, but the illusion that his Order was inwardly as beautiful as it continued to be on the surface prevents him from maintaining a beautiful society. In the end he must confess that there is less evidence of the divine within his Order than in external nature:

. . . I found Him in the shining of the stars,
I mark'd Him in the flowering of His fields,
But in His ways with men I find Him not . . .
O me! for why is all around us here
As if some lesser god had made the world,
But had not force to shape it as he would,
Till the High God behold it from beyond,
And enter it, and make it beautiful?
Or else as if the world were wholly fair,
But that these eyes of men are dense and dim,
And have not power to see it as it is—
Perchance, because we see not to the close. . . .
                ("The Passing of Arthur," lines 9-21)

Perhaps Tennyson has in mind Saturn's inability to make the Golden Age endure after he had tried to create it where men are barbarous. The "High God" (which alone is capitalized) is the divinity that shapes our ends. Arthur's utopian ambition rested upon a faith in a lesser god; Tennyson seems to be saying that the golden year is not within human power to maintain, since not even a perfect king can make men of beasts. The fool Dagonet correctly sees that Arthur's attempt to make society perfect has been a kind of overreaching; the king "Conceits himself as God . . ." ("The Last Tournament," line 365). He has tried to do the work that only the unfathomable deity can perfect, and like the imitations of that work by lesser gods, his Round Table was at the mercy of the High God, who made it perfect for a fleeting instant and pronounced judgment upon it through the holy grail when it failed.

Tennyson does not use a rich texture in the *Idylls* just for description but as a way to convey an important meaning. He implies to us the idea that man's desire for a union of sense and spirit, beauty and truth, cannot be fulfilled perfectly on earth but must remain a lofty ideal. Arthur and Guinevere are to be united in heaven as they could not be on earth, where the eyes of each were dim to the other's dreams. Tennyson uses the imagery of nature, which to the Victorians was recognizably English, to bring this universal idea to bear upon contemporary society, warning that blind moral purpose, whether it be evangelical reform or utilitarian progress, too often sacrifices beauty to its goals, but that the worship of beauty alone (perhaps Tennyson means the philosophy of sensationalism and the art-for-art's-sake movement) vitiates life by draining off its masculine energy. The Round Table is an ideal of both beauty and heroism; Guinevere is absolutely necessary to Arthur's dream of the Golden Age.

The *Idylls* as poetry remains beautiful, even while portraying the increasing corruption of Camelot. The poetry reminds us of the High God's power to incorporate ugliness within beauty (the king asks the churl, "Man was it who marr'd heaven's image in thee thus?"; the churl is still "My, churl, for whom Christ died . . ." "The Last Tournament," lines 62-64).

Tennyson's imagery is indeed complex, but the reviewers tended to see it as similar to Sir Walter Scott's lavish but simpler texture. Much of the criticism varied between two extremes—the aesthetes regarded the *Idylls* as beautiful pictures valued for their aesthetic properties (and even marred by moral significance)—and the puritanical critics disapproved of indulgence in the senses and wanted the *Idylls* to be an austere moral lesson. The dichotomy, ironically, is a symptom of the very failure that Camelot presents, the alienation of beauty from social purpose, or, figuratively, the failure to make culture prevail.

It is perhaps too extreme to argue that Tennyson's characters exist for the scenery, but on occasion his pictorial effects take on an importance that rivals that of the characters. Robert Browning was unhappy over this tendency in the *Idylls;* he wrote to Isa Blagden:

> Well, I go with you a good way in the feeling about Tennyson's new book: It is all out of my head already. We look at the art of poetry so differently! Here is an Idyll about a knight being untrue to his friend and yielding to the temptation of his friend's mistress after having engaged to assist him in his suit. I should judge the conflict of the knight's soul the proper subject to describe. Tennyson thinks he should describe the castle, and the effect of the moon on its towers, and anything *but* the soul. . . .[16]

But Tennyson could not make the moment in "The Coming of Arthur" that Browning disparages dramatically intense without marring his purpose to portray the life and death of the Round Table. Tennyson deliberately keeps the meeting of Lancelot and Guinevere at a distance from the happy founding of the Order; and we can never be sure at any moment how far the relationship of Lancelot and Guinevere has gone.[17] Otherwise, we should have a drama about Lancelot—a completely different kind of poem from the *Idylls.* The springtime setting is not irrelevant so much as deceptive.

Many of Tennyson's details troubled the reviewers. Some, for instance, were upset by the poet's emphasis upon Enid's dress. *Blackwood's* cryptically commented, "We should humbly beg the Laureate for the future to

tell us more of the maiden and less of her clothes—more
of the wedding, if he will, and less of the trousseau." [18]
Less typical was the praise of the *Macmillan's* writer,
which approaches the opposite extreme, arguing that
Tennyson puts man "more or less in the background; he
is studied rather as a part of the landscape than in himself.
So again, the passage in the *Mabinogion,* when Enid is
being arrayed for the wedding, . . . is the sole germ in
the prose story of all that beautiful portion of the poem
respecting the faded silk and the costly dress, so full of
meaning, and which brings out so exquisitely the character of Enid, and which connects so skillfully the two
phases of her history." [19]

Most of the reviewers were intent upon deciding
whether pictorial poetry was good or bad and not upon
determining what Tennyson does with his imagery. One
writer saw a moral lesson implied in such images as "the
useful trouble of the rain on the flat meadows and sedgy
streams of our midlands." [20] The *Times* praised Tennyson
for paring down the "gorgeous pictures" of his earlier
poems to achieve the "moral effect that belongs to genuine simplicity." [21] A Lincolnshire clergyman who signed
himself D. R. similarly praised Tennyson for his fidelity
to Lincolnshire landscape, but was unhappy to find such
images as that of great waters dropping flat for half a
league employed to dramatize the fall of such a wicked
man as the Red Knight. The reverend did not find an
appropriateness in Tennyson's describing the power of
nature just before he depicts Arthur's own knights pillag-
ing like beasts ("The Last Tournament," lines 460-480).[22]
Tennyson uses the images in the later *Idylls* to announce
the Nemesis overtaking Arthur: Arthur has ignored the
natural instincts of his queen and knights, and in the
end Nature takes its vengeance almost like a Satanic

personage opposing the Round Table. Bestial images in particular, as well as images of the omnipotent ocean, reappear like Wagnerian leitmotifs proclaiming the triumph of the beast in man over Arthur, who, like Saturn, prizes gentleness—"overprizes," says Balin "the Savage." ("Balin and Balan," line 180). The drama in the *Idylls* is not only within Lancelot's soul, but also beyond human action—a clash of Manichean forces of nature and civilization comparable to the gods and goddesses in the *Iliad*. Thus there is an element of truth in the *British Quarterly's* assertion that the poet holds his subject at "painting distance." [23]

Although the *London Quarterly* found his "formist discipline" of merit,[24] the more typical response was to notice the pictorial richness of the *Idylls*. Walter Bagehot was no doubt partly responsible for the widespread notion that Tennyson was a decorative poet. In his review of *Enoch Arden* Bagehot characterized Tennyson as an "ornate" poet, and the classification stuck.[25] Browning may have had Bagehot's view in mind when he disparaged the *Idylls*, and the *Quarterly* complained that the *Idylls* give the effect of "ornateness" because "the hand of the artist is manifest." [26] The reviewer holds up Malory's simplicity as a contrast to Tennyson. The critic of the *Times* in 1869, however, changed his opinion from what the paper had argued in 1859; he favored the "pictorial touches" in the *Idylls*, particularly in "The Holy Grail," over the simpler quasi-epic style of "The Coming of Arthur." [27] Although comment on the purpose of the imagery seldom was made, each reviewer had his opinion of the quantity of description poetry ought to contain.[28]

Swinburne, in his classic attack on the *Idylls*, plays the gadfly and does Tennyson a great service by pointing out the difference between the effect of his images and the meaning of his story. While his intention is to condemn the moral idea of the *Idylls* without appeal and then to find a redeeming element in the power of Tennyson's imagery, Swinburne unwittingly points up a fact about the *Idylls* that other critics in their adulation overlooked. First Swinburne unleashes his brilliant sarcasm on Tennyson's moral teaching:

> They [the real enemies of Tennyson] are the men who find in his collection of Arthurian idyls,—the Morte d'Albert as it might perhaps be more properly called, after the princely type to which (as he tells us with just pride) the poet has been fortunate enough to make his central figure successfully conform,—an epic poem of profound and exalted morality.
>
> It seems to me that the moral tone of the Arthurian story has been on the whole lowered and degraded by Mr. Tennyson's mode of treatment. Wishing to make his central figure the noble and perfect symbol of an ideal man, he has removed not merely the excuse but the explanation of the fatal and tragic loves of Launcelot and Guenevere. The hinge of the whole legend of the Round Table, from its first glory to its final fall, is the incestuous birth of Mordred from the connexion of Arthur with his half-sister, unknowing and unknown; as surely as the hinge of the Oresteia from first to last is the sacrifice at Aulis . . . Remove in either case the plea which leaves the heroine less sinned against indeed than sinning, but yet not too base for tragic compassion and interest, and there remains merely the presentation of a vulgar adulteress . . . Mr. Tennyson has lowered the tone and deformed the outline of the Arthurian story, by reducing Arthur

to the level of a wittol, Guenevere to the level of a
woman of intrigue, and Launcelot to the level of a
"correspondent." . . . The courteous and loyal
Gawain of the old romancers . . . is here a vulgar
traitor . . . The Vivien of Mr. Tennyson's idyl seems
to me, to speak frankly, about the most base and
repulsive person ever set forth in literature.[29]

But in his essay for the *Fortnightly* entitled "Tennyson
and Musset," Swinburne makes a favorable comment on
the imagery of the *Idylls*. After ridiculing Tennyson's
moral tone once again, he extols the unmatchable power
of the laureate's images:

Many years ago, as I have always remembered, on the
appearance of the first four *Idylls of the King*, one
of the greatest painters living pointed out to me,
with a brief word of rapturous admiration, the wonderful breadth of beauty and the perfect force of
truth in a single verse of "Elaine"—"And white sails
flying on the yellow sea." I could not but feel
conscious at once of its charm, and of the equally
certain fact that I, though cradled and reared beside
the sea, had never seen anything like that. But on
the first bright day I ever spent on the eastern coast
of England I saw the truth of this touch at once, and
recognised once more with admiring delight the subtle and sure fidelity of that happy and studious hand.
There, on the dull yellow foamless floor of dense dis-
coloured sea, so thick with clotted sand that the water
looked massive and solid as the shore, the white sails
flashed whiter against it and along it as they fled:
and I knew once more the truth of what I never had
doubted—that the eye and the hand of Mr. Tennyson may always be trusted, at once and alike, to see

and to express the truth. But he must have learnt the more splendid lesson of the terrors and the glories of the Channel before he caught the finest image ever given in his verse—the likeness of a wave "green-glimmering from its summit"—with "all/Its stormy crests that smoke against the skies." [30]

The terrors and glories of nature in the *Idylls* are as romantic as the storms of Shelley or the ocean of Byron. But the *Idylls* is not a romantic poem—to Swinburne's unspeakable dismay—because the human ideal Tennyson puts forth is a turning-away from the romanticists' identification of nature with morality and toward a view of man in opposition to nature. Matthew Arnold states the precise relationship of man to nature that Tennyson, with his realistic social conscience, sees:

> Know, man hath all which Nature hath, but
>   more,
> And in that *more* lies all his hopes of good.
> Nature is cruel; man is sick of blood:
> Nature is stubborn; man would fain adore:
> Nature is fickle; man hath need of rest:
> Nature forgives no debt, and fears no grave;
> Man would be mild, and with safe conscience
>   blest.
> Man must begin, know this, were Nature ends;
> Nature and man can never be fast friends.
> Fool, if thou canst not pass her, rest her slave!
>   ("To an Independent Preacher")

And that is why the Golden Age, where man is in harmony with nature, must always remain a myth.

Swinburne is unfair to Tennyson, for the moral intent of the *Idylls* is not simply to lionize Prince Albert or preach Victorian commonplaces. King Arthur embodies an ancient and enduring hope of man first expressed in the myth of Saturn—the hope for a just and beautiful society where man can be what the iron laws of nature will not allow him to be. The real fault of the *Idylls* may be quite the opposite of what Swinburne charges: King Arthur, instead of not being romantic and swashbuckling enough, may too often approach the character of a romantic hero, may lapse into emotions that make us long for an Othello, who he can never be. Tennyson's occasional wish to make Arthur more romantically appealing than the romantic Lancelot may harm his greater purpose of depicting the serene beauty of a perfect superhuman creature broken against the rudeness of the real world.

Swinburne's comment on Tennyson's images is the best example of one kind of criticism Victorians made of the *Idylls*. It brings to light the sharp difference in sensibility between the two poets (Swinburne's *Tristram of Lyonesse* glorifies the iron grip of nature and fate over man) as well as the inner processes of the *Idylls*. Tennyson, however, would no doubt have been more upset over Swinburne's praise of his imagery as a kind of romantic indulgence than over his scorn for the moral tone of the *Idylls*. The *Idylls* was the center of the controversy between Tennyson and the aesthetes. Tennyson repudiated their attacks upon his inclusion of a moral idea in the work by writing the rather petulant satire, "Art-for-Art's-Sake," which he aimed particularly in Swinburne's direction. Swinburne, in reply, called the satire an "idiotic eructation of doggerel" and lamented "the intelligence which could 'hail' a proposition or a definition of a principle common to all arts whatever as 'truest lord of hell' " as "simply putid: stupid is no word for it." [31]

In a literary climate more conducive to patient, objective examination of a poet's thought the controversy between Tennyson and Swinburne might have alerted Tennyson's admirers to the complexities of both the moral meaning and the nature imagery in the *Idylls* and led them to the awareness that Tennyson's pessimism, as expressed in *Maud,* had not changed but rather had increased to encompass an image of the whole Victorian world in dissolution. However, the *Edinburgh,* as sound and objective as any journal of the day, still continued, in 1886, to regard the *Idylls* as the reflection of a secure, beautiful, and happy England. Perfectly describing the imagery but not the spirit and meaning of the *Idylls,* its reviewer writes of Tennyson:

> If he has chiselled his clear-cut classic figures on the cold but lasting marble, he has also caught and transmuted into fixed beauty many of the shifting, shapeless features of modern society. If he has embodied abstract grace and goodness in an ideal world, he has yet painted realistic pictures of contemporary England, in which, amid a glow of local colour, he has caught the true spirit of rural life, and set them in frames jewelled with gems of natural description. . . . There runs through all his verse an identity of thought and treatment which proves this reproduction of different forms to be the exercise not of an imitative faculty but of a catholic sympathy, not merely the birth of a keen sensibility to beauty, but the outpourings of a heart which has pondered deeply on the prime duties and interest of mankind. . . . What seems to be mere description helps the general impression, and enforces the internal contrast. It is a fine accord between the world of

sense and the world of soul; the inward emotions are blended with the external signs.[32]

For a criticism of a work that, as the poet explicitly says, shadows "Sense at war with Soul," ("Epilogue," "To the Queen," line 37) this is rather wishful thinking. The poet described sounds like Wordsworth, and the romantic optimism of the writer belongs to a different world from that of Tennyson. The aesthetic criticisms of the *Idylls* were a collective exercise in self-delusion; the reviewers' love of what they wanted the *Idylls* to reproduce only furthers the truth of what Tennyson does imply about the England of his day.

Notes

1. *British Quarterly*, XXX (1859), 507.
2. Elizabeth Barrett Browning, "Aurora Leigh," Fifth Book, lines 151-222. *The Poetical Works of E. B. Browning* (London: Macmillan, 1897), 421-422.
3. Marshall McLuhan, "Tennyson and the Romantic Epic," *Critical Essays on the Poetry of Tennyson* (New York: Barnes & Noble, 1960), 86-95.
4. Stedman, *Victorian Poets* (New York, 1888), 205-233.
5. *Quarterly* (by Gladstone), CVI (October 1859), 471-483; the *London Times*, September 10, 1859, 5, and December 23, 1869, 4; *Edinburgh*, CX (July 1859), 247-258, and "The Epic of Arthur," *Edinburgh*, CXXXI (1870), 504-537.
6. "The Laureate and his 'Arthuriad,'" *London Quarterly*, XXXIX (January 1873), 400.
7. *Memoir*, II, 127.
8. *Ibid.*, II, 127.
9. *Ibid.*, II, 127.
10. Buckley, *Tennyson, the Growth of a Poet* (Boston, 1960), 176–177.
11. Pallen was rewarded with a note about the *Idylls* from the Laureate saying, "You see further into their meaning than

most of my commentators have done." Conde B. Pallen, *The Meaning of the Idylls of the King* (New York, 1904), 5, 15-19, 23, 104.

12. Paull F. Baum, *Tennyson Sixty Years After* (Chapel Hill, 1948), 176-213.

13. S. C. Burchell, "Tennyson's 'Allegory in the Distance,'" *PMLA, LXVIII* (1953), 418-424.

14. *Ibid.*, 424.

15. Alfred Austin, "The Poetry of Tennyson," *Temple Bar*, XXVI (May 1869), 181. Austin coined the phrase "exquisite cabinet pictures," and it expressed particularly well one (usually pejorative) notion of the *Idylls*. A writer in the *Spectator*, XLII (December 25, 1869), 1531, says that the *Idylls* have risen from "exquisite cabinet pictures" into a great epic.

16. Robert Browning, letter to Isa Blagden (January 19, 1870), printed for private circulation by Richard Clay & Sons, Ltd. (London, 1920).

17. Tennyson makes flaws in the ideal society much harder to detect than does Malory. In Malory Merlin even warns Arthur before he marries that Guenevere would fall in love with Launcelot.

18. *Blackwood's*, LXXXVI (November 1859), 611.

19. J. M. Ludlow, "Moral Aspects of Mr. Tennyson's Idylls of the King," *Macmillan's*, I (November 1859), 68. Chrétien makes a great deal more of Enid's apparel than does the Celtic story; Tennyson probably drew this detail from the French story instead of creating it wholly from the passage in the *Mabinogion*. "Erec et Enide," *Arthurian Romances of Chrétien de Troyes*, trans. W. W. Comfort (New York: Everyman Library, 1965), 6-7, 18, 21, 88.

20. *British Quarterly*, XXX (1859), 504-505.

21. *London Times* (September 10, 1859), 3.

22. "Lincolnshire Scenery and Character as Illustrated by Mr. Tennyson," *Macmillan's*, XXIX (December 1873), 140-142.

23. *British Quarterly*, XXX (1859), 504.

24. *London Quarterly*, XIII (October 1859), 66.

25. Walter Bagehot, "Wordsworth, Tennyson, and Browning: or Pure, Ornate, and Groteque Art in English Poetry," *National Review*, XIX (1864), 27.

26. *Quarterly*, CXXVIII (January 1870), 2-10.

27. *London Times* (December 23, 1869), 4.

28. Commentary on Tennyson's imagery is made in the following: *Quarterly*, CVI (October 1859), 481; *Bentley's Quarterly*, II (October 1859), 164; *Eclectic*, CX (September 1859), 292; John

Nichol, *Westminster*, n.s. XVI (October 1859), 504-528; *Dublin University Magazine*, LV (January 1860), 63; Henry Alford, *Contemporary*, XIII (January 1870), 104; James T. Knowles, *Spectator*, XLIII (January 1, 1870), 16; *Edinburgh*, CXXXI (April 1870), 502; T. H. Leary, "Tennyson's Last Tournament," *Gentleman's Magazine*, n.s. VIII (March 1872), 424-427; *Victoria Magazine*, XX (February 1873), 308; "The Meaning of King Arthur," *Contemporary*, XXI (May 1873), 939-941. The following books comment on the subject: John Churton Collins, *Illustrations of Tennyson* (London, 1891), 117-118; C. B. Pallen, *The Meaning of the Idylls of the King* (New York, 1904), 7-10; Henry Elsdale, *Studies in the Idylls* (London, 1878), *passim;* Walter Wace, *Alfred Tennyson, His Life and Works* (Edinburgh, 1881), 105-106. A number of these reviews and books discuss the seasonal imagery, Leary's article on "The Last Tournament" being apparently the first to mention it, followed by more lengthy comment in the *Victoria* review; the article entitled "The Meaning of King Arthur" in the *Contemporary;* Wace's book, which paraphrases the *Contemporary* article; and, most extensive of all, Elsdale's book.

29. Swinburne, *Under the Microscope* (London, 1872), 36-41.
30. Swinburne, "Tennyson and Musset," *Fortnightly*, XXXV (February 1, 1881), 152-153.
31. Swinburne, "Changes of Aspect," *New Writings by Swinburne*, ed. Cecil Lang (Syracuse, Syracuse University Press, 1964), 67. The satire is quoted in the *Memoir*, II, 92.
32. *Edinburgh*, CLXIII (April 1886), 488-489.

4.

The Gauntlet
of Criticism
II: Dramatis Personae

The "Bad" Characters

Tennyson makes his characters fit types or ego-ideals of the Victorian era. They tend to fall easily into the Victorian categories of good and bad, but an important fact about the *Idylls* is that Tennyson refuses to type the seemingly wicked characters as villains or to exempt the virtuous from error or defects. Although Tennyson's moral scheme has a clear polarity of abstract good and evil, and although the *Idylls* warns against both the neglect of Arthur's ideals and the dangers of figures like Modred and Vivien, an equally important implication of the poem is that in real society a melodramatic belief in heroes and villains is dangerously inadequate as a measure of human character. We are continually called upon to change our point of view while reading the *Idylls,* and

81

we also must reverse the moral relationships that seemed absolute a moment before. Tennyson has deliberately thwarted the Victorian tendency toward rigid moralism; hence most of the reviewers were convinced that Tennyson could have improved the poem by further punishing or removing the bad and rewarding and exalting the good.

A world of eminent Victorians, Arthur's kingdom is a land where people's minds are made up. Their rigidity is a partial cause of the tragedy. Edyrn's reform, Geraint's regaining of faith, both paralleled by Guinevere's repentance, stand out in contrast to Elaine's unquestioning love, Gareth's irrepressible devotion, the absolute vows of the grail knights, Vivien's incorrigible destructiveness, Enid's perfect honor, Ettarre's unyielding coldness, Tristram's unqualified cynicism, Modred's eternal sullenness, Arthur's impenetrable blindness.

These rigid characters always see half of the truth. Vivien obstinately ignores true goodness but understands the imperfections of the Order, as much as she exaggerates them, when Arthur does not. And the king's faultlessness seems to Tristram and momentarily to the queen all fault; from a purely naturalistic standpoint they are right. Yet they are as blind to the parts they have played in the downfall of the Order as Arthur is to fact that he has allowed it to happen. It is particularly ironic that King Arthur should criticize those who have no desire to see, for in judging others he condemns part of his own behavior.

Yet the *Idylls,* though the prophet proves a fool and jesters prove prophets, does not leave us in a morass of relativism. Tennyson reminds his reader of the complexity of modern life and the difficulty of maintaining an ideal where naive loyalties and commitments are dangerous. But this is only to underline the importance of an ideal, or at least of striving to find one. Tennyson seems to advocate a humanistic standard of flexibility and insight, of citizenship without utopian delusions, of intelligence without reliance upon rigid intellectual systems. The "golden" mean is Tennyson's intellectual ideal, and all things "golden" denote his ideal moral tone. Golden implies friendship instead of hostile rivalry, trustworthiness rather than betrayal, love and not hostility, heroism (the "golden deeds" of "The Last Tournament," line 100) instead of cowardice, charity as opposed to hoarding and wasting. The figures in the *Idylls* are ultimately judged by the quality of their characters and not by the defensibility of their acts.

But the reviewers tended to regard the characters as moral examples that could be taken out of context and praised or reprimanded for their behavior. "Vivien" was the first idyll completed, and Benjamin Jowett called it "the naughty one."[1] Although he liked it best, most reviewers did not; it was a daring beginning for a work that was expected to be the laureate's masterpiece and a tribute to the age. For even those who thought highly of the idyll tended to find Vivien deplorable. *Blackwood's* saw Vivien's "vulgarity" as one more sign of the corruption it saw everywhere; in a bizarre note of Victorian self-consciousness, its reviewer wrote:

We tremble now and then for the fate of the nineteenth century in the hands of some future Macaulay. He will have no difficulty in giving us a very bad character, if he ground his judgment on such facts as the admitted popularity of "Traviata," and the passing of the Divorce Bill. And we fear that he will find some additional evidence against us in the very book we are now considering; in those coarse passages in "Vivien," of which we have already hinted our strong disapproval.[2]

Vivien was a challenge to respectability, and many reviewers flaunted their respectability by belittling her.[3] The Victorian habit of eliminating all reference to sexuality from public discussion led many reviewers to remain silent about Vivien while extolling the dignity of the *Idylls* in general. "Subtle" and "art" were the words most often employed to describe Vivien when she was mentioned, both connoting an area of feelings that respectability feared.[4] The Victorians were really embarrassed by Vivien because they regarded the *Idylls* as a mirror of their own polite, moral, middle-class milieu and not as a larger humanistic work that might comment upon their narrowness. If the *Idylls* did not depart radically enough from middle-class morality for Swinburne's taste, it went rather too far for most other critics.

For the modern reader the appalling fact in the story is not the supposedly bad taste that would portray such a harlot as Vivien in serious poetry, but the idea that the great sage, whose combination of practical intelligence and idealism is the last hope for the Order, knowing the reason he must not yield the charm to Vivien, even sensing his own stupidity in not being able to resist her obvious gambits and erotic provocation, throws himself away and leaves his vast intellect in the rubbish heap with the other wasted human assets. The story shocks only by its irresistible truth.

The reviewers of the *Idylls* after 1869 tend to account for Vivien in terms of universals or parallels to un-English traits. One reviewer palliated the effect of her character by seeing her conquest of Merlin as "the story of Delilah with a difference." [5] This comment set the pattern for later criticism. The critics also likened Vivien to Milton's Satan (not his Sin, which is a closer parallel) and Keats' Lamia.[6] As Satan, she was the destroyer of the Golden World, or the "Eden of Camelot." [7] She is a potent force but not of the actively rebellious and heroic proportions of Satan; her nature is not that of a fallen angel but the portress of hell gate, able to seduce with attractive graces. Vivien's weapons are glib argument and sensuality.

One reviewer saw the relevance of Vivien to nineteenth-century society, but removed her from the Victorian world by saying she was a woman "of flesh and blood—alive at this hour in Paris." [8] Another writer decided that she was more fitted "for the court of Louis Quinze than for that of saintly chivalry." [9] One writer alone waggishly admitted to a "lurking kindness" for Vivien and found Merlin himself "worse than a rascal . . . namely, a bore." [10]

Swinburne again in his hostile way paid Tennyson the tribute of facing his work for what it was. Although it is amusing to hear Tennyson scolded for bad taste by the author of "The Leper" and *Lesbia Brandon,* Swinburne cuts through much of the hypocrisy of the Tennyson worshippers by pointing out that Byron and Musset had been reviled for portraying subjects less objectionable than "the cajoleries and caresses of a lissom Vivien." [11]

A number of Tennyson's other "bad" characters provoked hostile comment from the critics. Geraint, considered "utterly stupid" by one writer,[12] was condemned out of context as a bad human example. Some reviewers tried to find a respectable prototype for the Geraint idylls in Boccaccio's Griselda story.[13] Geraint is a kind of Victorian husband of the Murdstone variety; the reviewers either wanted to disclaim him or to overlook his suspicious, punitive character.

Tristram presented a different kind of problem for Victorian reviewers. The Tristram legend had already reached the height of its popularity as a romance with Wagner's opera in 1859. The public wanted the romance that Tennyson found lacking in the industrial world about him. Instead of portraying the love that overpowers the noblest impulses of a courtly hero and passionate woman, Tennyson presents a Tristram who is little more than a backwoods cynic. The romantic version of the story is implied as a contrast by the poet; his version is almost a Byronic wrecking of romantic sentiment, almost a travesty of the popular story. Its unpleasantness alone can reveal how bad Arthur's kingdom has become, and by voicing the cynicism of the idyll through the mouth of a famous romantic hero, Tennyson doubly underlines the condition of decay.

Swinburne charged that Tennyson "debased" the myth. (Again he ignores Tennyson's overall purpose in the *Idylls* while levelling a criticism that would be true of the story out of context.) Most critics ignored the character of Tristram; none praised Tristram, though he does defend himself well as a champion of free speech, free love, and worldly wisdom. The *London Quarterly,* which had become vitriolic in its criticism of the *Idylls,* wrote:

> Concerning the fine old romance of Tristram, and the inadequacy of such a treatment as the present to render the tragedy of the romance in its integrity, . . . we, with the reading world at large, must be content still to wait for *the* English version of

Tristram. . . . What Mr. Swinburne will make of
Tristram and Iseult he is at work upon, no one can
safely predict. . . . Whatever be the destinies of the
Tristram romance in the hands now reshaping it,
let us hope, at all events, that the chief character may
not be so depressed from all high standards of humanity as he is in this latest book of the Laureate's
. . . a commonplace man, of mere brute strength.[14]

A different critic, trying to save his milieu from Tennyson's censure as well, found a biblical prototype even
for Tristram: "Tristram comes next—with half of Lancelot left out of him—a second Esau—as bold, as careless,
as attractive, and as animal—and when he dies how fitting
is the swift, dark death that seems to abolish him and
his works." [15] But Tennyson's Tristram is not even as
romantic as the reviewer makes him; rather than a passionate force of nature, he is a modern man, a worldling
of the world, pretending to be a free, natural spirit and
debasing both the noble savage, which he can never be,
and the civilized man that he might have been. He embodies the self-deception Tennyson saw in the ethical
theories of naturalism.

Tennyson's queen was the greatest of challenges to
respectability, and despite the fact that she repents and
presumably goes to heaven, the reviewers tended to cate-
gorize her as a "bad" character. The climate of Victorian
England, still largely one of male dominion, tended to
react against Guinevere's beautiful plea for her own case.
No defense of her is necessary, for she is eloquent in her
own behalf:

Arthur, my lord, Arthur, the faultless King,
That passionate perfection, my good lord—

But who can gaze upon the sun in heaven?
He never spake a word of reproach to me,
He never had a glimpse of mine untruth,
He cares not for me. . . .
Rapt in this fancy of his Table Round,
And swearing men to vows impossible,
To make them like himself; but, friend, to me
He is all fault who hath no fault at all,
For who loves me must have a touch of earth;
The low sun makes the color. . . .

> ("Lancelot and Elaine," lines 121-134)

Even while she is repenting, Guinevere expresses compellingly the feelings that drew her away from the king:

I thought I could not breathe in that fine air,
That pure severity of perfect light—
I yearn'd for warmth and color which I found
In Lancelot—now I see thee what thou art,
Thou art the highest and most human too,
Not Lancelot, nor another.

> ("Guinevere," lines 640-645)

Her pleading itself was perhaps too outspoken for the reviewers, for the critics tended to blame the entire tragedy on the queen, as if the one sin that wrecked the dream of man in practical life were her doing and not Lancelot's as well, and as if Arthur's blindness and the whole social condition had nothing to do with the tragedy. Finding a scapegoat is a convenient way of rectifying a wrong that defies simple analysis.

The queen, in her defense of herself, as persuasive as it is, appears to be a sort of feminist. Lionel Tollemache, in an article dissecting Tennyson's political conservatism, disparages Guinevere in a way that ironically reveals Tollemache's own conservatism toward feminine rights. He cites a passage describing the repentant queen and foretelling her future in the nunnery. Tennyson sees in the queen a "golden" nature that, despite her errors, raises her above the commonplace. Tollemache sniffs, "Is it as a satirist that the poet tells us this; Doubtless, in those times, Guinevere's former rank would have told in her favor. Yet when we reflect how she had borne that rank, and why she lost it, it seems an odd reason for making her an abbess." [16] Many reviewers moralized in this fashion, though not often on political grounds.[17] The reviewers were often less willing to forgive Guinevere than is King Arthur himself, for she, in a different and still more telling way than Vivien, challenged their view of themselves and of their society.

The "Good" Characters

Tennyson wants us to remember that the Viviens, Modreds, and Marks, even though they triumph, are inferior to the golden race they bring to its destruction.

Lancelot was the most appealing character to the Victorians. "A man made to be loved," he resembles Shakespeare's Antony in having a high sense of honor that wars against his great capacity for pleasure. He is a complete man, without question a member of the golden race, and his salvation as a holy man in the end, although it seems an emasculation in human terms, is Tennyson's way of saving him from taint.

It is easy to sympathize with Browning's wish that Lancelot's conflicting emotions had been dramatized in the *Idylls*. But Tennyson has a wholly different purpose in mind. He makes Lancelot, like Arthur, a member of the highest clan; his similarity to Arthur is finally more important than his lapse into the ways of the iron age. Tennyson restores Lancelot with his character. For this reason his betrayal of Arthur, which he knows is beneath him, seems to be carried out without the passion of complete involvement. The most memorable scenes in which Lancelot appears show him less a demonic presence than a man out of his element—in fact, in disguise. In the garden scene in "Balin and Balan" he casts his eyes on earth before speaking to the queen, and his one discourtesy to Elaine is to look downward as she sees him depart. Arthur sees the homeless trouble in his eyes, for he is outside his true sphere, and in the scene where Guinevere casts the diamonds into the stream, he gazes downward in half disdain at all things in the world where even his good intentions destroy. Later the queen apologizes for her jealousy, and Lancelot, again with eyes cast down, forgives her. Unlike Malory's Launcelot, whose love for the queen is an ennobling experience and a chivalric example, Tennyson's protagonist is detached and a little passive, unable to change the fate that created a world which denies his wish for golden relationships. He does not delight in forbidden love, but yearns for a world where love and honor do not destroy each other. His sadness is Virgilian; his participation unwilling.

Blackwood's came close to describing how Tennyson conceived of Lancelot. Its reviewer wrote:

> Tennyson was no creator in the Shakespearian sense of the word . . . and yet to ourselves Lancelot gives place in the world, if to Hamlet, yet to him alone. There are some points in which he is more near and

touches us more deeply than even that prince of all our thoughts. . . . We know no such embodiment of high and fatal passion, of that extraordinary capacity of human nature, which sometimes can combine the sublime of noble character with deadly and degrading sin . . . as in the character of Lancelot of the Lake. . . . But Tennyson has dared to take up this blot and work it into the most noble, the most sad, the most wonderful of sinning men.[18]

One wonders if the reviewer really has Tennyson's Lancelot in mind, or the hero of the medieval romances, who is the combination of high passion and honor that is described. Tennyson's hero is not present often enough or vividly enough to merit a comparison to Hamlet, nor is he really a character of passion. He does not, as in Malory and the romances, fight desperately for the queen's life or live in constant apprehension of their guilt being discovered. "When did not rumors fly?" ("Lancelot and Elaine," line 1187) he asks Guinevere, his general malaise toward the fallen world preventing him from feeling great alarm, just as it prevents him from taking any passionate involvement in either love or honor.

The pejorative advice of the *Quarterly* had less praise for Tennyson than did *Blackwood's,* when their critic wrote:

Lancelot ought to have been much more seriously and fully drawn than he is: in his person is the centre of the tragedy; in his heart is the key of the failure of the ideal plan; we must needs sympathize with him, we must needs condemn him. Through him it is that, as far as the society around him is concerned, the evil is victorious, and chaos returns

where there had for a moment been a spark of
light. . . . The event, then, has the essence of tragedy;
Fate, that is something terrible and unknown, is
the agent of the calamity; . . . and it would have
been well worth the while of a poet to draw out
the terribleness of such a contrast, such a law as this;
to show the rigour of necessity as opposed to the
softness of our hearts. But this is beyond Mr. Tennyson's power.[19]

Had the reviewer said "different from his purpose" instead of "beyond Mr. Tennyson's power," his case would
have been stronger. Malory's story is much like that described by the writer. Launcelot is a passionate, dramatic
hero caught between two powerful impulses. But Tennyson portrays a Lancelot whose golden nature keeps him
from this passionate involvement. Lancelot remains aloof
because he has submitted to fate, mistakenly, and Tennyson proves that fate does not prevent human beings from
directing events. Lancelot allows Elaine to die and the
rumors to spread more easily than necessary (Balin's over-
hearing the garden conversation, for example, which was
not unpreventable, eventually brings about the death of
both Balin and Balan). Tennyson does not portray man
in the iron grip of fate because he does not believe that
man can ignore the power of his own choice. Both Guinevere and Lancelot choose their love for each other; they,
like Arthur, belong by nature to the golden world where
they can make free choices without incurring tragic consequences. They can be saved only by their natures and
by their transcendence of this world, for in real society
their acts are far from ideal.

In his lyric "Sir Galahad," Tennyson straightfor-
wardly idealizes Galahad, but in the *Idylls* he presents

him as only one of the several golden people whose presence in an imperfect society is out of place. Each has his own Victorian way of trying to live in a world below his greatness: Arthur's is the way of the evangelist; he tries to make men like himself; Guinevere is a kind of aesthete, wishing for a private cultivation of the feelings; Lancelot is a fatalist, aloof from a world he never made. Galahad does not compromise as Lancelot does; his is the way of the mystic—to make no terms with the world but to condemn it by leaving it for a better. King Arthur does not disparage Galahad for vowing to pursue the grail; its promise of the return of the Golden Age is not a delusion for him. Still, Galahad's ideality proves a destructive example for the other knights, whose hope for a magical return of the golden days of the Order through the healing power of the grail only makes recovery impossible.

Tennyson uses Galahad's disappearance not as an example but as a warning or judgment; he makes Galahad analogous to Astrea, the maiden deity who represents justice and flees the world after the passing of the Golden Age. For the Victorian readers to regard Galahad as the Victorian champion was to commit the very act of hubris Tennyson cautions against. Tennyson considers Galahad a rare kind of hero and a dangerous example for ordinary men. The fact that Galahad's perfection is gained only at great cost to the Order was of less interest to the Victorians than the goodness of Galahad in itself. Many reviewers regarded the moment of his disappearance as the high point of the *Idylls* and tended to see Galahad's purity rather than Arthur's ethic of work (which itself must even be seen as having its irony) as the finest ethical message in the *Idylls*.

Blackwood's implored Tennyson in 1859 to tell continued adventures of Galahad in the *Idylls,* or the "noble type of true Christian chivalry—of that work of heaven on earth which only pure hearts can love, only clean hands do!" [20] However, when Tennyson did include Galahad in the next series of idylls, he showed instead the inability of heavenly hands to do God's work on earth. Another reviewer erroneously conjectured that if Tennyson were to include Galahad in the *Idylls,* the grail story would fade into the background and Galahad's pure character would be seen "in conflicts and aspirations less exceptional than his ecstatic wanderings in search of the mysterious treasure." [21] The *British Quarterly* believed that Galahad if included would eclipse Arthur.[22]

It is a sad paradox that the laureate, worshipped by the larger part of the English-speaking world as the spokesman of current beliefs, should at last present the public with the large work it hoped for, and on the subject it loved, only to find his central passage disregarded and his social message generally misunderstood. Even Robert Browning wrote, "The old 'Galahad' is to me incomparably better than a dozen centuries of the 'Grail,' 'Coming of Arthur,' and so on. I ought to be somewhat surprised to hear myself thinking so, since it seems also the opinion of everybody: even the reviews hardly keep on the old chime of laudation." [23] Tennyson did not flatter his age or please the taste of his public by exaggerating the position of a Galahad in the real world; his public repaid him with its disapproval.

King Arthur drew a favorable response from almost all the reviewers, except Swinburne, who made discordant sallies against the "Morte d'Albert," or "Idylls of the Prince Consort." Swinburne closed his Tennyson and opened his Malory, there to escape from the "poor, mean, paltry, petty, almost base" king of the *Idylls* to find a "gallant, honest, kindly, sinful creature" who "strikes home to the human heart." [24] Again Swinburne sharply focuses the difference between his conception of the Arthurian tragedy and Tennyson's.

Swinburne envisioned a classical tragedy based on Malory, in which Arthur's initial sin (Modred is Arthur's illegitimate son in the *Morte Darthur*) overtakes him. He therefore regarded Tennyson's king as priggish rather than tragic and found Tennyson's dedication to Prince Albert as "Scarce other than my king's ideal knight" hilarious proof that Tennyson could not portray King Arthur tragically. Swinburne's case against Tennyson's use of Malory is cogent, but he did not first prove, as he should have, that his classical notion of tragedy could be applied effectively to the story of the Round Table. Modred in the *Morte Darthur* is not really an important agent of fate, nor does Malory emphasize Arthur's sexual immorality as a cause of his later downfall. Swinburne does not do justice to Tennyson's portrayal of nemesis overtaking the whole Arthurian society, including the king. King Arthur's weakness in the *Idylls*—his excessive idealism—is a more typically Victorian tragic flaw than the one act of self indulgence mentioned in Malory. Swinburne considered Arthur's effort to live above the moral norm of his society as an example of Victorian smugness, which he believed Tennyson shared, while ignoring the major admonitory intent of the poem.

Most Victorians saw and extolled Arthur as the idealist, refusing to stoop to lowly realism; the Evangelist, sacrificed as a martyr to cruel egotisms; and the Victorian husband, pontificating against wifely disobedience. Swinburne saw and despised the same image of the king. But what the reviewers rarely sensed is the irony that sets King Arthur at a distance from Tennyson's unquestioning approval. Arthur is not the villain of the poem, but he is pitiably in error. Tennyson was capable of regarding a man as a hero and yet seeing gross shortcomings in his actions. After meeting Garibaldi, for example, and being touched by his combination of nobility and ingenuousness, Tennyson remarked to Emily that Garibaldi had the "divine stupidity of a hero." [25] Tennyson sent him a copy of the *Idylls* but wrote to the Duke of Argyll that Garibaldi would probably not care much for it. Not given to false modesty about his work, Tennyson might have meant that a revolutionary hero would see in King Arthur an image of himself—and Don Quixote.

With Swinburne's almost sole voice of disparagement at one extreme and the nearly unanimous paeans of the other reviewers at the opposite, Tennyson faced his gauntlet of opinion without succumbing to either erroneous praise or mistaken belittlement. He created a King Arthur who is neither a crude moral example nor an imitation of classical heroes. In the face of such praise as he received, a lesser poet would certainly have followed up his success with more idylls bringing King Arthur to the fore as the champion of Victorian attitudes. Without exception the articles reviewing the first four *Idylls of the King* in 1859 lauded or quoted at length the farewell scene in "Guinevere." It was called "the crown of the work . . . the grandest thing that Mr. Tennyson has yet done," "more touching, I think, than any in our language, except King Lear's lament over Cordelia," "a magnificent burst of passion and pity," "that great forgiveness and solemn farewell," "a noble and tender reproof," "proof that the age . . . could not wholly be corrupt," "the last grand scene," "equal to the occasion and worthy the speaker." [26] Emily thought "Guinevere" "to my mind the grandest thing he has ever done"; it moved Macaulay to tears and so stirred Jenny Lind on hearing Tennyson read it that she refused to sing. Edward Lear could only "blubber bottlesful" and Dickens pronounced it "absolutely unapproachable." [27] Even Swinburne was later to be sufficiently moved to pause in his condemnation of the Albertine King and praise the speech for containing "such magnificent language that the reader is content and indeed thankful to take the manliness and propriety of such an address for granted." [28]

Tennyson, however, never again portrays the king in a like pose, and seldom is he given a speech at all. The later idylls tend to bring forward the society where the king is all too absent. He remains a distant reminder of what is being neglected. Occasionally he returns to the foreground for a moment, like conscience reawakening in a guilty self, too late—to find the knights already pledged to the grail quest or to find the queen's bower dark. A few reviewers began to notice paradoxes and ironies in the role Arthur plays, as his character developed differently than they expected. The *London Quarterly* in 1859 saw an "incongruous meekness and perfection" in the king, which "provides the tragic elements of discord, error, and misfortune." [29] The *Edinburgh* later recognized the utopian quality of Arthur's ideals, its reviewer writing that Arthur tries to make his realm a "paradise." [30] The *Victoria Magazine* saw the king as a Carlylean hero who gains his right to rule through the "call to labour that he might right the world." [31] But when we remember that Carlyle ridiculed the "inward perfection of vacancy" and the "lollipops" he found in the first four idylls,[32] we cannot see the poem as the vision of a bluff hero-worshipper.

Some critics of the later idylls besides Swinburne expressed dissatisfaction with Tennyson's portrait of the king. Perhaps Tennyson's independence of critics' advice added to the discontent. The *Quarterly,* although enthusiastic in 1859, complained ten years later of "that ostentatious cleanliness of the hands which indicates a desire to stand well with the respectabilities of the world." It was the first journal to criticize the sacrosanct farewell speech, finding it "too elaborate to be natural." [33] The reviewer in the *Literary World* wrote, "His majesty, we must confess, is one of those utterly proper, high-stalking, clean-shaved, rather albuminous personages in whom we fail to take a lively interest." [34] Such reviewers seemed to ignore Tennyson's focus on the society of the Round Table rather than the king, as well as the symbolic purpose Arthur serves. This purpose should have become particularly evident in "The Holy Grail," in which Arthur remains in the background to represent the ethic of social action that the knights have abandoned in favor of mysticism. It would of course have been inappropriate for Tennyson to make King Arthur conspicuous and triumphant in the idyll, for the poem portrays the crucial test and failure of his Order. Nevertheless, several reviewers maintained that Arthur, to be dramatically interesting, should have gone on the grail quest. [35]

Many reviewers continued to defend King Arthur against those who described him as an "impeccable prig," [36] but mistakenly regarding him as a kind of epic hero. Perhaps the majority of writers who reviewed the later installments of the *Idylls* would have agreed with the critic in the *Dublin Review* when he wrote, "If it had only been for what he has given us in King Arthur, the *Idylls* would still have been worth writing." [37] To remove the tragedy of the Round Table and leave King Arthur in a vacuum would erase the central idea of the poem. Of all the Victorian reviewers Walter Walsh of the *Gen-*

tleman's Magazine gave the most accurate summing up of the role the king actually plays in the poem; he recognized the irony of his idealism. "In our moments of weakness," Walsh wrote, "we could almost, as nearer to our common clay, long for the Arthur of the early romancists, the Arthur who errs and sins and is shamed." But Tennyson, he continued, gives us instead a blameless king who is the symbol of all "fanatical and impracticable heroisms"; we are left with "the crushing reminder of Don Quixote." [38]

Writing of the Victorian tendency to dogmatize, Walter Houghton says, "The voice of the Victorian prophet laying down the law; this sets our teeth on edge. Partly because it insults our intelligence, but much more because it rouses our righteous irritation. For if dogmatism, strictly speaking, is a matter of style, the style betrays—or seems to betray—an insufferable man." [39] The failure of the Victorian reviewers to discern the irony of King Arthur's role and his essentially symbolic character, together with the almost unprecedented popularity of the king's farewell speech, left the way open for twentieth-century critics to imagine Tennyson as just the sort of dogmatic prophet Houghton describes. The passage in "Guinevere" that left Victorian readers dissolved in tears and Victorian reviewers groping for adjectives of praise has fallen on some later ears with the clang of "tinny nobility." [40] In a later age Tennyson was repudiated for the same reason he was admired by the Victorians. Neither view quite captures the complexity of the poem. Arthur is not a Victorian cuckold threatening divorce but a mythical figure suffering the consequences of trying to live in a human society and yet maintain a superhuman ethical standard. His speech is not the huffing and puffing of a Josiah Bounderby, who has left our sympathies

long before he leaves his wife, but an attempt at the sublimity of a Wotan's farewell, the departure of a Wagnerian
demigod whose divinity has left him less free than lesser
mortals. He faces the ruin of his Order—all because of
him, because of his cosmic rightness, which has had the
effect of human rigidity. To reiterate: Tennyson spoke
of the "divine stupidity" of the hero. Our evaluation of
"Guinevere" and of the whole poem should keep this
paradox in mind.

Tennyson was indeed, as a *Punch* cartoon imagined
him, the self-chosen laureate of King Arthur—that is of
the "King within," or the ideal symbolized by the hero
of the *Idylls*. But the Victorian reviewers sought to es-
pouse the king as a human being acting out their conception of themselves—just as they wanted to see themselves represented in Galahad and Lancelot. Only by
ignoring the ethical contradictions involved could they
make the *Idylls* a favorable picture of Victorian England.

Despite the many fine things Victorian reviewers said
of the nobility and beauty of the *Idylls,* they could not
make the work conform to the popular image of Victorian England as the new Golden Age. For Tennyson
was a self-chosen exile from the *aetas aurea* that industrial, commercial England claimed for itself, and it, in
turn, could never meet his standard of the ideal society.
Tennyson's readers hoped to see their own age reflected
as a reality verging upon the ideal, but in the *Idylls* the
ideal is attained—if at all—for a fleeting moment only
before ideal and reality clash to the death. The widespread
puzzlement, disappointment, and even shock of the critics
over elements in the *Idylls* they could not easily understand is a better indication of the relation of the work
to the age, an aspect which Tennyson thought was not
often enough noticed,[41] than the overwhelming praise it

received. Far from catering to a demanding public, Tennyson created such a paradoxical and, in the finest sense, realistic work that any contemporary dogmatist—whether Evangelical, atheist, hero-worshipper, aesthete, cynic, or utilitarian—could see a reflection of his ideals in the story of the Round Table but could not read the *Idylls* as the Bible of his faction without finding that somewhere he had parodied himself.

Notes

1. See *Memoir*, I, 449.
2. *Blackwood's*, LXXXVI (November 1859), 624.
3. *Fraser's* passed rather stiffly over the Viven idyll, allowing it to be "astonishingly clever," but finding it impossible to look at Vivien herself without aversion. The reviewer in the *Dublin University Magazine* found "Vivien" "in many respects the poorest portion of this noble volume." The *New Quarterly* dismissed the "wily Vivien" as "such an exceedingly unpleasant subject that no art can redeem it." *Fraser's*, LX (September 1859), 306; *Dublin University Magazine*, LV (January 1860), 64; *New Quarterly*, VIII (1859), 346. See also *Dublin University Magazine*, LV (April 1860), 505.
4. See John Nichol, *Westminster*, XVI (October 1859), 512; *Quarterly*, CVI (October 1859), 471; *Saturday Review*, VIII (July 16, 1859), 76; *London Times*, September 10, 1859, 5; *Bentley's Quarterly*, II (October 1859), 180; *Eclectic*, CX (September 1859), 291.
5. *London Quarterly*, XIII (October 1859), 69. See also J. M. Ludlow, *Macmillan's*, I (November 1859), 64; the *North British Review*, XXI (August 1859), 165-168; *National Review*, IX.
6. *Eclectic*, CX (September 1859), 291; *Edinburgh*, CLXIII (April 1886), 495.
7. *Edinburgh*, CLXIII (April 1886), 495.
8. *Literary World*, n.s. I (December 24, 1869), 120. See also the comment in the *Contemporary*, XXI (May 1873), 946.
9. *National Review*, IX (October 1859), 381-383. See also R. H. Hutton, *Macmillan's*, XXVII (December 1872), 164.
10. *Literary World*, n.s. I (December 17, 1869), 98.

11. Swinburne, "Tennyson and Musset," *Fortnightly Review*, n.s. XXIX (February 1, 1881), 146-147.

12. *Blackwood's*, LXXXVI (November 1859), 613. See also John Nichol, *Westminster*, XVI (October 1859), 506, 512.

13. *Chamber's Journal*, n.s. XII (August 20, 1859), 122-123. The reviewer ignores Geraint's bad points by capsulizing the story myopically as "the brave Geraint—instructing his true wife Enid." See also *British Quarterly*, XXX (1859), 489; *Eclectic*, CX (September 1859), 291.

14. *London Quarterly*, XXXIX (January 1873), 402-403.

15. *Contemporary*, XXI (May 1873), 947. See also Walter Walsh, *Gentleman's Magazine*, L (May 1893), 504; T. H. Leary, *Gentleman's Magazine*, n.s. VIII (March 1872), 425-426.

16. Lionel Tollemache, "Tennyson's Social Philosophy," *Fortnightly Review*, n.s. XV (1874), 236.

17. *Fraser's*, for example, looked on Guinevere as the great "fatal influence" in the first four idylls and found her devoid of the "vital principle of honour" that Lancelot possesses. *Fraser's*, LX (September 1859), 301-314. The *Edinburgh* described her as "willful" and "self-indulgent" but defended her criticism of Arthur. *Edinburgh*, CLXIII (April 1886), 496-498. The writer in the *Literary World*, having played the devil's advocate in liking Vivien, asserts that Tennyson's "bad" characters in general, Guinevere included, are more memorable than the "good." *Literary World*, n.s. I (December 17, 1869), 97-98.

18. *Blackwood's*, CLII (1892), 761-764.

19. *Quarterly*, CXXVIII (January 1870), 1-17. See also: *British Quarterly*, XXX (1859), 487; *Quarterly*, CVI (October 1859), 473-478; J. M. Stone, "A Missing Page from the *Idylls of the King*," *Dublin Review*, CIII (October 1888), 260-262; H. D. Traill, "Aspects of Tennyson," *Nineteenth Century*, XXXII (December 1892), 962; "The Meaning of King Arthur," *Contemporary*, XXI (May 1873), 947; *National Review*, IX (October 1859), 383-384; *Edinburgh*, CXXXI (April 1870), 526-527. Many of these writers preferred Malory's Launcelot; the *Dublin Review* attacks Tennyson's "Protestant bias" in not having the Pope intervene and reconcile Arthur and Lancelot, as he does in Malory.

20. *Blackwood's*, LXXXVI (November 1859), 610.

21. *Saturday Review*, VIII (July 16, 1859), 76.

22. *British Quarterly*, XXX (1859), 485-486. A later review in the same journal, however, agrees that Tennyson successfully includes Galahad and does well to depart from the "dewy-fresh, serenely-pure, and saintly 'Sir Galahad' "—*British Quarterly*,

LI (1870), 205. Yet even this change of opinion evades the fact that not Galahad's character but his social role is changed in the *Idylls*. See also *Quarterly,* CXVIII (January 1870), 10; *Chambers's Journal,* XLVII (February 26, 1870), 140; *St. James Magazine,* n.s. IV (1870), 791-799; *London Times,* December 23, 1869, 4; *Intellectual Repository,* XVII (1870), 472-476, 522-524.

23. Robert Browning, letter to Isa Blagden, January 19, 1870, printed for private circulation by Richard Clay & Sons (London, 1920). See *London Times,* December 23, 1869, 4; *Academy,* I (January 8, 1870), 93. Hopkins, too, disparaged what he found "quite a fantastic charade-playing trumpery Galahad, merely playing the fool over Christian heroism."—Letter to R. W. Dixon, February 27, 1879, *A Hopkins Reader,* ed. John Pick (London), 1953), 95.

24. A. C. Swinburne, "Tennyson and Musset," *Fortnightly Review,* XXXV (February 1, 1881), 147-150.

25. *Memoir,* II, 2-3.

26. From (respectively): *London Times* (September 10, 1859), 5; *Macmillan's,* I (November 1859), 66; *New Quarterly,* VIII (1859), 344; *Chambers's Journal,* n.s. XII (August 20, 1859), 123; *Saturday Review,* VIII (July 16, 1859), 76; *Blackwoods,* LXXXVI (November 1859), 624; *London Quarterly,* XIII (October 1859), 78. Patmore in the *Edinburgh* found "Guinevere" the best of the first four *Idylls;* the critic in the *North British Review* considered it his best poem. Favorable comments also appeared in the *Westminster, Fraser's, Quarterly, Spectator, Dublin University Magazine, Athenaeum, Irish Quarterly, Tait's,* and the *Eclectic.*

27. See Joanna Richardson, *The Pre-eminent Victorian* (London: Cape, 1962), 101-117.

28. Swinburne, "Tennyson and Musset," *Fortnightly,* XXXV (February 1, 1881), 148.

29. *London Quarterly,* XIII (October 1859), 76-78.

30. *Edinburgh,* CXXXI (April 1870), 504.

31. *Victoria Magazine,* XIV (February 1870), 381-382.

32. See *Correspondence of Thomas Carlyle and Ralph Waldo Emerson* (Boston, 1892), II, 339-340.

33. *Quarterly,* CXXVI (April 1869), 337; CXXVIII (January 1870), 4.

34. *Literary World,* n.s. I (December 17, 1869), 97-98.

35. See *St. James Magazine,* n.s. IV (1870), 807; *Quarterly,* CXXVIII (January 1870), 11-12.

36. See *Contemporary,* XXI (May 1873), 944-945.

37. *Dublin Review,* CIII (October 1888), 260. See also *Macmillan's* XXVII (December 1872), 156-161.
38. Walter Walsh, "Tennyson's Great Allegory," *Gentleman's Magazine,* L (May 1893), 503-504.
39. Walter Houghton, *The Victorian Frame of Mind* (New Haven: Yale University Press, 1957), 137.
40. See Valerie Pitt, *Tennyson Laureate* (London, 1962), 184.
41. *Memoir,* II, 129, 134. If further proof were needed of the difficulties reviewers had in sensing the real relation of the *Idylls* to their own milieu, Roden Noel's article in the *Contemporary* serves to settle the case rather convincingly. Noel's review is a compendium of many misunderstandings befogging the *Idylls* criticisms: He sees the work as romantic rather than historical, a fairy tale rather than a reflection of human life, an analogue to *The Faerie Queene* in ornament and unreality rather than in social significance. Like Swinburne, Noel quarrels at length with the depiction of Vivien (a "too real and unlovely harlot") and the ethical idea of the *Idylls,* arguing, "I would suggest that the poet might have represented suffering and disappointment, not as a penalty apportioned to particular transgressions, rather as integral elements in that mysterious destiny which determines the lot of man in his present condition of defect, moral, physical, and intellectual." (Certainly this is what Tennyson does in fact portray, for Arthur's inability to transcend human limitations is evident throughout the poem.) Noel argues as well that nature in the *Idylls* is "a symbol and embodiment of the soul's life, . . ." in "consanguinity with our own desires, aspirations and fears. . . ." "The Poetry of Tennyson," *Contemporary Review,* XLVII (1885), 202-224. It is not surprising that Tennyson, in writing to Noel, told him, "You are wrong about the 'Idylls of the King,' but wrong in a gracious and noble way, for which I am obliged to you." *Memoir,* II, 311.

5.

Rival Visions

Lowell

Of the nineteenth-century writers who employed Arthurian legend for the chief purpose of social criticism, Tennyson is the greatest poet. Conversely, of those who achieved poetic success in reshaping the myth of the Round Table, Tennyson remains most relevant to the character and problems of his milieu. Lowell, Arnold, Swinburne, and Morris are his peers and his rivals; each in his way creates a version of the story that commands major attention. For all but Tennyson, and perhaps Arnold, however, Arthurian legend remains what it had been in the romantic period—a glorification of nature and fantasy. Poetic success is a kind of *tour de force* for Lowell, Swinburne, and Morris. They proved that the romantic conception of the Round Table might, after all, be shaped into effective poetry by the writers who could believe in the advent of the millennium or embrace the state of nature.

James Russell Lowell's "Vision of Sir Launfal" (1848) is deeply rooted in romanticism—in the romantic conception of the Round Table and the romantic period in general. Unlike Tennyson, Lowell pays little heed to the traditional myth. He removes the grail story entirely from the central story of the Round Table, chooses a new knight to be his protagonist, and sets the tale in a time somewhat later than the days of King Arthur. His story, his ethical idea, and his poetic method are eminently romantic. The story bears greater resemblance to Wordsworth's "Resolution and Independence" than to Tennyson's "Holy Grail" or to any of the traditional stories written by Malory, Chrétien, or Wolfram von Eschenbach about the quest.

Sir Launfal, a proud, rich, and selfish earl, in Lowell's version, encounters an old leper, much as the self-concerned poet in Wordsworth's lyric meets an ancient leech-gatherer. Both poets use a natural setting of a morning landscape with beautiful wildlife to contrast the protagonist's lack of natural piety. Sir Launfal unfeelingly casts the leper a gold coin, which is shunned.

The knight then goes on the grail quest, during which he loses all he has—his earldom and his wealth. On his return he again finds the leper who scorned his token offering before; now Sir Launfal gives, or shares, the little he has, and the leper becomes Christ, who tells him,

> Lo it is I, be not afraid!
> In many climes, without avail
> Thou hast spent thy life for the Holy Grail;
> Behold, it is here,—this cup which thou
> Didst fill at the streamlet for me but now; . . .
> Not what we give, but what we share,—

For the gift without the giver is bare;
Who gives himself with his alms feeds three,—
Himself, his hungering neighbor, and me.
              (Part Second, Stanza Eight)

After his vision of Christ, Sir Launfal shares his castle with the poor; and the summer, which had laid siege to the wintery fortress for three centuries, at last enters it in disguise with the first of the poor. The Golden Age returns: each man is now lord of the earldom as much as Sir Launfal, and nature smiles upon the new order. Like Tennyson's Galahad, Sir Launfal loses himself to save himself.

Lowell's poem is a romantic appeal for the millennial utopia; he urges us to break the bonds of social institutions and create the heaven on earth where man can find his natural self. Lowell castigates the new Golden Age with its obedience not to Saturn but Mammon:

The priest hath his fee who comes and shrives
        us,
We bargain for the graves we lie in;
At the devil's booth are all things sold,
Each ounce of dross costs its ounce of gold;
For a cap and bells our lives we pay,
Bubbles we buy with a whole soul's tasking:
'Tis heaven alone that is given away,
'Tis only God may be had for the asking;
No price is set on the lavish summer;
June may be had by the poorest comer.

And what is so rare as a day in June?
              (Prelude to Part First, lines 21-31)

Utopia is an order without a code, ruled only by the spontaneous wisdom that nature gives. The leper and the grail quest have a miraculous effect upon the realm. Whereas for Tennyson the grail quest is the symptom of a social disease and the cause of social death, for Lowell the grail brings an unexpected beneficial influence. Lowell's leper is quite different from the hermit in Tennyson's grail idyll, being not a spokesman of traditional religious wisdom, but an agent brought suddenly into the natural world by God. He is precisely parallel to Wordsworth's leech-gatherer—"A man from some far region sent,/To give me human strength, by apt admonishment."

Lowell optimistically imagines a social miracle that is to endure indefinitely. He is not centrally concerned with social criticism or with historical probability but with human morality in the abstract. Like the romantic poets, he regards human nature as predominantly good if uncorrupted by social artificialities. He is convinced that the golden world is at the doors for those who deserve it. In "Gold Egg: A Dream Fantasy," Lowell writes,

> Each day the world is born anew
>   For him who takes it rightly;
> Not fresher that which Adam knew,
> Not sweeter that whose moonlit dew
>   Entranced Arcadia nightly.[1]

Tennyson saw the devastating effect of factory smoke, child labor, Darwin's theory, the Crimean war, rigid factionalism, and the prospect of a collapsing empire, and such benign hopefulness would have strained his credulity.

As a comment upon nineteenth-century society, Tennyson's "Holy Grail" immeasurably surpasses "The Vision of Sir Launfal." Lowell's ending is sentimental and unconvincing. The reader is persuaded by the poem's moral idea, but when he attempts to imagine Sir Launfal acting out his newly found charity in real society, he remembers how King Lear's foolish charity is rewarded. Christlike humility could not, as Tennyson convinces us in his portrait of King Arthur, make a utopia of society as it exists. It is perhaps a mistake for Lowell to involve himself in Sir Launfal's social role at all. From the viewpoint of individual morality, Lowell is convincing when he asserts, "He gives nothing but worthless gold/Who gives from a sense of duty." (Part First, Stanza Six) But society, as Tennyson reminds us, relies upon the duties of its citizens, even if it is a mistake to believe, as King Arthur does, that a man's duty is his whole being. Lowell characterizes Sir Launfal's initial lack of faith through the same metaphor that Tennyson employs in the grail idyll; Sir Launfal's pride is a kind of moral waste land: "The heart within him was ashes and dust." (Part Second, Stanza Six) Lowell does not consider, however, the possibility that Tennyson envisions, of a society, its lepers as well as its earls, becoming a waste land in which Sir Launfal's spiritual regeneration would have no effect on others.

Swinburne

At the opposite extreme from Lowell's romantic spiritualism is Swinburne's equally romantic espousal of a sublime, tragic, Godless nature. Swinburne's key images —the turbulent ocean, fire, light and darkness conquer-

ing each other, the soaring of birds—suggest a wish to
dissolve into the elements of nature, to participate in the
motions of the nonhuman world and be an agent of fate.
Lowell and Swinburne depart in opposite directions from
the balance of reason and emotion, idealism and practical insight that Tennyson's social commitment requires.
Each makes of Arthurian legend his romantic view of
man's place in the world. In poetic power, ethical meaning, and treatment of Arthurian romance, Swinburne is
the leading challenger to Tennyson as the great Arthurian
poet of the nineteenth century.

Tristram of Lyonesse (1882) is, as it were, a rebuttal
to the *Idylls*—to the entire work and not just to the
portrait of Tristram in "The Last Tournament." Swinburne attacked Tennyson's most fundamental assumptions
regarding the modern treatment of Arthurian romance
in *Under the Microscope*. He felt that Tennyson's modern moral ideal, his attempt to make a single story out
of apparently heterogeneous material, and his conception
of tragedy were utter failures. Swinburne praised Tennyson's nature imagery, the one redeeming element for
Swinburne, but by doing so he overlooked the great difference between the moral value of nature in the *Idylls*
and in Swinburne's poetry. In every possible way, except
in the close observation of nature, Tennyson and Swinburne are directly opposed. No doubt Swinburne hoped to
make the *Idylls* seem priggish by telling the story of a
great romantic love and to expose the diffuseness of
Tennyson's composite work by vivifying a single romance.

But what Swinburne gains in freedom and emotional
intensity, he loses in modern relevance and social realism. Where Lowell radically alters a legend only as a
way of expressing his individual view of the world, Swinburne remains meticulously loyal to the traditional myth

of Tristram and Iseult. Tennyson recasts Arthurian myth,
but Swinburne retells it.[2] In itself, such an attempt would
seem far less valid than Tennyson's, for if the original
romances have the value Swinburne attributes to them,
a modern copy could not be of more than derivative
value. Swinburne does, however, accomplish a great deal
more than retelling the Tristram story. He imparts to the
legend the flavor and spirit of his best poetry, making it
an individual poetic vision painted upon the canvas of
myth with a daring that indeed challenges Tennyson's
ideal of moderation.

Swinburne used nature to express his own Byronic
rebellion against the bonds of civilized society and the
God that he thinks man has created in his own pale
image. The love of Tristram and Iseult is as wild and
inevitable as nature—powerful like the ocean, overwhelming human control like storms. Society and history are
nearly obliterated in the onrushing lyric imagination of
the poet, but a social ideal is contained within the tempest
of *Tristram of Lyonesse*. Strangely at odds with his own
republicanism. Swinburne adulates the aristocratic splendor of the Round Table:

> . . . too late
> The sacred mouth of Merlin set forth fate
> And brake the secret seal on Arthur's birth,
> And showed his ruin and his rule on earth
> Inextricable, and light on lives to be.
> For surely, though time slay us, yet shall we
> Have such high name and lordship of good days
> As shall sustain us living, and men's praise
> Shall burn a beacon lit above us dead.
> And of the king how shall not this be said
> When any of us from any mouth has praise,

That such were men in only this king's days,
In Arthur's? yea, come shine or shade, no less
His name shall be one name with knightliness,
His fame one light with sunlight.
    ("The Sailing of the Swallow," lines 384-398)

The golden days have a pagan, ritualistic glory; Arthur's leadership has a totemic force. The idolatry which Tennyson sees blinding the eyes of the knights to moral ideals Swinburne extols as savagery expressing itself through the forms of civilization. He rejects the character of Tennyson's "blameless" king, seeing the fall of the Round Table as the fated outcome of Arthur's former sin:

His age shall bear the burdens of his youth
And bleed from his own bloodshed; for indeed
Blind to him blind his sister brought for seed,
And of the child between them shall be born
Destruction: so shall God not suffer scorn,
Nor in men's souls and lives his law lie dead.
    ("The Sailing of the Swallow," lines 399-404)

In its individualism, its sense of doomed love, its evocation of the sublime, and its yearning for the unattainable—in every way *Tristram of Lyonesse* is a romantic poem. Swinburne continues to adhere to the escapist desire inherent in Arthurian poetry of the romantic period. His utopia is the Spenserian bower of bliss, in which Tristram and Iseult escape from social restriction, and Avalon.

Tennyson exposes middle-class society to the fact that it is not living by its professed ideals of justice, peace, reason, purity, and love; Swinburne confronts middle-class respectability with scorn and radically different values. Tennyson subordinates the Tristram story and deprives it of its romance to make it serve to point out a social failure caused by the same behavior that Lancelot and Guinevere reveal. Swinburne conversely subordinates the story of the Round Table to make its downfall parallel to the fated deaths of Tristram and Iseult. Knighthood itself seems a reckless, passionate commitment. Tennyson chooses the least romantic death for his Tristram, Mark sneaking from behind and killing him instantly. Swinburne's ending—in which Tristram and Iseult both die upon a kiss—is the most romantic conclusion of the legend.

Swinburne showed the faintest trace of social meaning in his undergraduate Arthurian lyrics, "Queen Yseult" and "Lancelot," and in his "Joyeuse Garde." He contrasts the good knight, Roland, to the tyrannical Moronde; "Ermonie the happy land" is Roland's country, where Blanchefleur lives with him in exile from her husband's cruelty. Swinburne's utopia here, too, is the wilds rather than the court. He lays heavy emphasis upon Blanchefleur's golden ring and Yseult's golden hair as symbols of the true, passionate self opposed to the oppressions of society.[3]

Swinburne admitted that there was an "admixture of modern thought" in the poem, about Arthur as well, but his notion of fate is modern only because it is also universal and timeless. His sense of time is much closer to that of Shelley in "Ozymandias"—time as the inevitable conquerer over all human pride—than to the distinctive Victorian vision of evolving patterns of growth and decay. Rather than the rapid and complex movements of life in the machine age, as suggested in the constant failures to keep up with change in the *Idylls*, Swinburne depicts an impulsive and relentless current moving toward an obvious end.

He too employs seasonal images to suggest the passing of time, but not to indicate social change. The seasons are the periods of individual human life only: Queen Morgause was in

> the green middle Maytime of her life,
> And scarce in April was our king's as then . . .
> But cold as rains of autumn was King Lot
> And grey-grown out of season . . .
>   ("The Sailing of the Swallow," lines 375-380)

The instability of the human personality is sometimes conveyed through seasonal imagery:

> And all her Mayday blood as from a swoon
> Flushed, and May rose up in her and was June . . .
> Then with half summer in her eyes she turned,
> And on her lips was April yet, and smiled . . .
>   ("The Sailing of the Swallow," lines 472-476)

Swinburne rounds off a cycle of events in the final poem, "The Sailing of the Swan," just as Tennyson uses "The Passing of Arthur" to remind us of the first idyll. For Swinburne the end is in the beginning: when Tristram and Iseult first kiss, "their four lips became one burning mouth." At the end, still in the power of fate, "their four lips became one silent mouth." Tennyson prophesies his ending in the beginning as well, but as an ironical contrast to the expected future of Arthur's Order. Swinburne mentions only briefly Lancelot, Pelleas and Ettarde, Arthur and the Round Table, and Nimuë to provide a social background for the love story of Tristram and Iseult.

For Tennyson chivalric society is the authority from which Tristram and Iseult have the choice to escape, and chivalry itself fails only because of such desertions. For Swinburne, society is a death cell in which the only human choice is to face doom with heroism and passion or with cowardice. In *The Tale of Balen* (1896) Swinburne accentuates the power of fate still further. Nowhere is the contrast between Tennyson's emphasis upon choice and Swinburne's upon fate more evident than in the two poets' versions of the Balin story.

Tennyson departs widely from Malory's story of the Dolorous Stroke and almost creates his own plot, bringing to the foreground the mistaken choices in the tale— Balin's decision to bear the queen's crown as his insignia, Arthur's giving him permission to do so, Balin's enraged rejection of the Order and his trampling on his shield, Balan's decision to attack him, and the conviction Balan reaches that the queen is innocent. Swinburne sees the story as a perfect example of man's fate. Again he follows his source assiduously. Malory and Swinburne present the story essentially as a series of revenge slayings, beginning with Balin's slaying of a knight in Arthur's court (Arthur's cousin in Malory), his six-month imprisonment for the murder, Balin's smiting off the head of the Lady of the Lake, who had slain his mother (Balin, she claims, killed her brother), Balin's slaying of Lanceor when the knight tries to punish Balin for killing the Lady of the Lake, the suicide of Lanceor's lady, Balin and Balan's slaughter of forty of Rion's followers, Garlon's killing of two knights who at separate times accompany Balin, Balin's conquest of Garlon, and his slaying of Pellam with a spear. This last act is the Dolorous Stroke, which will lay three counties waste for twelve years; the spear is the one that wounded Christ. Balin then meets Garnish, a knight who finds his bride sleeping with a foul knight and kills them both. Finally, Balin fights against Balan, who does not recognize him because he is not using his own shield; both knights die, fulfilling a prophecy made at the beginning of the story: a damsel bearing a heavy sword had appeared at the court, saying that only the purest knight could draw it from its scabbard; all fail, even Arthur, but Balin, just out of prison and in poor clothes, draws the sword; he refuses to return it as he is told, whereupon the lady warns him that with the sword he will kill the one he loves most on earth. Swinburne omits a few proper names, the funeral services (which Malory considers important for religious reasons and Swinburne does not), and Balin's squire, whom Malory has carry the news of Balin's exploits to his friends in Northumberland. Swinburne eliminated the squire to accentuate Balin's romantic solitude, leaving him no close friend but Balan, from whom he is separated, and the two knights who briefly accompany him. Just as Tristram is doomed to a love that society forbids, Balin is banished from the Round Table, and whatever good to society he might have been is cancelled by his early death. For Swinburne the tragedy is not the outcome of a lapse into error and bestiality but a necessary and right event in the ordering of fate:

> Both came we out of one tomb,
> One star-crossed mother's woful womb,
> And so within one grave-pit's gloom
> Untimely shall we die.

Images of the tempestuous sea and the iron hardness of the North convey the force of fate in the story, as does

the rushed quality of the narrative, in which events tele-
scope into each other.

   Swinburne sees the Golden Age as a laughable delusion: after all the knights except Balen have been proved
impure by failing to draw the sword, Arthur, who has
failed himself, laments,

> Methought the wide round world could bring
> Before the face of queen or king
> No knights more fit for fame to sing
> Than fill this full Round Table's ring
> With honour higher than pride of place:
> But now my heart is wrung to know,
> Damsel, that none whom fame can show
> Finds grace to heal or help thy woe:
> God gives them not the grace.

Swinburne adds this lament to the original story. It is
quite similar to the many pasages in the *Idylls* wherein
characters realize that reality is much worse than they
imagined it. The king realizes, for example, as the laureate hopes his readers will realize about their own society, that his Order is not of the Golden Age and, given
its real moral condition, could never have been.

   But Swinburne remains a thorough romantic in his
more typical view of the golden days. Before Balin dies,
he recalls his happy life as a creature of nature; almost
in the spirit of *The Prelude* he relives the pleasure nature
has given him in solitude:

> And there low lying, as hour on hour
> Fled, all his life in all its flower
> Came back as in a sunlit shower

Of dreams, when sweet-souled sleep has power
On life less sweet and glad to be.
He drank the draught of life's first wine
Again: he saw the moorland shine,
The rioting rapids of the Tyne,
The woods, the cliffs, the sea.

The joy that lives at heart and home,
The joy to rest, the joy to roam,
The joy of crags and scaurs he clomb,
The rapture of the encountering foam
Embraced and breasted of the boy,
The first good steed his knees bestrode,
The first wild sound of songs that flowed
Through ears that thrilled and heart that
      glowed,
Fulfilled his death with joy.

Again Swinburne adds to his source a reminiscence parallel to the visions in the *Idylls*. But the passage is mark-
edly different from the familiar "passion of the past." In
the *Idylls*, and even in "Break, Break, Break," and "Tears
Idle Tears" Tennyson evokes his poignancy by showing
the gulf between nature and human feelings; the happy
autumn fields cannot erase the knowledge of death or
the deadness of the past, and the cold waves breaking on
the crags dully mock the living sorrow of the dreamer.
Swinburne's hero seems perfectly attuned to nature, much
like the child in "Tintern Abbey," to whom nature was
an "appetite, a feeling, and a love." He never becomes
the mature narrator like the one in Wordsworth's lyric, to
whom nature reveals a "sense sublime, of something far
more deeply interfused. . . ." Balen seems to face death
with the joy of natural exhilaration.

Tennyson follows Malory in calling Balin "the Savage." Swinburne changes the epithet to the less pejorative "the Wild." Tennyson's knight tries unsuccessfully to achieve the "golden earnest of a gentler life." But Swinburne's is romantically sublime, identifying with the wind of fate and the iron tide of battle rather than "the golden calm of summer." A northern individualist, Balen asserts, "I ride alone afar/And follow my soul for star." [4]

Morris

William Morris, in *The Defence of Guenevere and Other Poems* (1858), was as clearly influenced by romanticism as were Lowell and Swinburne, though he differs from both stylistically. Rather than make his Arthurian vision a judgment of the dehumanized society he brilliantly criticizes in his prose writings, Morris employs the story of the Round Table almost as a vacation exercise. "The Defence of Guenevere," the best of his Arthurian poems, is a story about frivolous chance rather than the direction of social tendencies. Morris has Guenevere gamble rather than choose, as Tennyson portrays her. Morris shows that her choice of Lancelot is not a moral error but is based on the best guess she is capable of making; she likens her decision to an imagined predicament of selecting one of two ribbons, a red or a blue, to determine her eternal fate. Like the blue cloth, "heaven's color," Lancelot's appearance seemed to make him the better man; She could not believe in the king's perfection, having been "bought/ By his great name and his little love." In a sense, she had no choice, not being able to know the ultimate meaning of her alternatives. Morris portrays man in a world that he cannot control or understand; Tennyson shows that he could be blind to the control he might exert.

Instead of retelling Malory's heroic romance, Morris extracts from the flow of events a single moment in which he reveals Guenevere's character by allowing her to defend herself. The surprise ending is not in Lancelot's appearance—which is predictable even to those not familiar with the story—but in the revelation that Guenevere's passionate apologia has been the carefully timed artifice of a superior mind. Her lying nearly reaches the truthfulness of artistic illusion, for it attacks and defies her listeners' desires to know the literal account of things. Her being is a reproach to the meagerness of the pedestrian moral climate in which she is forced to live. Morris' golden race are the last romantics; their sin is made goodness by their characters. They are the begetters of value and not defendants to be judged. Guenevere defends, or rather discloses, literally herself and not her acts to the knights:

> The shadow lies like wine within a cup
> Of marvelously colored gold; yea, now
> This little wind is rising, look you up,
>
> And wonder how the light is falling so
> Within my moving tresses, Will you dare
> When you have looked a little on my brow,
>
> To say this thing is vile? or will you care
> For any plausible lies of cunning woof,
> When you can see my face with no lie there
>
> Forever? Am I not a gracious proof? [5]
>   (lines 232-241)

In Malory's version of the story Lancelot upbraids
Mellyagaunce for disturbing the queen's chamber to prove
her guilty, telling him that even King Arthur would not
open her bedcurtains unless to sleep with her. Perhaps
Morris recalls this admonishment, for Guenevere's parad-
ing of her own beauty before the knights seems to bait
their vulgarity. She challenges them to prove themselves
the coarse inquisitors of their queen that they seem in-
clined to become. At the appearance of Lancelot she seems
to rise to her full pride, which seems the natural majesty
of a superior instinct. She listens "like a man who hears/
His brother's trumpet sounding through the wood/Of
his foes' lances." Lancelot seems her kin, a member of
her superior species in the wood; she "gave a slight spring
sometimes" and her cheeks grew crimson as Lancelot
on his roan charger "drew all men to see. . . ." Guenevere
and Lancelot seem to possess a natural power and freedom that make the concluding images of vital animality
fitting and joyous.

Malory saw the love of Launcelot and Guenevere as
a perfect example of the courtly, or what he calls the old
love. He says that because the queen was a true lover, she
had a good end. Tennyson rewards Guinevere with the
rank of abbess in a nunnery after her years of "good deeds
and . . . pure life"—quite the opposite reason from Malory's. Morris saves the queen—figuratively and literally—
because of what she is and not what she does. She implores the knights for sympathy by reliving the "wild
day" when she, "half-mad with beauty," and Lancelot
kissed in the garden. She appeals to their whole sense of
life, asking ". . . must I prove/Stone-cold forever?" Romantically, she and her knight had hoped to be "Like
children again, free from all wrongs/ Just for one night."
She belongs to the golden world which the poets, as Sid-

ney says in his *Apology for Poetry,* create to judge our
brazen world, and she is a silent judge of her prosecutors
as well as an eloquent witness in her own behalf. The
defense *of* Guenevere is both her verbal plea and the
poet's vindication of what she is. For Tennyson the "wild
hour coming on" is the nightmarish end of the queen's
misdeed, but for Morris the abandon of the "wild day"
is Guenevere's salvation.

Morris' Arthurian poetry is romantic in both the
general sense that it idealizes nature, individualism, and
passion and the specific Arthurian sense that it visualizes
the golden days of chivalry through the eyes of wonder.
In *Ogier the Dane,* the last story in the second part of
The Earthly Paradise (1868-70), Morris revives once more
the fairy mythology that the romanticists without exception coupled with Arthurian legend. Keightley mentions
the story of Ogier in his *Fairy Legends;* Spenser's influence on the poem is clear in the name of the first fairy,
Gloriande, named of course after the Fairy Queen. Ogier
is carried away from the troubles of the world by Morgan
le Fay, traditionally Arthur's wicked sister, and he remains in Avallon with her for a century. She tells him,

> I, who longed to share with thee my bliss,
> Am of the fays and live their changeless life,
> And like the Gods of old, I see the strife
> That moves the world, unmoved if I so will.[6]

Avallon is perfectly parallel to Saturn's isle and to the
abode of King Arthur after his passing from the society
of men. Like Arthur, Ogier returns to put down the
heathen. After a century, however, the France he returns
to has to so declined from its first heroism that he seems

quixotic; calling himself the Ancient Knight, he strikes
awe into the hearts of his followers in much the way Tennyson's king does, yet he seems strangely incongruous:

> . . . his fair armour shone
> With beauty of a time long passed away,
> So with the music of another day
> His deep voice thrilled the awe-struck listening
>   folk.[7]

Ogier wins the victory for France by reviving the spirit of
ancient heroism, but the night before he is to marry the
French queen as his reward, the fairy guardian appears
and vanishes with him again. Never again, even in time
of trouble, will France be saved by his return. Like
Tennyson, Morris does not employ the miraculous return
of the hero as a symbol for the nation's ability to meet
any crisis without planning. Unlike the laureate, however, Morris concentrates upon a pastoral world apart
from contemporary life, and not upon his society and its
struggles.

In the short poems of the *Defence of Guenevere* volume Morris continues to reveal two strains of what could
be called his romantic conception of Arthurian legend—
the Spenserian fantasy of "Ogier the Dane" and the commitment to passion as the highest human experience expressed in "The Defence of Guenevere." Rarely do the
stresses and anxieties of Victorian England intrude upon
the pastoral setting of these poems, and Morris portrays
in them little serious conflict between social responsibilities and personal desires. In "King Arthur's Tomb" he
depicts Launcelot recalling the love that was once a necessity to his being and that carried him and the queen be-

yond social reproof. Romantic passion dictated by fate, coupled with a sense that existence is unreal, makes the poem convey quite the opposite meaning from that of Tennyson's use of Arthurian legend:

> A lady dwelt, whose name was Guenevere;
> This he knew also; that some fingers twine,
> Not only in a man's hair, even his heart,
> (making him good or bad I mean) but in his life,
> Skies, earth, men's looks and deeds, all that has
>   part,
> Not being ourselves, in that half-sleep, half-strife,
> (Strange sleep, strange strife) that men call living.[8]

Instead of emphasizing the importance of men's choices in determining the quality of society, Morris makes Arthurian legend a pleasing diversion from the malaise of existence, which seems no different from the anxiety and alienation the individual suffers in his dehumanized modern environment.

Yet the "strange disease of modern life," as Matthew Arnold describes the malady, is not the focal point of the poem. Launcelot and Guenevere as timeless lovers are the heart of Morris' poetic impulse. Their love evolves naturally, in spite of their attempts to live according to their society's mores. When the queen first heard the crowd crying for Launcelot, who had just slain the Roman emperor, Lucius, she saw only King Arthur; but the years of watching Launcelot excel in tournament and hearing about his conquests in battle bring her closer to him and at last create an unbreakable bond of passion. She and Launcelot are caught in a predicament that is as timeless as the tragedy of Tristram and Iseult; their inability to realize their dreams without the intrusion of society is a comment upon man's inevitable circumstance rather than upon the specific conditions of nineteenth-century life. The poet is not a social critic except in the broad sense Arnold intends when he says that all poetry is a criticism of life.

Morris seems to place Launcelot and Guenevere on a higher moral plane than the king. They live on after his death, seeming properly destined for each other. The fall of the king seems to be fated and not to be blamed upon Launcelot and Guenevere; references to it are subtly woven into the poem: Launcelot, for instance, gazes upon an arras "where the wind set the silken kings a-sway." [9] Guenevere, rather than repent and go to heaven with Arthur, is willing to join Launcelot even in hell. Arthur seems, in comparison to the fated couple, a silken figure indeed. At the end of the poem Morris tries to effect a repentance scene, with Guenevere calling down upon them both a terrible feeling of guilt, which strikes down Launcelot in a swoon. She believes she has killed him, but he awakes at the ringing of bells, at last welcoming the moral order which he has denied. But the conclusion belongs to a different poem; there seems to be no real guilt in the lovers, no nemesis, and certainly no new moral perception that could crush Launcelot. Morris seems to be searching for the sense of purgation and renewal that Tennyson creates at the conclusion of the *Idylls,* but he has eliminated from the beginning any evil to be purged.

"In "Sir Galahad: A Christmas Mystery," Morris tells a version of the quest for the grail which belongs in between Lowell's Christian parable and Tennyson's symbolic portrait of the modern wasteland. As in "The Vision of Sir Launfal," Christ appears to the protagonist of the poem—Sir Galahad—not to warn him against his former vanity but to reassure him that his chastity will prove a greater love than the earthly passions of the other knights, who will "come foil'd from the great quest, in vain." [10] Christ's celestial love will be found more rewarding than courtly love: Galahad alone will achieve the holy grail. Morris keeps the failure of the grail quest and its deleterious effect upon the Order as only a vague idea in the background of the lyric, whereas Tennyson and Malory make the adventure of Galahad secondary to the larger collective failure of the quest.

The otherworldliness that Morris seems to idealize in his portrait of Galahad is at odds with his own social principles. In his challenging essay, "Useful Work versus Useless Toil," Morris contradicts the values Galahad represents, asserting that the product of work should be that "worth having by one who is neither a fool nor an ascetic." [11] His point in the essay is not far from the point of Tennyson's "The Holy Grail." Work can be pleasure, he writes, only when "Social morality, the responsibility of man towards the life of man, will, in the new order of things, take the place of theological morality, or the responsibility of man to some abstract idea." [12] Tennyson sees no discrepancy between social and theological morality properly understood. Through the words of King Arthur at the end of the grail idyll, however, he does assert that theological morality must normally arise out of social morality, and not the reverse.

In "Sir Peter Harpdon's End" Morris again seems to posit values other than the betterment of society—the highest value in his essays of social criticism. Sir Peter Harpdon has personal ambition, a love of beauty, and romantic love for Alice de la Barde, but no utopian visions. The golden moments of his life are his happiness with Lady Alice, who imagines herself asleep in Avalon

"Among the poppies and the yellow flowers." [13] Sir Peter Harpdon admires the men of ancient Troy for striving to uphold an impossible ideal—not a social ideal but their devotion to Helen's beauty. Though "wrong as men could be," [14] they are justified, in the knight's eyes, by their loyalty to aesthetic perfection. The Morris of the prose works, the critic of industrialism and social injustice, seems at the moment to be absent.

In "Art and Industry in the Fourteenth Century," Morris makes it clear that he does not measure ultimate values by the scale of beauty alone. In this essay he departs sharply from the view that the middle ages could serve as an anodyne for the imagination, which his Arthurian lyrics misleadingly suggest. Here he presents his concrete image of the *aetas aurea* by which he measures the shortcomings of industrial society. The town of Medehamstead, called in the Middle Ages the Golden Burg, flourished for a short time like the Round Table but remained after its decay a light and symbol for centuries. Its rich shrines and St. Peter's Church lent a beauty to the community that modern towns lack. But Morris insists,

When I had the Golden Burg in my eye just now, it was by no means only on account of its external beauty that I was so impressed by it, and wanted my readers to share my admiration, but it was also on account of the history embodied in it. To me it and its like are tokens of the aspirations of the workers five centuries ago; aspirations of which time alone seemed to promise fulfilment, and which were definitely social in character. If the leading element of association in the life of the medieval workman could have cleared itself of certain drawbacks, and developed logically along the road that seemed to me it could scarcely have stopped short of forming a true society founded on the equality of labour: the Middle Ages, so to say, saw the promised land of Socialism from afar, like the Israelites, and like them had to turn back again into the desert.[15]

As for Tennyson, whose ideal is quite different from modern socialism, the perfect Order of the Golden Burg decayed as competitive hostilities overwhelmed a once cooperative society. The lust for gold and the striving of each man to maximize his own power impoverished and weakened society as a whole. Perhaps Morris chose the age of Chaucer rather than the age of the Round Table to use as an example in order to present a more authentic historical vision than he could do using the myth of King Arthur. His dream of a utopia where all work is creative expression could not, indeed, be envisioned through the metaphor of knights errant, whose vocation is more constabulary than creative.

When Morris does make the order of knighthood a social ideal in his poetic fragment "In Arthur's House" (c. 1865-1870), he shows a marked influence from Tennyson, which conflicts with his desire to uphold a pastoral way of life. Morris depicts Arthur's court, in the "midmost glory" of its days, and the contrasting life in rural nature. The knights and ladies, while on a hunting party, meet an old man who possesses the miraculous sword Tyrfing and has a gift for seeing into the past and future. He tells Arthur a story set so far back in time that the land was then populated by "fearful things by lake and fen,/And manlike shapes that were not men." Recalling the wilderness in "The Coming of Arthur," Morris imagines ancient Britain beset by beasts: the old man says, "no holiday/It was to chase the wolves away." Although the tale is not finished, it was to relate, as the ancient storyteller says, "The first recorded deed that drew/My father's house from the dark to light." [16] The imagery of wolves, light from darkness, the Round Table's moment of glory, and the house of God the Father may all derive from the *Idylls.* Morris' only departure from Tennyson —but an important one—is his switch to using the woods as a setting for moral influence rather than the court. Despite the images of destructive nature, which contradict a pastoral ideal, Morris desiderates the state of nature. The young, ignorant man of the woods at the beginning of the story happens upon a group of knights and ladies, much the way Perceval in Chrétien's romance encounters a knight for the first time. Not knowing what they are he believes he has seen "the household of the Gods." [17] He is morally superior to them, having lived innocently; only after he becomes the victim of their mocking does he feel hate for the first time. For Tennyson the woodsman is the greatest cynic, but Morris identifies sarcasm with the court and purity with nature.

The fragment takes place entirely in the woods, and its implicit Golden Age is the mythical state of nature. Even the glory of Arthur's days occurred before the recorded period of the Round Table:

> He held his court then in a place
> Whereof ye shall not find the name
> In any story of his fame:
> Carliel good sooth men called it not,
> Nor London Town, nor Camelot;
> Yet therein had we bliss enow.[18]

Like the Golden Burg, the obscure community of knights is a version of the static utopia, which Morris envisioned more fully in *News from Nowhere*. Graham Hough, in *The Last Romantics*, described *News from Nowhere* as "a modern reshaping of the ancient myth, in legend named the Golden Age, in political philosophy the state of nature" It is a "sketch of an idealized suburban life, in which there is no painfully hard work, no poverty, no passion that cannot be fairly contained by the social organism. . . ." [19]

Morris chose obscure historical examples for his utopia for the same reason that Tennyson divorced his Camelot entirely from historical reality. Both writers believed that the ideal community has a kind of simplicity that really never has been achieved. They envisioned a society based upon a unity of moral values; both turned to the middle ages for their examples, both refusing to see medieval times as wholly uncivilized and refuting the official dogma of evolution that places value upon complexity for its own sake. In his prose romance, *The Hollow Land*, Morris, too, turned against the modern myth of progress as the return of the golden world. Here once more he employed a medieval setting. His hero, Sir Florian, after a life of bloodshed and revenge, finds himself in The Hollow Land, where he meets his love, Margaret. The two linger in this Elysium and finally come upon

a fair palace, cloistered off in the old time, before the city grew golden from the din and hubub of traffic. Those who dwelt there in the old ungolden times had their own joys, their own sorrows, apart from the joys and sorrows of the multitude: so in like manner was it now cloistered off from the eager learning and brotherhood of the golden dwellings:

so now it had its own gaeity, its own solemnity apart
from theirs; unchanged, unchangeable were its marble walls, whatever else changed about it.[20]

The Hollow Land is the golden city, whose life has taken
the print of the new golden age. Morris idealized the
ancient marble palace instead: Sir Florian and Margaret
see two faces wrought in marble—ancient as in a dream,
yet their own faces; together they walk toward the golden
gates, open them, and see a great space of flowers, having
reached the true realm of gold.

Arnold

As an Arthurian poet, Matthew Arnold is outshone
but not entirely obscured by Tennyson. Unlike their more
romantic contemporaries, Tennyson and Arnold wanted
to make a modern poem out of Arthurian romance rather
than to revive the charm of the original legends. They
depicted the strange disease of modern life that sets in
when Merlin, who for Arnold is Goethe, "physician of the
Iron Age" ("Memorial Verses"), no longer exercises a
vital influence upon society.

The critics did not like Arnold's "Tristram and
Iseult" (1852) any more than they did the modern aspects
of the Idylls; its modern element was so clear that the
reviewers did not even try to bring it into accord with
their notion of Arthurian romance as an antidote to the
world of "Empedocles on Etna" and Maud.[21] Arnold in-
stinctively draws the least romantic elements from the
Tristram legend, as does Tennyson. He began the poem
with Tristram, who is in effect the romantic self in mod-

ern society, on his sickbed. The real sickness in the poem,
as Lionel Trilling writes, "is not the suffering of any
of its three characters but the despair of the poet himself,
speaking in his own person on the conditions of human
life that erode and deaden the human spirit." [22] Illness is
seldom an element in the lives of romance heroes, but
Tristram lives in the real world, where the sleet whipping
the window pane, the sea-gale which "nips too keenly the
sweet flower," and the "fierce Atlantic deep" greet his
tired eyes.[23] Wind, ocean, and fire—Swinburne's images
—recur in the poem, but the fire is dying and the elements threaten to upset the mind instead of stirring it.
Arnold's full, adjectival verse conveys the richness of the
life Tristram has lost. The description of the sick man
and Iseult of Brittany almost belies their malaise:

> Over the sick man's feet is spread
> A dark green forest-dress;
> A gold harp leans against the bed,
> Ruddy in the fire's light.
> I know him by his harp of gold,
> Famous in Arthur's court of old;
> I know him by his forest dress—
> The peerless hunter, harper, knight,
> Tristram of Lyonesse.
>
> What lady is this, whose silk attire
> Gleams so rich in the light of the fire?
> The ringlets on her shoulders lying
> In their flitting lustre vying
> With the clasp of burnish'd gold
> Which her heavy robe doth hold.
> Her looks are mild, her fingers slight
> As the driven snow are white;
> But her cheeks are sunk and pale.[24]

"Tristram and Iseult," like "The Last Tournament," portrays only the end of the Tristram story. The passion is over, and life itself is nearly gone. The heroic strength which Tristram in his delirium still imagines he possesses is long lost:

> At Arthur's side he fights once more
> With the Roman Emperor.
> There's many a gay knight where he goes
> Will help him to forget his care;
> The march, the leaguer, Heaven's blithe air,
> The neighing steeds, the ringing blows—
> Sick pining comes not where these are.[25]

Arnold's vision of the golden days includes Geoffrey's notion of Arthur as the conqueror of all Europe who triumphs even over Lucius in Rome. The two segments of Tristram's life seem to imply not only the present and past in his life but the present and past of Europe—its past vital, heroic and unified; its present disintegrating and deriving its only vital power from the spirit of the past. The poem is the work of a man conscious of living in an age of transition. When Tristram and Iseult meet, they are between two worlds—the past which they lived passionately and the future, told in Part Three, in which Iseult of Brittany lives quietly as a widow with her children. Sitting with her gold curls sweeping her broidery frame, Iseult of Brittany will light her silver lamp for fishermen on the iron coast. Being out of her golden element, she will not be happy, not at least able to feel the joy that Tristram and Iseult of Ireland felt in the springtime of their prime. But in the late winter, which seems to bear promise of spring, she tells her children,

with their bright blue eyes and flushed cheeks, the story
of Merlin and Vivien; it is a fairy tale to them, but to
the reader it is only another instance of the ennui that
weighs down the poem. The bright prospect of the future
that the children seem to promise is refuted by Vivien's
"fresh clear grace," which proves treacherous, "for she
was passing weary of his love." [26] The children seem to
lack the intense passion of their elders but have a kinder
light shining in their eyes. They are spirits of nature,
screaming in mad delight among holly-clumps and juni-
per, but Vivien too has the "spirit of the woods" in her
face, and the children's mother "seems one dying in the
mask of youth." [27] Life does not fulfill the promise of
youth, Arnold implies, and nature's infinite powers of
renewal do not always act upon society.

The first two parts of "Tristram and Iseult" portray
the effects of a single obsession upon the emotions—

> some tyrannous single thought, some fit
> Of passion, which subdues our souls to it,
> Till for its sake alone we live and move—
> Call it ambition, or remorse, or love—
> This too can change us wholly, and make seem
> All which we did before, shadow and dream.[28]

The last section of the poem pictures the effect upon
Iseult of Brittany that a different power has over human
life, which takes away just as completely the happiness
man desires. Not tragedy or deep sorrow causes her death-
in-life;

> No, 'tis the gradual furnace of the world,
> In whose hot air our spirits are upcurl'd

Until they crumble, or else grow like steel—
Which kills in us the bloom, the youth, the
    spring—
Which leaves the fierce necessity to feel,
But takes away the power—this can avail,
By drying up our joy in everything,
To make our former pleasures all seem stale.[29]

She avoids the noisier life that might take away her delight in the old tales she gleaned from Breton grandames,
but she has not been able to elude the pressure of life
and time entirely, and her features are fatigued; her voice,
which "alone/Hath yet an infantine and silver tone," [30]
comes languidly. Neither the obsessive passion, which is
like the Victorian rigidity Tennyson criticizes, nor the
gradual wasting away of a passive life (perhaps Elaine
symbolizes the same trap) can be a rewarding escape from
the sterility of a social waste land.

When Matthew Arnold first heard *Tristan and Isolde*
in Germany, he thought that he had managed the story
better than Wagner.[31] An extravagant opinion, no doubt
—for an opera lover an incredible one, but Arnold, who
was not particularly musical, referred probably to intellectual honesty rather than artistic impact. His "Tristram" as he said of his poetry in general, was an attempt
to capture the main currents of thought in his age. If he
does not match the scope and power of the *Idylls*, he does
at least honestly express the spirit of the age. He finds no
return of the Golden Age in the era of industrialism and
as Tennyson did refuses to follow in the direction of
Wagner or of his own English contemporaries who still
belong to the romantic movement. Not fantasy, not
single-minded passion, not living "in harmony with nature" could offer him hope; only the hope for change and

the enduring qualities of character gained through humanistic culture might have some chance of carrying society through the darkling plain of the present, where ignorant armies, as in Arthur's last battle, clash by night.

Notes

1. Quotations from Lowell are from *The Poetical Works of James Russell Lowell* (Boston and New York: Houghton Mifflin & Co. 1885), 107-112, 369-371. Lowell refers explicitly to "our iron age" and his correspondent in the *Biglow Papers* says he must check his own tendency to believe that "the happy sceptre of Saturn is stretched over this Astraea-forsaken nineteenth century." *Works*, 197-198. Lowell wrote "The Vision of Sir Launfal" during the time he was preparing a review of Tennyson's *The Princess* for the *Massachusetts Quarterly Review*. See Leon Howard, *Victorian Knight-Errant* (Berkeley and Los Angeles: University of California Press 1952), 269-273.

2. Sir Walter Scott's edition of the English *Sir Tristrem* was Swinburne's primary source; he possibly did not know Gottfried's version. See Samuel C. Chew, *Swinburne* (Boston: Little, Brown & Co., 1929), 168. Swinburne follows Malory in the Balen story but not in the Tristram legend; Tennyson does exactly the reverse. Swinburne chooses the more romantic version of both stories; Tennyson the less romantic.

3. Gosse and Wise, eds. *Works* (Bonchurch Edition, London: Wells, 1925-1927), Vol. I, 9-62, 63-73, 104-106.

4. "The Tale of Balen," *Works*, Vol. IV, 44-47, 179, 229, 243, 245. See also Swinburne's references to the hero-age of ancient Britain in *Locrine*. *Works*, Vol. X, 143.

5. "The Defence of Guenevere," *The Collected Works of William Morris*, with an introduction by his daughter, May Morris (New York, 1966), Vol. I., 8-9.

6. "Ogier the Dane," *Works*, Vol. IV, 230.

7. *Ibid.*, 236.

8. "King Arthur's Tomb," *Works*, Vol. I, 11.

9. *Ibid.*, 13-14.

10. "Sir Galahad: A Christmas Mystery," *Works*, Vol. I, 30.

11. "Useful Work versus Useless Toil," *Works*, Vol. XXIII, 99.

12. *Ibid.*, 112.

13. "Sir Peter Harpdon's End," *Works,* Vol. I, 55.
14. *Ibid.,* 42. "Near Avalon," too, expresses a sort of aesthetic escapism, six knights in the poem wearing locks of golden hair in their heumcs—their adoration of the queen being again much like the Trojans' sacrifice for Helen's beauty. *Works,* Vol. I, 140.
15. "Art and Industry in the Fourteenth Century," *Works,* Vol. XXIII, 387-388.
16. "In Arthur's House," *Works,* Vol. XXIV, 325.
17. *Ibid.,* 327.
18. *Ibid.,* 316.
19. Graham Hough, *The Last Romantics* (London, 1961), 111-112.
20. "The Hollow Land," *Works,* Vol. I, 290.
21. See Lionel Trilling, *Matthew Arnold* (Meridian edition; New York; World Publishing Co., 1965), 73-74, 130.
22. *Ibid.,* 122.
23. Arnold, "Tristram and Iseult," *Poems by Matthew Arnold* (Macmillan edition, New York, 1923), 198-202. Arnold derived the outline of his story from Dunlop's *History of Fiction. Poems,* 272-273n.
24. *Ibid.,* 199-200.
25. *Ibid.,* 209.
26. *Ibid.,* 233-234.
27. *Ibid.,* 228-233.
28. *Ibid.,* 230.
29. *Ibid.*
30. *Ibid.,* 228.
31. See Lionel Trilling, *Matthew Arnold,* 368.

6.

A Pyramid of Caveats: The Idylls *in Chronological Sequence*

No poem of Tennyson's relates more closely to the social meaning of the *Idylls* than "The Golden Year." What Tennyson called "The dream of man coming into practical life" to be "ruined by one sin" is the dream of the golden year, which Arthur tries but fails to actualize. He learns that such an effort is God's work ("The Passing of Arthur," line 22) and that the arrogation of such a responsibility in human society may lead to temporary improvement but will end in destruction. The fact that the Round Table, a symbol of the Victorian dream of the golden year, collapses is not a melodramatic sermon against Guinevere's sin but a reminder that the dream is hopelessly fragile—like the Lady of Shalott's fancy. Tennyson implied that Victorian optimism, with its apocalyptic sense of divine mission, would, if tested by the actual condition of existing society, be exploded as easily as

Arthur's Order. In the *Idylls,* Tennyson warned against
the social tendencies that belie the dream of the new
utopia. Tennyson sees the potential fate of society following a dialectic closely parallel to that described by
Marx, although he relies on a moral dialectic rather than
an economic, and it is a direction to be avoided. But
Tennyson, like Marx, envisioned a widening breach between a blind, increasingly small minority and the majority that comes to have fewer and fewer possessions (of
golden virtues for Tennyson) as it multiplies in numbers.
Like Marx, Tennyson saw as well a colossal conflict between the opposing factions and a new order succeeding.
But for Tennyson the last battle is not a revolution and
the new order is no utopia.

Tennyson clarifies his position toward utopian thinking in "The Golden Year." The poet Leonard, who has
written a lyric on the golden year, expresses Tennyson's
conviction that human betterment comes as a nearly in-
visible inching forward at the same time that the more
obvious cycles of change take place. He believed that
human progress was guided by divine purpose. The visible changes in human history he felt were like the cycles
of the earth or the ebb and flow of the tide as the ocean,
over the eons, gains slowly on the continents. The temporary increases, such as Victorian prosperity and Victorian peace, are delusive: in the golden year itself
"Wealth no more shall rest in mounded heaps" and "all
men's good" will be "each man's rule"; "universal Peace"
will at last be achieved. As for the present, "setting the
how much before the *how,*" it is a feverous age, in which
the forms of art to be newly attempted and the scientific
ideas to be discovered have already been exhausted.

To point up the characteristic impatience of a Victorian moralist with processes beyond our knowledge,

Tennyson answers Leonard's gradualism with a rebuff
from Old James, the narrator's travelling companion.
James is a sort of Carlyle, "full/Of force and choler"; he
mimics Leonard's visionary patience, then breaks his staff
against the rocks, as if to break the evolving cycles and
to explode Leonard's dreaming. "What stuff is this!" he
retorts;

> Old writers push'd the happy season back,—
> The more fools they,—we forward; dreamers
>   both—
> You most, that, in an age when every hour
> Must sweat her sixty minutes to the death,
> Live on, God love us, as if the seedman, rapt
> Upon the teeming harvest, should not plunge
> His hand into the bag; but well I know
> That unto him who works and feels he works,
> This same grand year is ever at the doors.
>   (lines 64-72)

But James in turn is mimicked by the blasting of a slate-
quarry nearby, and we return to the work of changing
and subduing nature (and not just living, as in the golden
year, from its fruits)—a task which continues into the
indefinite future.

King Arthur's ambition to found a perfect social
order is much like Old James' wish to break the continuity
of history and live autonomously in the present. He too
speaks of tilling fields and weeding gardens as our responsibility of the moment. But we live in a world of
becoming, and our largest responsibility is to assure that
the drift of society is toward improvement and not disaster. "All things move," says the poet Leonard, but in
Camelot Arthur attempts to keep them as they are through

the unchanging seasons of the golden year. Not he, nor
any man, can approach success in that attempt; man is,
in fact, constitutionally unsuited to a world of being.
Ulysses, who cannot rest from travel, is man; Telemachus,
"most blameless" like King Arthur, is a subduer of a
rugged people—either more or less than man. Old James
ridicules living in dreams of a golden past or future;
King Arthur warns against pursuing unattainable grail
visions: both overlook the need in man for an unattainable goal toward which to strive. They ignore the vital
power of dreams. The problem of Arthur's Order is not
that it could not attain the ideal, but that it *was* ideal for
a short time: all things change and any change from the
ideal is downward. Arthur attempts the impossible task
of restoring his Order to its original pattern and does not
see what it is becoming. The *Idylls* tells us why society
cannot and should not be perfect for men, who cannot
live as if time were nothing. Time destroys both Arthur
and Saturn.

The *Idylls,* as it appeared in separate volumes or
parts of volumes from 1859 to 1885, belongs with a whole
minor library of works dedicated to combatting the Victorian tendency toward rigidity. The habit of seeing in
one's moral arrangement, as King Arthur does, the final
design of God in the world, is a characteristically Victorian trait that a number of Victorian writers—perhaps
no less characteristically—criticized. "The Victorian,"
writes Houghton, "tends to divide ideas and people and
actions into tight categories of true-false, good-bad, right-
wrong; and not to recognize the mixed character of human experience." [1] The opposite intellectual current
which moved toward the ideal of seeing all sides of a
question, suspending judgment, and being critical of specious dogmatisms is no doubt, as Houghton suggests,

typical of the Victorian period as well; but it is a temper
of the best minds and not so much a quality of life in
Victorian society. In innumerable ways Tennyson challenges set Victorian ideas of morality, character, Arthurian
legend, and contemporary society. Even the Round Table
fell, Tennyson reminds us, although it was part of a far
more glorious Golden Age than modern society; far less
chance has Victorian society, threatened by the same temptations that destroyed the Round Table, to maintain or
even achieve the perfection that it would like to claim for
itself. Tennyson encouraged his readers to avoid sitting in
judgment or merely correcting minor deviations from
their codes, but to see the directions that changes were
going and to keep changes from becoming betrayals of
the larger human values.

Like Dante's *Inferno* (which one acquaintance said
that Tennyson knew by heart in the original), the *Idylls*
portrays a scale of excesses, the consequences of which
Tennyson considered to be social rather than metaphysical. Like Matthew Arnold, Tennyson was alarmed over
the prospect that the people of the modern world would
become enlightened without gaining essential understanding, informed but valueless, progressing quantitatively
but decaying in quality. Through the fatalist in "Despair"
Tennyson says what the dark side of the *Idylls* warns
against: "For these are the new dark ages,/You see, of
the popular press." The answer, if there is one, must be
found not in information and wealth but in culture.

1859: Four Women: The Betrayal of Love

Tennyson began his first four *Idylls of the King* soon after he had become involved in the feminist controversy. *The Princess* was published in 1847, but he continued to revise it and add to it well into the fifties; the link between the two works is important. In the *Idylls* Tennyson takes up with complete seriousness, although not without irony, the question of woman's role in private and public life—a topic that in *The Princess* he treated half seriously, half satirically. *Idylls of the King,* as the first volume was entitled in 1859, contained the stories of Enid, Vivien, Elaine, and Guinevere. In final form these would become five poems: "The Marriage of Geraint," "Geraint and Enid," "Merlin and Vivien," "Lancelot and Elaine," and "Guinevere." Actually all of the ten poems that comprise the Round Table series relate events that reflect modern relationships between men and women. This may be the reason that the Victorian novelists tended to respond far more favorably to the *Idylls* than did the poets.[2] Each of the four women in the first group of poems bears some resemblance to a character in Victorian fiction: Vivien is a kind of Becky Sharp, associated with all things French, exploiting others for her own aggrandizement, often by feigning helplessness; Elaine recalls Amelia Sedley and little Emily, a genuinely helpless creature ready to follow throughout the world the man she mistakenly loves; Enid, despite the differences in their husbands, is a sort of Dorothea Brooke, a provincial woman committed to upholding her husband's heroic calling; and Guinevere, returning in a destructive romance to a man who first appealed to her senses, because she finds her hsuband's idealism boring, is a Eustachia Vye. The first four idylls, which many reviewers were wont to regard as one continuous epic, are more appropriately classed as novelistic portrayals of nineteenth-century women.

An important aspect of Tennyson's Golden Age is the concept of ideal womanhood, the great principle of Goethe. Just as in the Golden Age not only Saturn but Astrea, the maiden goddess and principle of justice, presided, Arthur needs the feminine to inspire his Order. Arthur taught his knights

> To lead sweet lives in purest chastity,
> To love one maiden only, cleave to her,
> And worship her by years of noble deeds,
> Until they won her; for indeed I knew
> Of no more subtle master under heaven
> Than is the maiden passion for a maid,
> Not only to keep down the base in man,
> But teach high thought, and amiable words
> And courtliness, and the desire of fame,
> And love of truth, and all that makes a man.
> ("Guinevere," lines 471-480)

Woman symbolizes all that civilization means, but paradoxically the ideal civilization fails because of a woman. Each of the four women in the original idylls, either through the behavior she chooses or the role forced upon her by an imperfect society, proves how impossible is Arthur's ideal in real society.

The king clearly believes in what John Killham has termed the "doctrine of Female Influence." The betrayal of this principle makes Tennyson's warning relevant specifically to the Victorian era, though his larger point is not confined to his own times. Killham describes as an *idée fixe* of the Victorian era, the tenet that a woman's destiny is to exert moral influence through her role in Christian marriage, being educated properly with this guiding principle in mind.[3] King Arthur wrongly expects a real woman to live as if she were part of a code and had no individuality of her own. The doctrine of Female Influence, taken in its extreme form, is another of the rigid codes which people in reality cannot live up to. Rather than inspire ideal womanliness as part of the perfect order, the doctrine forces the four women to betray love.

Each of our four women embodies a cluster of ironies and moves in an element of paradox. Each is a real woman and not to be blamed for her individual failure to be an ideal influence for chivalry. The effect of each should discourage any simple belief in the possibilities for ideal love in real society, where even a well-intended virtue can have destructive social consequences.

Irony in its literary usage customarily involves more than an unexpected twist of fate: it emerges when a situation is complicated by two or more conflicting truths. We label a literary idea ironic if its is apparently true but actually false, or if it is true in a sense different from that intended. The double vision of irony requires flexibility, an openness to what Houghton called the "mixed character of experience."[4] Anyone reading Tennyson must have the ability to distinguish between the validity of behavior or ideas in the abstract and their applicability in a social context, for Tennyson has presented us with situations in which human actions and traits have effects opposite to their abstract value.

Elaine, the nearest to Tennyson's ideal as the paragon of womanly innocence, is no less blind in her devotion than the king in his idealism. Her love in fact causes Lancelot momentarily to become doubly disloyal: his "honour rooted in dishonour stood/And faith unfaithful kept him falsely true" ("Lancelot and Elaine," lines 871-872). In utopia, however, she might have exerted the perfect influence upon Lancelot: "And peradventure had he seen her first/She might have made this and that other world/Another world for the sick man. . . ." (lines 868-870). Arthur, in his illusion that he has created utopia, hopes that Lancelot does love Elaine (lines 598-599); and, to double the irony, well he might if he knew the real situation. Both Elaine and Arthur reveal their foolish trust through the most ironic utterances that are made in the idyll. Elaine's letter implores Guinevere to pray for her and asks Lancelot by his peerless honor to do as well (lines 1270-1274). The king then asks that she be buried like a queen (she has threatened to supplant the queen in Lancelot's life), and he tells Lancelot that free love, bound in ideal marriage, is for the best (as his own is not) and would have been so for Lancelot, who is, Arthur thinks unbound (lines 1370-1376). In the context of the situation, Elaine's love only intensifies Lancelot's anguish and causes her own death; her love is betrayed by reality. She lives and dies "in fantasy," the phrase referring in the beginning of the idyll to her daydreams (line 27) but later with ironic force to her illusions about Lancelot and life in general (lines 396 and 1125).

Elaine suffers from the shortcoming of taking true for false and false for true (lines 1, 4). Her dream of ideal love is a touching parallel to Arthur's dream of the golden year; both fantasies are too naive to endure the test of reality. She, like Arthur, departs at her death on a barge; the people of Camelot believe she is the fairy queen come to take Arthur to Fairyland. Without knowing it, they reveal an ironic link between Elaine and Arthur—their fitness for an unreal world.

The Elaine idyll contains a wealth of minor ironies. Elaine loves an anonymous knight who is given a blank shield by her brother, Sir Torre; the great knight's wearing a shield as blank as the villain Modred's (blankness signifying lack of heroic accomplishments) ironically reminds us of Lancelot's fall from knightly perfection. His disguise, too, reminds us that in the court his actions have been hidden. Elaine's dream about receiving the diamond comes ironically true at two moments—she is presented with the diamond by Gawain, who is the opposite of her ideal knight, and as her corpse passes under the window of the castle the queen flings the diamonds unwittingly at her, out of jealousy now made pointless by her death. The great diamond, Sir Torre (one considers the German *der Tor,* or "the fool" and in the Harvard Notebook Number 16 Tennyson referred to "Sir Tor") has told her, is for queens (line 230)—as indeed it is and is not—and not for "simple maids," which the queen is certainly not, though in a sense not intended by Sir Torre.

Ironies beget fresh ironies. The king hopes that Lancelot is no more a lonely heart; the irony is pathetic. Arthur's reassurances now seem like the efforts of a child to comfort an adult in sorrow over the child's own fated death. The king continues in his dream of making the world right, just as Elaine dreams of traveling to Camelot, where the queen will pity her distress and where, after her long voyage, she will rest. The queen does pity her after her voyage down what becomes the river of life leading to her permanent rest.

All of these ironies undermine the reader's admira-

tion for Elaine's kind of unqualified commitment in a
social situation. Elaine's altruism, which in the Golden
Age might have made her a disciple of Astrea, is in the
real world a self-denial so extreme as to kindle a passion
for death, which calls to her "like a friend's voice from a
distant field/Approaching thro' the darkness" (lines 992-
993). By her refusal to compromise her fantasy, she makes
it impossible for herself to live; she loves death and illusion rather than herself and life. The refusal to compromise in a complicated social situation can be the result
of childish stubbornness or sublime rightness, both of
which necessitate escape or tragedy. Elaine escapes in
death.

Guinevere is Elaine's opposite. A self-emancipating
woman, she too refuses to compromise her fantasy of a
bower of bliss with Lancelot. Like Elaine's dream, her
desires cannot coexist with an acceptance of social reality.
But rather than turn the conflict upon herself in suicide,
the queen turns her hostility outward in displays of
jealous temper against Lancelot and outbursts of mockery
against the king's social vision. She helps to prove the
power of Female Influence in a negative way: by thinking
only of her feelings and ignoring her influence upon
society, she gains unintended revenge upon the Round
Table for its violation of her emotions. The influence
of her adultery is very great indeed. Although she does
not live in fantasy, as Elaine does, she is guided by the
illusory premise that life is, as Edgar says in *The Promise
of May,* "an automatic series of sensations." Sensations
tell her that Lancelot is a better man than Arthur, and
she believes her senses to be self-justifying. She betrays
not just Arthur but her social responsibility as the greatest female example in the realm—a duty, however, that
she never freely chose. Although far from a militant femi-

nist, she enacts the extreme condition of feminine emancipation. Her independence goes beyond rebellion against repressive codes and role-playing; it is a denial of the feminine as a spirit of civilization. Guinevere is beautifully female by nature; but her womanliness remains only a phenomenon of nature—a priceless potential for making society better and more beautiful, an influence not only on her own world but for the ages, wasted by her living according to her own impressions. She is able to defend her feelings convincingly; but her actions she finally repudiates, for they are guided by the impossible wish for an escape from society.

The contrast between Enid and Vivien, suggested in Tennyson's subtitle, "The True and the False" in the first edition of the poems, is somewhat different from that between the queen and Elaine. Both Vivien and Enid are fully conscious of Female Influence and employ it to the limit of their ability to achieve opposite goals. Although Tennyson carefully avoids absolute categorizing, he seems to make a categorical judgment of Enid and Vivien. He introduced a redeeming irony to prevent their being taken for Virtue and Vice. Vivien, the worst of slanderers, hits nearer to the truth about the realm than her virtuous opposite. Vivien and Enid participate in society, not forcing illusions upon themselves; Vivien understands the wickedness of society and Enid the goodness. Enid is a female Gareth, appearing early in the story of the Round Table, coming from the provinces untainted by the rumors of guilt at the court, maintaining the idealism of the king and, through persistence, effecting a good influence upon others. But the Geraint idylls come after "Gareth and Lynette," and Enid's good influence upon Geraint is undermined by the irony that Geraint must return with her to the provinces to keep her away from the rumored guilt of the queen.

Vivien appears later than Enid as a consciously destructive spirit in an Order that has declined a step further. She has the persuasive charm of cosmopolitanism, and from it she derives her airy contempt for morality. Enid, with her provincial goodness, in contrast, is too tongue-tied and helpless to have a lasting influence upon her surroundings. She simply must endure Geraint's rigid suspicions until he regains belief in her. She succeeds because the world around her is still predominantly good. It has become bad enough, however, to require her to persist heroically to effect good; in "Merlin and Vivien" the realm has become worse; Vivien strives with no less persistence and overcomes the moral wizard. Elaine and Guinevere, with great potential for good influence upon society, fail to exert their power; Enid and Vivien, one with inadequate power for good and the other with power for only evil, strive to the limit to exert the power they have. Thus love is betrayed in all four stories.

Enid's power is slight, and her verbal impotence parallels Elaine's inability to find ideal love in the world. Society betrays the best ideals and efforts of both weak individuals. Enid's inability to employ the instruments of vice in the cause of virtue is a different form of the inability Elaine suffers from. Enid is inexperienced in courtly styles. Geraint forces her to wear her faded old dress until she reaches the court, possibly with the idea that until she becomes courtly in her being and able to deal effectively in surfaces, she should put up with the awkwardness of her provincial dress. Vivien wears ideas as she wears clothes—to seduce. Her capture of Merlin's charm marks the passing of intellectual persuasion from

the forces of truth to the voices of slander. Society is becoming the world pictured in *Maud,* the "Wretchedest
age, since Time began" where language is babble and the
only redemption is that not all men lie. Images of human
talk in the first four idylls carry forward through the
force of irony the rage against the abandonment of honesty and social responsibility expressed in *Maud.* Elaine's
servant has had his tongue cut out by enemies of civilized
order; he represents, as Enid does, mute virtue in the
face of whispered slander, sophists' arguments, and brazen
insult. Guinevere's death is looked forward to as a libera-
tion from the noises of this world to "where beyond these
voices there is peace" ("Guinevere," line 692). Arthur
speaks rarely, only when delivering judgment. Tennyson
seems to question Mill's notion of argument as the path
toward truth, for in the society envisioned by the *Idylls,*
real argument has deteriorated into hypocritical persuasion. When Gawain in "The Holy Grail" swears "louder
than the rest," we are prepared by the *Idylls,* in the edition of 1859, to expect folly or betrayal.

Vivien is an accomplished sophist armed with the
verbal weapons of nineteenth-century intellect. She appeals to the clichés of romantic love, though no romanti-
cist herself, imploring Merlin to "trust me not at all or
all in all ("Merlin and Vivien," line 396). She likens herself to a "summer fly," and Merlin repeats the phrase,
which echoes Burke's famous statement that men without
tradition are as flies of a summer. (Tennyson employs the
image in *In Memoriam,* Section L, as well.[5]) She appeals
through the image to a false sense of life's insignificance
as a way of inveigling from Merlin the charm which he
considers, as she does, important indeed. She mockingly
assents to Merlin's belief that silence is love and wisdom.
She plays the psychologist, analyzing his reticence as "sel-

fish" (line 335) and diagnosing his refusal to give her the charm as a symptom of his general mistrustfulness. He is a prophet, but not one of those "that can expound themselves" (line 316). Vivien appeals to Merlin through feigned avowals of religion, swearing by heaven that she would not prove traitoress to him, and calling down a thunderbolt from heaven if she lies. She employs the rhetorical technique of confusing categories, insisting that she cannot give Merlin all her love unless he give her all his by yielding the charm—a strange love token. She idealizes Elaine's kind of Evangelical altruism when she reminds Merlin that she has followed him at the sacrifice of her own welfare, even washing his feet (no more biblical gesture could be imagined) when she was "faint to swooning" (line 279). He should "sacrifice" the charm in return. Or, she can play the feminist, accusing Merlin of not acknowledging woman's intrinsic nobility: "Lo now, what hearts have men! they never mount/As high as woman in her selfless mood" (lines 440-441). From feminism she proceeds to utilitarianism, a movement closely tied to it, insisting that Merlin's desire for fame, a typically masculine illusion, is a denial of love. Woman "wakes to love," however, and love is of the moment; it "carves/A portion from the solid present, eats/And uses, careless of the rest. . ." (lines 459-461). Like the great philosophy of Use, in its Benthamite extreme, Vivien's supposed philosophy of love denies historical continuity and all sense of time but the moment. Vivien triumphs by appealing to Merlin through Guinevere's philosophy of love as momentary sensations, and by her facile persuasion, which is no different in essence from her exploiting sexuality.

The betrayal of love is most evident in "Merlin and Vivien," but it is the central breakdown in all of the four stories that make up the first group of idylls. To point up the parallel between Guinevere's betrayal of wifely love and Vivien's pretended love for Merlin, Tennyson links the farewell scene in "Guinevere" with the ending of "Merlin and Vivien" through similar details: in both scenes there is a waving of hands and a profession of one's fate to love the other still. The parallel is ironic, for Vivien's hands do not bless Merlin, nor did she ever love him. But on the important second level of truth Tennyson equates Guinevere with the harlot, Arthur with the foolish sage.

1869: The Waste Land: The Betrayal of Faith

Tennyson, like Arnold, shows increasing alarm at the breathtaking Victorian gains in scientific knowledge and technology as a threat to a culture not ready for shocks to its religious beliefs. The holy grail volume and *Culture and Anarchy* stand together as two classic manifestos against cultural sterility and intellectual chaos. The poet, in his four new idylls—"The Coming of Arthur," "The Holy Grail," "Pelleas and Ettarre," and "The Passing of Arthur"—brought to the fore his conviction that a society without faith in metaphysical principles is like a band of lost travellers in a desert. Neither Tennyson nor Arnold felt his own beliefs threatened by *The Origin of Species* (1859), for neither had the kind of fundamentalist belief that cannot endure scientific truth; but both writers, perhaps because of the passing of the Second Reform Bill in 1867, feared a kind of cultural "Jacobinism"—a term that Arnold employs to denote the "fierceness" and "addiction to an abstract system" that he sees as the spirit of the liberated but largely uneducated working class.[6] Tennyson, dismayed particularly by the fundamentalist tendencies of the populace, with their anti-Babylonian fervor and uncritical devotion to dubious beliefs, wove into the *Idylls* of 1869 a warning against the betrayal of society's organic faith. Such a betrayal, he makes clear, can manifest itself in apocalyptic visions as well as sterile materialism.

Tennyson included four visions of the Second Coming in "The Holy Grail" to caution against excesses which actually betray religion while they seem to further it. The holy grail itself, the cup used at the Last Supper, appears again on earth as a test of the moral condition of the Order; its reappearance suggests Christ's second coming, Arthur's legendary return, and the myth of the new golden age. Tennyson reserves judgment as to the veracity of such myths. In the broadest sense a Christian, he nevertheless conceived of the time scheme of the universe as a geologist or astronomer might rather than according to the biblical pattern; King Arthur himself is uncertain of his destiny in "The Passing of Arthur"; the golden age is primarily an ironic superstition in most of Tennyson's poetry; and he doubted for a long time whether he could portray the grail vision "without incurring a charge of irreverence."[7] The possible ambiguity of this statement is often missed. On one hand, some scholars, such as Algernon Herbert, regarded the myth itself as "a blasphemous imposture, more extravagant and daring than any other on record, in which it is endeavoured to pass off the mysteries of Bardism for direct inspiration of the Holy Ghost."[8] At the opposite extreme were those who, like Robert Stephen Hawker and Henry Alford, both acquaintances of Tennyson and poets who wrote about the grail (see Appendix), held the supernatural elements of the legend in great esteem. Tennyson averted irreverence by surrounding the grail in layers of uncertainty and leaving its moral value dependent upon the moral condition of those who seek it. The destructive effect of the quest could confirm the suspicions of Herbert, while the success of Galahad and, in another sense, of Bors, leaves open the alternative of revering the grail itself for those who wish to do so.

A glance at the process by which the grail idyll came into being may help to disclose the delicate balance Tennyson sought and achieved in it. Although created, according to Emily Tennyson, "like a breath of inspiration," [9] "The Holy Grail" required unusually refined judgment and conscious craftsmanship. The manuscript of the idyll, partly prose draft and partly verse, in the Harvard Notebook 38 reveals at least one important fact about the composition of the poem. The episode of Sir Bors was not part of Tennyson's initial plan for the poem. The prose draft omits Bors' adventure, and Arthur does not mention him after the quest; perhaps this is one reason why in the published idyll Arthur does not refer to Bors when summing up the negative results of the quest (lines 892-898). Tennyson seems to have added the episode involving Bors, since the prose sketch for it is written in the same notebook across the page from passages already in verse. In the verse manuscript Bors tells Arthur, "I have seen it," but the account of his imprisonment among the Druids is not versified in the notebook, except for the few snippets on the same page as the incomplete prose draft.

Tennyson must have felt he needed to include the episode concerning Bors to provide something that otherwise would be missing in the idyll. If he had not included Bors, the grail quest might have seemed an error *per se* rather than an admirable effort made at the wrong time and mostly for the wrong reasons. Arthur's confirmation of the truth of the unseen at the conclusion might appear too nearly refuted by the previous action. Without Bors, the failure of all the grail knights except Galahad would make the state of the Order seem completely decayed; Bors, however, does see the grail and return to Arthur's service, proving that at a better time the test brought by the grail might have been faced successfully by modest and dedicated men. Ironically, the attempt to face the challenge only depletes the already impoverished energies of the Order beyond redemption. Because Tennyson added the episode of Sir Bors the grail quest became the point of no return rather than the end itself, and the total chaos remains to come. Bors' character adds a touch of humanity to the religious ideals symbolized by the grail, which Tennyson does not find incompatible with Arthur's social ideals. Bors is, on the other hand, the only knight to serve both the grail and Arthur—to uphold both his faith and his social principles. For the other knights to have done the same would have required a much higher moral level in the Order than is present when the grail quest occurs. The grail itself is left neither the object of the poet's ridicule nor the emblem of his idolatry.

Tennyson used the grail quest to reflect the tendency some people have to favor belief which is spectacular and exclusive to one's self or one's special sect over a faith that can enrich a whole society. Throughout the four idylls of 1869 Tennyson employs a motif that is familiar in religious thought: life without faith is a waste land. For Tennyson faith can bring light to the dark land, making a garden of the wilderness, awaken life in the desert. Culture is not faith, but it is the fruit and sign of faith. A land without culture is necessarily a land without faith.

Tennyson's outlook on faith forms the basis of his quarrel with Evangelicalism. "On one of its sides," writes G. M. Young, "Victorian history is the story of the English mind employing the energy imparted by Evangelical conviction to rid itself of the restraints which Evangelicalism had laid on the senses and the intellect; on amusement, enjoyment, art; on curiosity, on criticism, on science." [10] Narrow religion, Tennyson believes, is rigid, sterile, uncreative; it does not have an organic function in society nor "grow" out of the human instinct for bettering social relations. The dogmatic or fundamentalist assurances, being faith imposed from without and not emerging from within a rich life, have the effect that John Henry Newman derived from rational arguments in proof of God: "they do not," he writes, "take away the winter of my desolation, or make the buds unfold and the leaves grow within me, and my moral being rejoice." [11]

King Arthur first brings to a land that is kept in a state of wilderness by the heathen invaders a faith that is so powerful that it makes utopia of his realm for a moment. He is both a religious leader and a culture hero in "The Coming of Arthur." He is challenged by a society that had "made/Their own traditions God, and slew the Lord" ("Aylmer's Field," lines 794-795). The skepticism of those who reject Arthur on the basis of his lineage is a reflection of Tennyson's bitterness toward Victorian lineages of wealth and name. Arthur routs the beasts from the gardens of the king ("The Coming of Arthur," lines 20-25), and clears the forest to let in the sun, and thereby manifests his power of bringing faith. With Guinevere he could have "power on this dead world to make it live" (line 93). The three colors of light falling on the three queens who bless

Arthur at the moment of the vows taken at his coronation suggest the rainbow in Merlin's song—a symbol of
the covenant, suggesting the superhuman origin of his
power.

In the grail idyll Tennyson shows the extent to which
Arthur's power of inspiring the knighthood has dimin-
ished by a new cluster of images that depict a waste land.
Lancelot, the greatest knight, whose failure in chivalry
is a crucial test of Arthur's Order, passes through "waste
fields far away" (line 785). He reaches a "naked shore,/
Wide flats, where nothing but coarse grasses grew" (lines
790-791). The other knights have similar experiences;
Percivale traverses a land of sand and thorns, where he
is thirsty unto death and sees mirages of the world's richness—a brook with lawns and apple trees, a kind woman
spinning, and a knight in golden armor—all of which
crumble to dust. Tennyson perhaps had in mind the
parable of the sower in St. Matthew. The seeds in the
parable, which are cast in diverse places, some in stony
regions, some on fertile ground, some among thorns, are
figuratively the word of God. The seeds that fell among
the thorns were choked by them.

The waste land in the grail story symbolizes the
sterility of materialism. The knight of gold, whom
the plowman leaves his plowing and the milkmaid her
milking to idolize, seems the "lord of all the world" (line
414). He is the central symbol of the Victorian golden
age that Tennyson bitterly mocked in *Maud* and ridiculed
by implication in the *Idylls*. The knight is a mirage that
crumbles to dust, a lord among the dead, leaving the
plowman and the milkmaid as foolish as the knights who
abandon Arthur's duties of plowing the "allotted field"
(line 904). When the knights return after seeing the
mirages in the waste land, they find the Order lean and

barren as well, greeting them is a heap of broken images;
Percivale relates:

> O, when we reach'd
> The city, our horses stumbling as they trode
> On heaps of ruin, hornless unicorns,
> Crack'd basilisks, and splinter'd cockatrices,
> And shatter'd talbots, which had left the stones
> Raw that they fell from, brought us to the hall.
>
> (lines 712-717)

Arthur has proved a dark prophet but a true one. His
religious role has changed from that of Moses, the law-
giver and the leader of his people, to the voice in the
wilderness.

Tennyson omitted the magical elements of the bleed-
ing lance and the fisher king from the story of the grail,
for he finds no such magical means of salvation for a
society that has become a waste land. The paradox of the
grail is that it can "cure" only those like Galahad who
need no cure. The grail vision gives Galahad power to
express what is already within him. The grail appeared
to him;

> And in the strength of this I rode,
> Shattering all evil customs everywhere,
> And passed through Pagan realms, and made
>   them mine,
> And clashed with Pagan hordes, and bore them
>   down,
> And broke through all, and in the strength of
>   this
> Come victor.
>
> (lines 476-481)

Galahad's purity was tested and proved true; the grail gave him power to further Arthur's purposes in the world.

Percivale, caught up in the vanities of the world, becomes delirious under the influence of the grail. He remembers,

> I was lifted up in heart, and thought
> Of all my late-shown prowess in the lists,
> How my strong lance had beaten down the
>   knights,
> So many and famous names; and never yet
> Had heaven appeared so blue, nor earth so
>   green,
> For all my blood danced in me, and I knew
> That I should light upon the Holy Grail.
>
> (lines 361-367)

His heart leaps again when he meets his sweetheart of old, now widowed and prosperous, and the people of her town implore him to stay and rule them, "as Arthur in our land" (line 605). He tears himself away and continues the grail quest. The grail only brings out in Percivale the worldliness that is already in him; we are not convinced by his supposed self-conquest and the fact that he becomes a monk. As he retells the story to Ambrosius, he reveals a great involvement in the world and considerable vanity over his rare experience.

Lancelot's experience brings out what is within him as well; his madness only intensifies the inner conflict which he has tried to keep at a refined distance, and his being conquered by little men on the quest only proves the fact that he cannot serve Arthur greatly any longer. Man's word, Arthur has told Lancelot, is God in man;[12] having broken his word beyond repair, Lancelot has be-

trayed the faith that would make the grail vision a positive
influence upon him.

The grail is a kind of premature last judgment, a
comment perhaps upon the fundamentalist's claim to
salvation by faith alone, as if faith could exist without
ethical action. The knights look to the grail as a panacea,
but Arthur, knowing it is primarily a test and not a cure,
is troubled at its appearance. The grail comes because of
the growing evil in the realm, a sign to maim the Order,
a touchstone to reveal it to itself. Accordingly, "Pelleas
and Ettarre," the next idyll following, reveals the realm
in the dark wood, largely without faith. The barrenness
of the idyll recalls the depletion of the Order by the grail
quest; the lack of faith, of keeping one's word, is now
the norm. No longer have emotions simply slackened
from the energetic dedication of "The Coming of Arthur,"
but they have become intense in the opposite direction.
Pelleas' persistence in courtly love arouses no love or
even tolerance from Ettarre; she is first coldly gracious,
then angry, then totally hostile. Pelleas' misguided faith
in her only leads him to frustration, hatred of her, and
finally opposition to the Order of chivalry. Pelleas is not
only lost to the Order, but he becomes a powerful enemy
against it as the Red Knight.

Pelleas first believes that Ettarre's coldness is simply
one of the "ways of ladies," "To those who love them,
trials of our faith" (lines 202-203). But she is simply
faithless, and Gawain is her perfect match. When Gawain
sees Pelleas thrust out of doors in bonds, he utters the
strange oath, "Faith of my body" (line 311)—a peculiarly
suitable defamation of *faith* for expressing Gawain's surprise at seeing an Arthurian knight humiliated. But on
learning the reason for Pelleas' degradation, Gawain
pledges his word to Pelleas that he will work his work

(an echo of Arthur's phrase in "The Coming of Arthur"). Moments after he gives his word to Pelleas, he breaks it, not bringing the news of gold from Ettarre, but remaining with her in a cynical affair. Pelleas is left in Arthur's position, but he is not blind to the truth: Gawain parallels Lancelot in his mission to bring Guinevere to the king, the hinted betrayal in "The Coming of Arthur."

Equally as destructive of the Order as the grail quest is the spreading corruption symbolized by the worm within the rose, which burdens Pelleas' mind as he recalls the "tender rhyme" he overheard in Camelot. Ironically, just when Pelleas leaves his musing on the song of the rose, he enters the castle of Ettarre to find a rose garden, above which are lying Gawain and Ettarre. Pelleas leaves his naked sword across their naked throats, and his imagination thereafter is infected by snakes, dung, nettles, and poisonous winds. He suffers the shocks of the court's general betrayal of the word and the queen's disloyalty. Knowing that he who loves the rose must die, if the worm be there, he joins the forces of hatred: hissing like a snake at the queen and springing from her door back into the dark wild, he repudiates his name, his sword, and his faith.

Too late Percivale tells Pelleas that the king himself is true, or else "let men couple at once with wolves" (line 526). Pelleas is one of the latter-day knights, created like the demigods in the vain attempt to restore the golden world that is long past. He was not at the Round Table when the original vows were taken, nor was he active in Arthur's heroic conquests over the invading hordes and encroaching wilderness. Percivale knows how necessary Arthur is to the existence of civilization; he is saved from Pelleas' flight into satanism by the spectre of wolflike men, "worse than wolves" ("The Coming of Arthur," lines 32-33). He remembers as Pelleas cannot the golden days when the king had not yet become a fool in the eyes of the knights. Perhaps Percivale's vision of the grail has told him that Arthur's faith will win out over a betrayal much greater than the scorning of Pelleas' golden circlet, which is a minor reflection of the crown.

In "The Passing of Arthur" no faith is left in the realm to bring the return to spring; only a different order can bring hope of renewal. Arthur has become what he explicitly hoped not to be: "a lonely king . . ./Vext with waste dreams" ("The Coming of Arthur," lines 81, 84). Tennyson intended in this concluding idyll to make Arthur seem both a Christlike savior and a human sufferer, or, what Guinevere finally acknowledges him to be, the "highest and most human too" ("Guinevere," line 644). To emphasize the point further, Tennyson added a line to the epilogue in 1891 describing Arthur as "Ideal manhood closed in real man" (line 38). If in "Guinevere" the human qualities of the cuckold clash with the dignity of a demigod, in "The Passing of Arthur" the human and the divine merge effectively in the portrayal of Arthur as simultaneous victim and savior. Tennyson added to the human appeal of the king in "The Coming of Arthur" by having Bellicent reminisce on the "golden hours" of her childhood (line 356), when she had been unjustly punished and Arthur comforted her. In the concluding idyll, however, Arthur is the victim of injustice himself; but there is no one to comfort him.

Arthur's divine and human qualities merge especially in the conception of him as the *pater familias* or head of a household. When Bedivere warns that "yonder stands/ Modred, unharm'd, the traitor of thine house," the king replies,

My house hath been my doom.
But call not thou this traitor of my house
Who hath but dwelt beneath one roof with me.
My house are rather they who sware my vows,
Yea, even while they brake them, own'd me
    king.
              ("The Passing of Arthur," lines 152-158)

Arthur himself extends the notion of the household beyond personal relations to the realm of spirit. Tennyson no doubt had Christ's prophecy to the apostles in mind: "A man's foes shall be they of his own household" (Matthew 10:36). The fall of Camelot also fulfills the warning of St. Mark: "And if a house be divided against itself, that house cannot stand" (Mark 3:25). In betraying Arthur's household, the knights betray their faith as well. St. Luke makes the analogy between a house without a foundation and a man without faith; when a stream beat against the house, he warns, "the ruin of that house was great" (Luke 6:49).

Arthur, like Christ, is a victim of his own household; and he is also a redeemer. The core of Arthur's final wisdom, made ironic by its repetition of Arthur's optimistic words in the first idyll, is that

The old order changeth, yielding place to new,
And God fulfils himself in many ways,
Lest one good custom should corrupt the world.
              ("The Passing of Arthur," lines 408-410)

Through his role in history, perhaps in ways beyond his immediate vision, the king has worked for the betterment

of man. The faith still expressed in the tragic ending of
the *Idylls* resembles that which Christ asked of his apostles when he said, "Let not your heart be troubled: ye
believe in God, believe also in me. In my father's house
are many mansions: if it were not so, I would have told
you" (John 14:1-2). In the midst of many betrayals,
symbolized by the "waste land, where no one comes,/
Or hath come, since the making of the world" (lines 370-
371), faith returns. The "fresh beam of the springing
east," which makes the king's forehead "like a rising
sun" (lines 382, 385), promises a redemption for Arthur
and, in some inexplicable way, for mankind.

1872: Spring and Fall: The Betrayal of Society

Like the first two groups of idylls, the penultimate
addition to the series, comprising "Gareth and Lynette"
and "The Last Tournament" (first published in the *Contemporary* in 1871), centers on a single pattern of betrayal.
The two idylls, which were intimately connected with
each other in composition,[13] add to the series a warning
against the betrayal of the social order. Tennyson believed
that the loss of faith in his own time might loosen the
whole social fabric; the betrayal of society is in his eyes
a predictable consequence of the betrayal of faith. In
"Gareth and Lynette" he portrays the individual knight
Gareth, nearly an ideal follower of Arthur, finding fulfillment through service to society, protecting the innocent (Lynette) from harm. In "The Last Tournament"
Tennyson shows the repudiation of the social order by

Tristram, Mark, the participants in the tournament, and the queen.

Tennyson introduces several new themes in both idylls to reinforce the concept of social betrayal. He describes Camelot in "Gareth and Lynette" as a city "built to music" (line 272); the social unity thus signified has disintegrated in "The Last Tournament," and Tennyson accordingly has the fool Dagonet chide Tristram for breaking Arthur's music (line 266). Tennyson also refers in both idylls to the vows taken by the knights and then broken. Merlin, who appears to Gareth as an unnamed ancient seer, warns him that Arthur will bind him by "such vows, as is a shame/A man should not be bound by, yet the which/No man can keep" (lines 266-268). These vows represent the basic responsibility of man to society; it is fitting that the anti-social Tristram should dismiss them as "the wholesome madness of an hour" ("The Last Tournament," line 670). Tennyson considered this theme important enough to add in 1873 the exchanges of vows between Arthur and Lancelot ("The Coming of Arthur," lines 130-133) and between the king and queen ("The Coming of Arthur," lines 464-469).[14]

Certain other common elements bind the two idylls as contrasting portraits of society. King Mark and the seneschal Sir Kay figure in both idylls. They are both vulgar and egotistical, both opponents of the social order Arthur is trying to maintain. In "Gareth and Lynette" Mark's attempt to buy his way into the knighthood is scorned by the king, and Sir Kay's ridicule of Gareth is itself made the object of ridicule when Gareth proves himself a great knight. In "The Last Tournament," however, Sir Kay's spirit of cynicism prevails, with Tristram as its chief spokesman. King Mark, who surpasses even

Tristram in disloyalty, reappears in "The Last Tournament" to kill Tristram. The story of the mountain treasure told by Gareth resembles the Nestling story in "The Last Tournament," both of them involving treasures found on mountaintops. In the latter tale, however, as is suited to the waning spirit of the Round Table in "The Last Tournament," the final outcome is that the child which had been rescued by Arthur and Lancelot later idylls reflect each other in still another way: he contrasts the vernal optimism of the Gareth story, conveyed dies under Guinevere's care. Tennyson makes the two especially through images of birds,[15] to the autumnal setting of "The Last Tournament," which suggests social decline.

Tennyson makes Lancelot significant in both idylls, since his breaking the vows of the Order is one of the most crucial social betrayals. Lancelot or his legend is omnipresent in "Gareth and Lynette." Tennyson adds to Malory's essential story, the tale of Beaumains, a number of details that make the bond between Arthur and Lancelot stronger. Only in Tennyson's version of the story is the king said to confide all his secrets to Lancelot, and Tennyson has Lancelot admonish Sir Kay for going against Arthur's orders and pursuing Gareth. Malory has Beaumains ask that Lancelot follow him and knight him at the appropriate moment, but Tennyson makes it seem that Lancelot is closer to Arthur by having the king, unknown to Gareth, ask Lancelot to follow Gareth in case he needs help. Tennyson also has Gareth overhear kitchen talk about exploits in which Arthur and Lancelot saved each other's lives. The social bond between the king and Lancelot is so strong in "Gareth and Lynette" that when Lancelot violates it, as he has already done in "The Last Tournament," he has exiled himself from society. He presides over the last tournament so absent-mindedly that Tristram replaces him as the controlling spirit of the idyll. Lancelot is significant more because of his improper absence than by his presence in "The Last Tournament." His troubles circle his "sick head" (line 138) all night, but Tristram, "half plagued by Lancelot's languorous mood" (line 194) bears his own disloyalties lightly

Lancelot's languid alienation affects the tone of "The Last Tournament." The sense of betrayal is modern rather than medieval. Tennyson intends it to resemble the decadence he finds to be overtaking Victorian culture. Ruskin in *Modern Painters* describes this malaise perfectly when he writes, "On the whole these are much sadder ages than the early ones; not sadder in a noble and deep way, but in a dim wearied way,—the way of ennui, and jaded intellect, and uncomfortableness of soul and body. The middle ages had their wars and agonies, but also intense delights. Their gold was dashed with blood; but ours is sprinkled with dust." [16] In "The Last Tournament," the most beautiful of the idylls in its setting of "death-dumb autumn-dripping gloom" and the ugliest in its unremitting cynicism, Tennyson depicts the lost glory of the past and the decadence of the present. Society, like the wine fountain in Camelot, seems to have "run itself/All out like a long life to a sour end" (lines 287-288). Dagonet, offered a drink from the fountain by one of the twelve damsels in white, finds "the cup was gold, the draught was mud" (line 298). The inner loyalties that held the society together have been betrayed, and only the external rituals of tournaments and prizes remain.

Tennyson displays his greatest lyric gift as he expresses this sense of betrayal and loss, the most genuine passion of the *Idylls*. It is not what he called his "passion of the past" but the poignancy of fleeting happiness at the moment its loss is realized. The greatest passages in the *Idylls* describe shining moments as they drift beyond grasp —Merlin's moment of weakness, Arthur's awareness that the knights have already pledged their vows to the grail quest, the knights' realization that they have returned to a ruined Order, Lancelot's divine despair when Elaine's body floats by on the barge, the universe of sadness contained in Dagonet's words when Arthur returns to the queen's darkened bower, Guinevere's wild regret when the golden days have passed, replaced by nightmares, King Arthur's sight of his whole Order passing and yielding to a world not his own, Bedivere's sense of his identity crumbling as the Round Table dissolves. Often with the loss of happiness comes the sensation, sometimes the real awareness, that the moment of joy was only a happy dream based upon misunderstanding, and even the pleasure of remembering happy days is tarnished by reality. The many references to *gold* and *golden* in the *Idylls*[17] create an illusion of splendor, but the cold realism of the Camelot society dispels the dream.

As in the first two series of idylls, in the penultimate group Tennyson portrayed a specific kind of betrayal, this time one still more fundamental and drastic in effect— the rejection of social identity itself. The intellectual concept on which "Gareth and Lynette" and "The Last Tournament" are based is freedom; like love and faith it is ambiguous, which allows us to rationalize the betrayal of ideals even while it serves as an ideal in itself. The liberty which Tennyson idealized is the freedom of the citizen in an ordered society. In "Of Old Sat Freedom on the Heights" he personified it as the custodian of tradition and honesty: "Her open eyes desire the truth./The wisdom of a thousand years/Is in them." She is "Godlike" and "king-like," revealing herself to the human race "part by part" from above, and standing as a check upon "the falsehood of extremes."

The personification of liberty seems to be present to the greatest extent in societies that are most civilized and peaceable. In "You Ask Me, Why, Tho' Ill at Ease," the poet envisions a stable land "Where Freedom slowly broadens down/From precedent to precedent." Although often criticized by the radicals of his day as hypocritical, Tennyson's combination of paternalistic welfare and centralized control is in many ways more like twentieth-century notions of liberalism than the laissez-faire principles of the Victorian industrial middle class.

King Arthur is a champion of true freedom, and if the world were a realm of gold, his effort to make all men free at once would succeed. Arthur is wrong not in what he wants to do but in believing that he can accomplish it. He allows too much freedom in his realm because he is not himself passion's slave and projects his unique self-control on others. The freedom which he makes possible for the Knights of the Round Table is, in the familiar categories posited by Erich Fromm, the "freedom to." Fromm's analysis provides the key to understanding the ambiguity of freedom in Tennyson's 1872 volume. "Freedom from," according to Fromm, is the first step in man's emancipation from tyrannical authority. This Arthur accomplishes by putting down the oppression of the invaders and driving back the intruding wilderness. Fromm believes, however, that "freedom to," the capacity for developing human individuality, has lagged behind the acquisition of "freedom from" in societies where Protestantism (ironically the champion of political freedom) has exercised strong moral control. The Evangelical restraints that Tennyson criticizes are the object of

Fromm's denigration as well: too often, Fromm main-
tains, the Protestant ethic stresses man's weakness and
his presumed need to submit to forces larger than himself.[18] King Arthur, with Evangelical zeal, frees the land
from oppression, but he cannot free the knights from
the tyranny of their passions. Freedom from must be
complete before freedom to can be exercised. The knights
become one will with Arthur in the fervor of the moment—he, believing that it is their power over themselves
and their capacity to express freedom, they instead sub-
mitting their wills to a force beyond them. He exercises
over them the charismatic force of a dictator, but he is
not a dictator. He relies, in fact, upon their own moral
consciences to subdue their passions while he tends to
what he thinks are the more important tasks of subduing
external threats to his Order.

Underestimating the power of the emotions, Arthur
unwittingly makes himself the scapegoat of the Order.[19]
He tries, like Milton's God, to make men strong enough
to stand yet free to fall, but he is not God and cannot
change the fact that the majority of knights cannot stand.
Merlin, the wisest of Arthur's followers, is not strong
enough; his fall is the most dramatic proof of Arthur's
error. Because he is removed from the private happenings
of his realm, Arthur is like a Victorian moralist who
believes in the concealment of sexual knowledge or the
laissez-faire economist who abandons ethics to the Invisi-
ble Hand and unwittingly betrays society to its baser
tendencies. If there is to be a central principle of freedom, there must, in real society, be a maximum of central
awareness and, to the extent of the need, a measure of
central control. Tennyson is quite in accord with Mill's
notion that individual freedom is limited only by the
rights of other individuals, but he is more alarmed than

Mill over the possibility that a decadent social climate will invite the domination of the weak by the powerful and encourage apathy toward violations of human rights.

Gareth, unfortunately, is the only free knight because his passions are in accord with his social responsibilities. He seems to confirm Arthur's faith in human strength and prove the viability of the Order. He is capable of living by high principle without being watched. Gareth's notion of freedom is patently biblical: "Who should be king," he demands, "save him who makes us free?" (line 136). He echoes the words of Christ, "And ye shall know the truth, and the truth shall make you free" (John 8:32). Gareth seeks in Arthur's Order a release from the bondage of instinct, freedom from the dependency of childhood, and freedom to break the bondage of wickedness everywhere. The paradox is that one can gain from the Order only an expression of what one brings to it, and Gareth's desire for freedom from himself, like Galahad's power to die into life, is exceptional.

Gareth, however, is plagued by his mother's wish to keep him free from the dangers of a knightly calling; this "freedom from" is a bondage to him. It seems an excessive protectiveness, because the realm is at the height of its goodness, but a similar protectiveness in the Geraint idylls—Geraint's shielding Enid from the taint of the queen—may already be justified. The conditions that Gareth's mother sets—that he serve a year and a day as a kitchen boy—are a further imposition upon his freedom rationalized in the name of protective freedom. Gareth replies that "The thrall in person may be free in soul" (line 163). Gareth finds greater freedom to act within the strict bonds of Arthur's Order than in an unregulated life, for the bondage is his own mastery of his psyche, not an imposition from without.

In the social climate of "The Last Tournament" the predominance of Tristram's cynicism and his triumph over knights loyal to Arthur prove that the knights were not ready to uphold Arthur's ideals without his supervision. Tristram's sudden humiliating death cancels any belief that he offers a viable alternative.

To intimate Tristram's perversion of freedom as a motive for behavior in "The Last Tournament," Tennyson relied on a new pattern of ironies. The situation of the tournament itself provides the central irony. It establishes the perfect condition of "freedom to" for the knights, where each can demonstrate his individual power without hindrance from arbitrary human judgment or external interference. Tht concept of the game, as Johan Huizinga points out, is a sign of man's attainment of freedom. Play, he writes, "is free, is in fact freedom." It is a "disinterested" activity.[20] The game is a microcosm of free society in its pure state. To participate in the tournament is to affirm the values of freedom and equality (Arthur is sometimes ousted himself in tournaments) and the universal applicability of rules. Analogous to the free "play" of the mind in culture, the tournament simulates the condition of the Golden Age; in Arthur's realm it is a utopia within a utopia.

But society, like a game, requires the general assent to rules and the watchfulness of objective umpires. The breakdown of Arthur's Order is manifested in the unruly last tournament. The spirit of the game vanishes when society ceases to value the rule of law; intellect is no longer the free pursuit of truth but a rationalization of selfish ends.

A German biographer and critic of Tennyson, T. A. Fischer, points out a number of ironies in the idyll which illustrate that freedom has deteriorated into a breaking of rules. First is the irony of the tournament's title, the "Tournament of the Dead Innocence." Although Tennyson derived its name from the child that died under Guinevere's care (itself a significant comment), he used it to betoken the loss of innocence in the realm, also indicated by the queen's unfaithfulness and subsequent betrayals. A second irony lies in the fact that the king should choose Lancelot to preside in his place, since Lancelot has, without Arthur's knowledge, usurped the king's place in Guinevere's heart. It is ironic that the rules of the most important tournament are broken, as the arbitrator, himself a breaker of social rules, ignores offenses (as Arthur remains blind to the breaking of his vows) and presents the gems to the red hand (a symbol of God's vengeance to come) of the least pure of the knights, Sir Tristram. It is ironic that the fool should call Arthur the "king of fools." [21] He is indeed that in many senses: the epitome of all folly; the king for those who are fools enough to follow him; still the king for the fool himself, who remains loyal in his folly and ultimate wisdom; the King Fool among a world of fools; the King Fool for the small band of men who in their folly wish to right the evils of the world.

In the midst of this irony lies the central fact that freedom, worshipped in Tristram's song, has deteriorated into a rationalization for its opposite, an escape from freedom. Freedom means breaking the rules of the tournament while the king is away. Freedom is the "Brass mouths and iron lungs" that jar the golden dream of the follower of the vision, "expecting all things in an hour" ("Freedom"). It is the liberty of broken music to escape the bonds of harmony. It is the "thralldom who walks with the banner of Freedom, and recks not to ruin a realm in her name" ("Vastness"). Freedom is Tristram

and Isolt's unloving escape from the tyranny of King
Mark and the license of Arthur's knights to shout down
the admonitions of the king and butcher the followers
of the Red Knight and their families. Freedom is the
specious wisdom that "we love but while we may." It is
to be an animal without even the animal's capability for
maintaining the spirit of a game. It is freedom from
society.

1885: The Night Cometh: The Betrayal of Self

"Balin and Balan" was completed in 1874, but Tennyson chose not to publish it as the last addition to the
Idylls until 1885, when he included it in *Tiresias and
Other Poems*. In it Tennyson presented a vision of society
in civil war and returned to the theme of madness presented in *Maud*. Tennyson used the motif of fratricide—
or, figuratively, any violation of the unseen brotherhood
of man—to bind together several other stories of violence:
Leodogran is assailed by his brother, King Urien; Tennyson mentions the two brothers, one a king, that slew each
other and left the crown of diamonds that Arthur discovers; Lancelot's own kin set upon him in tournament
when he is disguised: and in the blind, savage hacking
of the last battle, no one knows whether he is attacking
friend or enemy, for friends have become enemies. "Balin
and Balan" is perhaps fittingly presented along with
"Tiresias" as emphasizing the contraries of physical sight
and moral insight. Although belonging rather early in the
entire series, it expresses powerfully and richly a crucial
last caveat of the laureate to his age.

The most fundamental betrayal of all, which makes all loyalties groundless, is the disavowal of the "King within." Central to Tennyson's criticism of the new golden age is its betrayal of selfhood, its primitive reduction of man to inert machines, its setting all against all. In "Locksley Hall Sixty Years After," published in the Tiresias volume, Tennyson continues his challenge to empire and industrialism: "Have we grown at last beyond the passions of the primal clan?/'Kill your enemy, for you hate him,'/Still, 'your enemy' was a man." In the deepest philosophical sense, for Tennyson, no death is ever escaped: any homicide is a fratricide, even a suicide. Brotherly love is only a pale reflection of the ideal betrayed when society becomes civil war. Balin and Balan die, locked in each other's arms, having judged, as did Guinevere, by the evidence of the senses. Too late, they too learn the reality of the unseen. Behind the veil of individual difference and temporal physical life lies the realm of eternal being: Balin and Balan seem to suggest not just two members of a family or even two members of the human family but two parts of the self—Balan, the rational, controlled knight, behaving as the code demands, resembles the conscience; Balin, "the savage," unable to live within a code, suggests the aspect of the self that Tennyson calls in "Lucretius" the "brute brain within the man's"—the darker force of the id. Not just brotherhood but selfhood disintegrates in the fratricides depicted in the *Idylls;* the metaphor for its destruction is madness, which in *Maud* Tennyson links explicitly with suicide. The poet's moral idea is perfectly expressed in the words of John Donne's seventeenth meditation: "Any man's death diminishes me, because I am involved in mankind." Like the cycles within cycles of his time scheme, Tennyson's patterns of inward-turning violence seem to involve the different spheres of self, society, and mankind.

Violence in all three spheres, of self, society, and mankind, is accompanied and partly caused by lack of insight. No amount of information and no degree of idealism can make up for the errors committed by Arthur and his knights. The many patterns of reverse errors already present in the *Idylls* are now brought together, around a core of confusion in "Balin and Balan." Throughout the *Idylls* men take true for false and false for true, faith for superstition (the "fancy" of Arthur's Table Round), and superstition for faith (the grail). They take freedom for bondage, and the reverse. Wisdom and folly are mistaken for each other. Slanderers are convincing but the honest are not believed; the noble are taken for their inferiors (Arthur and Gareth) and lesser men for greater (Lancelot and Gawain). Finally, vision (which is, as Arthur says after the grail quest, the world of the senses) is believed real, and reality is dismissed as vision. In the "spiritually central" lines of the *Idylls,* the king's speech after the grail quest, Tennyson made it clear that he believes the individual self and God to be the final reality. This is betrayed in "Balin and Balan." The idyll is a test of the society that places its trust in the unreal.

Tennyson, who was one of the chief founders of the Metaphysical Society, believed that the fundamental purpose of intellect in his time was to transcend the differences in sects and ideologies and pursue the metaphysical question—to define, that is, the nature of reality, or, in Matthew Arnold's phrase, "to see the object as in itself it really is : . ." [22]

Social decline makes the reverse errors mentioned above prove ironically true. The queen, for instance, incorrectly thinks that Arthur lives in superstition, being

"Rapt in this fancy of his Table Round" ("Lancelot and Elaine," line 129). Ultimately, Arthur is the greatest realist, for he remains loyal to metaphysical reality; but in the decaying society he rules, his utopianism indeed becomes fanciful. But Balin and Balan commit reverse errors by believing what they see and hear. Their trust in appearances is revealed in their childlike attempt to pose as "mightier men than all/In Arthur's court." (lines 31-32). Fittingly, Arthur himself disproves their claim by overthrowing them. He remains unrecognized until after their defeat, since it is his principle to trust only inner reality rather than overpower them with his outward authority. Ironically, in "The Coming of Arthur," when he makes no attempt to impress Guinevere by his appearance, assuming she will love his inner worth alone, he commits a more fatal error than Balin's.[23]

Balin has done violence to one of Arthur's knights because he heard that the man had slandered him. Balin is welcomed back to the Order like the prodigal son, but he again shows his concern for appearances by asking the queen for permission to wear her crown as the symbol on his shield. The king assents to the idea reluctantly, not eager to rely upon appearances to inspire chivalric behavior. The king wrongly considers the request harmless, as merely an appearance. The crown does not represent to him Balin's ambition to usurp royal status.

Balin trusts his impressions in all things. For example, he overhears Guinevere and Lancelot in their garden meeting. He is instantly sure of their adultery—when even the reader cannot be. Then, hating the queen's symbol, he tramples upon his shield. Balan sees him doing so, but thinks he is an unknown knight repudiating his own honor (which he is doing). He attacks him and they wound each other fatally. But before dying, Balan assures Balin that the queen is loyal, and once more Balin trusts his ears. We are left not knowing whether Balan is right or wrong, aware only of the confusion and tragedy that result from trusting in appearances.

In "Balin and Balan" Tennyson includes all the themes present in the earlier idylls. The betrayals of love depicted in the first group of idylls are recalled: Elaine's self-denial, for example, is mocked in "Balin and Balan" by the foolishness of Vivien's squire, who is ridiculously eager to die for her. Elaine's self-destruction and Vivien's destructiveness portrayed in the four idylls of 1859 are reflected in Balin's oscillation between savagery and self-reproach, which makes love impossible for him. Balan's quiet nobility recalls Enid's tongue-tied honor. Balin's quick suspicion, his rash trust, and his dying in the belief that his idol, Guinevere, is true parallel the blindness already portrayed in Geraint, Elaine, and Arthur. Guinevere's infidelity—the most blatant betrayal of love in the first group of idylls—also provides major ironies in "Balin and Balan," one of which is that the reader cannot even be sure the queen is actually unfaithful yet, while the effect of rumors has made the truth almost a matter of indifference. Camelot could fall without Guinevere's infidelity when slander and suspicion become widespread.

The central motif of the "Holy Grail" volume—the betrayal of faith—is recalled in King Pellam, who pollutes pure ideals by claiming descent from Joseph of Arimathea, collecting fraudulent religious relics, and adopting an ascetic life style only for the sake of competing with Arthur's Christian ideals. Pellam's celibacy, even his casting aside his wife, are reminiscent of Percivale in "The Holy Grail," who turns away from his former love while on the quest and becomes a monk after he returns. The betrayal of society—the theme of the two idylls published in 1872—is suggested as well in Pellam, one of the ancestral voices prophesying war, who originally lost with Lot against Arthur and still repudiates Arthur's leadership. His refusal to pay tribute recalls the Red Knight's opposition to Arthur. The demon of the woods, anonymous like the Red Knight, was once driven from society by its evil and returns to oppose it. His story parallels Pelleas' exactly. And in the hissing Garlon is another Modred.

Nature and civilization are clearly at war in "Balin and Balan." The good and bad forces of the Arthurian world are all in evidence; collapse seems distant in the mid-May setting, but threats are coming more frequently. Instead of Gareth's idealization of Arthur, we have Balin's ironic worship of the queen. Tristram's freedom of the woods is foreseen in Balin's flight from the Round Table. The idyll shows the society of Camelot poised at the moment when it could go either way: the idylls before it show good triumphant, but Balin's reform is not lasting like Edyrn's; and the idylls after it show continuous decline. The errors, if not the wickedness, are becoming the norm and are now committed by groups rather than individuals: Pellam has a minor society of his own, and Balin and Balan stand together against Arthur for a moment. The need for truth is now urgent, but truth is difficult to attain. The one seer who understands both the value of Arthur's ideals and the real situation is still to be ensnared by Vivien. But "Balin and Balan," the last written of the *Idylls,* is an introduction to the first, "Merlin and Vivien." The wheel has come full circle; the crucial failure of the whole series is the immediate outcome of the social condition in "Balin and Balan." A violent oscillation between faith and doubt is setting in, and human conflicts are overthrowing the spirit of the game. The mist of the last battle has yet to take physical form, but the misunderstandings it symbolizes are already numerous. For Balin and Balan "The night has come" (line 610). For Victorian society, Tennyson implies, the crisis is at hand.

Notes

1. See Walter Houghton, *The Victorian Frame of Mind* (New Haven: Yale University Press, 1957), 162.
2. Not only Swinburne, but the Brownings and Hopkins, spoke disparagingly of the *Idylls;* but Dickens, Eliot, and Thackeray seem to have been overwhelmed.
3. John Killham, *Tennyson and the Princess* (London: University of London, 1958), 101-102. In *The Princess* Tennyson portrays the lady "rapt in glorious dreams, the second-sight of some Astraean age" (lines 419-420), recalling the feminine element in the Golden Age.
4. Houghton, *The Victorian Frame of Mind*, 162.
5. Be near me when my faith is dry,
    And men the flies of latter spring,
      That lay their eggs, and sting and sing
    And weave their petty cells and die.
6. Arnold, *Culture and Anarchy*, edited by R. H. Super (Ann Arbor: University of Michigan Press 1965), 109. Tennyson commented that the key to the grail idyll in particular lay in "a careful reading of Sir Percivale's vision and subsequent fall and nineteenth century temptations. . . ." *Memoir*, II, 63. Some sort of spiritual extremism is no doubt implied.
7. *Memoir*, I, 456.
8. Herbert, *Britannia After the Romans*, i, vii.
9. *Memoir*, II, 57.
10. G. M. Young, *Victorian England* (Oxford Paperback Edition, London, 1963), 5.
11. Newman, *Apologia Pro Vita Sua* (Garden City, 1956), 319-320.
12. This passage was added in 1873.
13. This is evident from Harvard Notebook 40, which contains seven pages of prose draft for "Gareth and Lynette" and considerably more verse manuscript, along with a short prose sketch upon which "The Last Tournament" was based, ac-

cording to Sir Charles Tennyson.—See Ricks, ed., *Poems of Tennyson*, 1705. This manuscript was written between 1869 and 1872. A reference to Tristram in the Gareth sketch may have provided the first link to the Tristram story in "The Last Tournament." Although published earlier, "The Last Tournament" seems to have been conceived later than "Gareth and Lynette," as a bleak counterpart to it. The changes Tennyson made in the Gareth story—particularly his removing Bellicent's liason with Lamorack from the prose draft of both idylls—sharpen the contrast between the loyal and innocent knighthood of "Gareth and Lynette" and the pervasive disloyalty in "The Last Tournament."

14. He also omitted from "Gareth and Lynette" Gareth's repudiation of the "foolish vows" to his mother, which appears in the prose draft. He did this no doubt because "Gareth and Lynette" portrays the *keeping* of vows. Bellicent in the prose draft sends Gareth to Arthur's kitchen to overhear gossip about the queen's infidelity, which she thinks would justify her own affair with Lamorack. This, too, did not belong in the innocent world Tennyson wanted to portray in "Gareth and Lynette."

15. Neither Malory's story of Beaumains nor Tennyson's own prose draft contains these images; he seems to have added them consciously for the purpose of sharpening the seasonal contrast between the two idylls. The setting of "Gareth and Lynette," including the birds singing, could have been suggested by Chrétien's *Perceval*, which also begins with a widow in the forest looking after her only son.—See R.S. Loomis, trans., "Perceval, or the Story of the Grail," *Medieval Romances* (New York: Modern Library, 1957), 9.

16. Ruskin, "On Modern Landscape," *Modern Painters*, III, in *Works*, ed. Cook and Wedderburn (London, 1902-1912), Vol. IV, 321-322.

17. Baker in the concordance lists forty references to "golden" and twenty-six to "gold" in the *Idylls*.—*A Concordance to the Poetical and Dramatic Works of Alfred, Lord Tennyson*. (London: Kegan Paul, Trench, Trübner & Co., Ltd., 1914), 271-272.

18. Erich Fromm, *Escape from Freedom* (New York: Holt, Rinehart & Winston, Inc., 1941), 37.

19. Clyde de L. Ryals even sees King Arthur as a villain because he deprives the knights of their individual wills and drives them into madness, though his intention is to make free will possible.—*From the Great Deep*, 90.

20. Johan Huizinga, *Homo Ludens: A Study of the Play-Element in Culture* (London, 1949), 1-14.

21. T. A. Fischer, *Tennysons Leben und Werke* (Gotha: Friedrich Andreas Berthes, 1899), 208-210. Sir Dagonet figured in the first prose sketch of the idyll and was important to Tennyson.

22. Arnold views the main effort of the critical mind in all areas of knowledge to be the effort to define the object in itself. "The Function of Criticism at the Present Time," *Viking Portable Arnold*, 234-238.

23. Tennyson possibly recalled the scene in *Troilus and Cressida,* which he called Shakespeare's best play, where Cressida first sees her destined lover. Pandarus tries to arouse her romantic interest, but when Troilus appears, she asks, "What sneaking fellow comes yonder?"—Act I, Scene II, line 214. The extent of Arthur's fatal blindness is suggested in "The Passing of Arthur," where the king says that "The king who fights his people fights himself./ . . . the stroke/ That strikes them dead is as my death to me."—(lines 71-73) Therefore he seems to be "king among the dead" after his former knights fall. (line 146). The many misunderstandings and the general climate of mental confusion in the *Idylls* provide a telling linkage between the Arthurian tragedy and the intellectual milieu of the poet. Clyde de L. Ryals gives a remarkable enumeration of the elements conveying the idea of misunderstanding (which he interprets as a metaphysical theme rather than a comment upon Victorian culture) in *From the Great Deep,* 191-192.

7.

The Dissolving Image: Patterns of Meaning in the Completed Poem

The *Idylls* became an organic whole when Tennyson added "Balin and Balan" in 1885. In 1888 he divided the Geraint story into two separate idylls to give a mechanical completeness to the structure, and in 1891 he added the final touch, a single line in the epilogue. The poem had become an intricately developed tragedy stressing man's inability to remain civilized without the guidance of a metaphysical ideal. Overcoming many inauspicious circumstances—a difficult topic, diverse sources, an uncomprehending public, and a serial method of composition—Tennyson achieved a stunning artistic triumph. The *Idylls* is the central work of his career; it expresses an intellectual seriousness commensurate to the more than sixty years he spent on the subject of Arthurian legend. Yet it is one of the best organized of long poems, seeming in its unity to be almost the outpouring of a single gust of inspiration. An appreciation of the poem must involve both its artistic patterns, particularly the development of its imagery, and its comment on man and society. I shall consider in turn the light imagery, the nature imagery, and the changing conceptions of utopia closely connected to the image patterns.

The Shining Moment

Light images in the *Idylls* often have the evident meaning of spiritual or metaphysical influence on human action. As the story moves from the utopia of Arthur's court in "The Coming of Arthur" to the jungle and waste land of the concluding idylls, there is a general darkening of the landscape accompanying the loss of Arthur's ideal in Camelot. At the same time there is a fragmenting of white light, suggesting wholeness and perfection, into the broken lights of the spectrum, generally suggesting sensuality or at least a love of surface impressions. As Camelot darkens and becomes more colorful, so to speak, the characters of the knights worsen; and to them, in their human weakness, the world sometimes appears more beautiful than before. For Guinevere, too, "That pure severity of perfect light" in Arthur's character is too much to bear; and she longs for the "warmth and colour" that she found in Lancelot ("Guinevere," lines 641-642). In the prologue to *In Memoriam* Tennyson expresses the hope that men will learn to bear the divine light; the *Idylls* is a lament over the fact that the light is often too strong for human eyes. In "The Coming of Arthur" the knights arise from having taken their vows, some dazed "as

one who wakes/Half-blinded at the coming of a light"
(lines 264-265). The light, to follow the simile, seems to
issue from outside the dream of this life—as in fact Arthur
himself seems to do. Excalibur is a blade "so bright/That
men are blinded by it" (lines 299-300). Tennyson continues to mention errors and limitations of sight throughout the *Idylls* as a reminder that a belief in the reality
of the unseen is necessary. At the moment of the king's
coronation honor shines through the "listening eyes" of
the knights ("The Coming of Arthur," 1. 320), as if for
the moment they have transcended ordinary vision. The
light of Guinevere's eyes smites "on the sudden" into
Arthur's life; and with her he hopes to "Have power
of this dark land to lighten it" (line 92). Ironically, however, Guinevere's eyes missed seeing Arthur's greatness
on first impression; and later in the story the king himself will feel the need to be enlightened. At the triumphant beginning of his reign Arthur's eyesight is keen:

> . . . the world
> Was all so clear about him, that he saw
> The smallest rock far on the faintest hill,
> And even in high day the morning star.
>   ("The Coming of Arthur," lines 96-99)

But after the downfall of his Order, just before the last
battle, it seems to him

> . . . as if the world were wholly fair,
> But that these eyes of men are dense and dim,
> And have not power to see it as it is:
> Perchance, because we see not to the close. . . .
>   ("The Passing of Arthur," lines 18-21)

And in the battle "even on Arthur fell/Confusion, since he saw not whom he fought" ("The Passing of Arthur," lines 98-99).

Many images of light occur in "The Coming of Arthur" to suggest the momentary perfection brought by Arthur's creation of the Order. "Gareth and Lynette" portrays the kingdom still in a predominantly civilized state; the "Sun of Glory" is said to be still at its height. When King Mark sends a golden cloth that shines like "the sudden sun/Between two showers" in the hope that Arthur will include him in the Round Table, a mute reproof of the gesture is given by the shields of the knights, some "blazon'd rich and bright" in remembrance of their accomplishments ("Gareth and Lynette," lines 380-410). Camelot is still bright, and its light is generally symbolic of virtue, but deceptive images also occur. Gareth's opponents are named the Morning Star, the Noonday Sun, and the Star of Evening; but all are villains. On the other hand, Death, advancing fearsomely in half-light, proves to be only the disguise covering "the bright face of a blooming boy" (line 1373).

In the idylls immediately following, eyesight becomes noticeably less trustworthy as the world of Camelot darkens. In the Geraint idylls a moral decline is suggested in the recurring preference for varied colors over pure white. Enid, for example, must dress "In crimsons and in purples and in gems" to "please her husband's eye" ("The Marriage of Geraint," lines 9, 11). The women in the fall of the wicked Earl Doorm are "dressed in many hues" ("Geraint and Enid," 1. 597). The moral condition of the Order is still good enough in the Geraint idylls that Edyrn "drew himself/Bright from his own dark life. . . ." ("The Marriage of Geraint," lines 594-595). But at this point in the poem the balance of good and evil has almost been reached, for the next idyll, "Balin and Balan," is the first to have a tragic ending; furthermore, the scarcity of light images and the multiple errors of the eye in "Balin and Balan" reinforce the impression of growing evil. A lovely simile of a distant fire reflected in a cabin window suggests how remote and indirect the influence of the ideal has become in the Order (lines 226-232). Pellam's idolatrous chapel is gloomily nocturnal. Vivien appears in the idyll, singing mockingly of the "fire of heaven" and the "old sun-worship." Connected by her original name, Nimuë, with the Lady of the Lake, she is actually a parody of Arthur's spiritual protectress: in the following idyll, "Merlin and Vivien," she is described as wearing "a robe/Of samite without price, that more exprest/Than hid her, clung about her lissome limbs" (lines 219-221). Merlin tells her the story of "A maid so smooth, so white, so wonderful,/They said a light came from her when she moved" ("Merlin and Vivien," lines 564-565). Such, he allows himself to see in Vivien, as she glitters like a serpent in the "glare and gloom" of the storm (line 957). Merlin's failure of vision is the turning point of the *Idylls*.

"Lancelot and Elaine" contains light images that suggest an ideal already lost. Often they occur in someone's memory. Lancelot recalls an emerald Arthur wore "centred in a sun/Of silver rays, that lightened while he breathed" (lines 294-295). Elaine remembers the "shining flood" (line 1036) that seemed in her childhood to offer a route to court. One of the most memorable flashes of light in the *Idylls* accompanies the disappearance of the diamonds into the stream. Again the light suggests an ideal lost—Elaine's pure life, the diamonds as a reward for knightly greatness, Lancelot's loyalty to Arthur. In this scene, the queen, angrily believing that Lancelot's

heart has not been given with the diamonds, declares
that Elaine shall never have them:

> Saying which she seized,
> And, thro' the casement standing wide for heat,
> Flung them, and down they flash'd, and smote
>   the stream.
> Then from the smitten surface flash'd, as it were,
> Diamonds to meet them, and they past away.
> Then while Sir Lancelot leant, in half disdain
> At love, life, all things, on the window ledge,
> Close underneath his eyes, and right across
> Where these had fallen, slowly past the barge
> Whereon the lily maid of Astolat
> Lay smiling, like a star in blackest night.[1]
>
> (lines 1225-1235)

Lancelot sees the truth distinctly but can do nothing
about it, and it seems to mock him: the reflections mock
the real diamonds, and Elaine's death-smile mocks Lancelot's disdainful glance.

Light as mocking illusion in "Lancelot and Elaine"
introduces the climactic light-image in the poem—the
holy grail. Arthur warns the knights that they will follow
wandering fires, as they do; the grail itself is a deceptive
promise of redemption for all but Galahad. It appears
on a beam of light reminiscent perhaps of the spiritual
light that once inspired the Order. On the quest the
various knights frantically pursue false lights in many
forms, but only Galahad is surrounded by the pure white
light of truth. Those who return find a Camelot darker
than before the appearance of the grail, and from that
point darkness ceases to be a mere lack of light but

gathers into a devilish energy. Thus, Pelleas, as innocent as Gareth had been, brings the sunshine to Camelot
("Pelleas and Ettarre," lines 21-22); but darkness finally
claims him for its own. "Pelleas and Ettarre" takes place
mostly at night; after his frustrating love for Ettarre,
Pelleas journeys from the physically dark field to the
morally benighted Camelot, where he hisses at the queen
and returns to the dark, preferring true darkness to false
lights.

In "The Last Tournament" the Order has become
so immoral that goodness seems a minor flaw spoiling the
homogeneity of evil. One snowdrop throughout the year,
cries "the swarthy one," would make the world "as blank
as winter-tide" (lines 216-221). The image of autumn
leaves links the varied colors suggesting sensuality with
decay; the ladies at the feast "cast the simple white" (1.
232) and glitter "variously gay" (1. 226). The active power
of darkness emerges in "Mark's way," which is to creep
out of the night and slay Tristram. Innocence is suicidal:
the ptarmigan that "whitens ere his hour/Woos his own
end" (lines 693-694). Arthur at the end of "The Last
Tournament" returns to find the queen's bower dark:
truth, now found only in darkness, confronts him; the
final calamity approaches.

In "Guinevere" the darkness becomes surrealistic.
The queen dreams, in the "dead night" (line 70), of the
blackening shadow her guilt casts upon the kingdom. She
flees all night long to Almesbury, where she hears a
novice sing a song of night and disappointment. Guinevere later answers the novice's pert moralizing with the
question, "What knowest thou of the world and all its
Lights/And shadows, all the wealth and all the woe?"
(lines 341-342) In the depth of her moral experience sug-

gested by the darkness as well as the light the queen at this moment surpasses the dramatic force of her earlier passions; her dignity rivals the king's. He enters in darkness; she shadows her face from him (lines 414-415). In the darkness over her head his hands wave a blessing and farewell. Through the "thick night" (line 566) Arthur hears the sound of the trumpet. The creeping mist obscures the one low light, which no doubt recalls the lamps of the foolish virgins in St. Matthew. Only recollections of the shining past brightens the night, and the blurred phantom of the king, departing in mists and moony vapors.

The *Idylls,* a tragedy of human shortsightedness, ends fittingly at night with the forces locked in the "last, dim, weird battle of the west" ("The Passing of Arthur," line 94). A white mist, blanker and more suggestive of nothingness than the vivid blackness of "Guinevere," makes the battle a confusion in which everyone's sight fails: "And some had visions out of golden youth,/And some beheld the faces of old ghosts/Look in upon the battle" ("The Passing of Arthur," lines 103-105). There are "cryings for the light" (line 116), but none comes. Although a hush falls at last and the wind blows away the mist, human sight remains unreliable to the end. Bedivere attempts to keep Excalibur to please men's eyes, trusting what he can see more than Arthur's command. Arthur confesses that even his mind is "clouded with a doubt" (line 426), but he knows that men must keep their faith in the unseen lest, like animals, they "nourish a blind life within the brain" (line 419).

The shattering of his utopian dreams helps him reach a stronger faith through the experience of doubt. In *In Memoriam* Tennyson writes of Arthur Hallam:

He fought his doubts and gathered strength,
  He would not make his judgment blind,
  He faced the spectres of the mind
And laid them: thus he came at length

To find a stronger faith his own;
  And Power was with him in the night,
  Which makes the darkness and the light,
And dwells not in the light alone. . . .
                              (Section XCVI)

Hallam's mythical namesake in the *Idylls* finds that this Power remains with him through the darkest of his experiences. The queens that once stood by him "clothed in living light" ("The Passing of Arthur," line 454) now return to carry him to his symbolic destiny, the rising sun. But Bedivere's straining eyes cannot discern the place to which Arthur vanishes. Then, in the epilogue, Tennyson links the idea of limited vision to the social meaning of the poem for his own era: faith must be kept, he urges, even though the Victorians have not found their utopia, and "the goal of this great world/Lies beyond sight" (lines 59-60).

The Reversion to Nature

Tennyson used a succession of nature images which parallels and reinforces the light imagery in the *Idylls*. The Round Table dissolves as nature overwhelms the work of a king. Nature proves a far more subtle adversary than the king expects: Guinevere's love for Lancelot, a perfectly natural instance of sexual selection, easily escapes his notice. This one flaw is adumbrated and ramified in countless ways throughout the *Idylls;* it is nature's most important triumph, and the many images of nature foretell the coming tragedy.

The *Idylls* vividly illustrates a conception of nature common to the Victorian era. Darwin's theory only added impetus to the trend toward distrusting the natural as a norm for behavior and regarding the term *nature* in a pejorative way. John Stuart Mill's essay *On Nature,* first written at almost the same time Tennyson published *In Memoriam,* is an important manifesto marking the Victorian departure from the romanticists' view of nature as a source of moral good.[2] Tennyson showed nature in the *Idylls* as a force corresponding to the spirit of evil in a Manichean universe, impelling man downward into bestiality.

Tennyson gave an exact image of man's place in the natural world in his lyric "The Kraken," which appeared in *Poems, Chiefly Lyrical* (1830). The Kraken, a mythical marine creature, lies asleep in a seascape of sponges that swell to "millennial growth and height" amid "many a wondrous grot and secret cell" that give the environment, like the landscape of the *Idylls,* a deceptively pastoral ambience. At the end of the world the Kraken will emerge, like man's bestiality in the Armageddon of the last battle, to be seen by "man and angels," constituting the lowest part in the scale of being which circumscribes man's potential.

Tennyson inherited from the renaissance the view of man "divided against himself by divine strivings and a bestial predisposition."[3] The four zones of sculpture on the hall of Camelot could be taken for a conventional representation of the renaissance scheme:

And in the lowest beasts are slaying men,
And in the second men are slaying beasts,
And on the third are warriors, perfect men,
And on the fourth are men with growing
    wings . . .
           ("The Holy Grail," lines 234-237)

But Tennyson implied that Arthur's attempt to make men from beasts is an acceleration of evolutionary processes. The knights' relapse into bestiality is a slipping backward as well as downward. Tennyson converts the beast image of the renaissance from the subhuman to the prehuman.

Man reverting to nature is not an animal but a monster. He possesses too great a destructive power to be merely bestial, and he is too much aware of his powers of choice to see himself as a simple instrument of nature. His lapsing from civilization is a tragic mockery: the feral children in Cameliard before Arthur came "grew up to wolf-like men,/Worse than the wolves" ("The Coming of Arthur," lines 32-33). Wolves, as Thomas Huxley writes, "could not hunt in packs except for the real, though unexpressed, understanding that they should not attack one another during the chase." [4] Man is not furnished with social instincts strong enough to allow him to live in a state of nature without government, yet nature has given him too much aggressive and erotic instinct to abide easily by the rules of civilization. Tennyson envisions man in nearly the same way that Freud does in *Civilization and its Discontents:* civilization demands from man a repression of his instincts and creates, to the extent of the repression, a residue of frustration that poses a permanent threat to the continuance of civilization. In this tragic paradox Tennyson finds the only answer to be a realistic social arrangement that does not depend upon human perfection for its stability—and a cautious hope for gradual improvement.

"Arise and help us thou!" cries Leodogran to Arthur, "for here between the man and beast we die" ("The Coming of Arthur," lines 44-45). Arthur meets the paradox with a simple solution: He demands perfection of his followers. His ideal admits of no compromise; Arthur himself—"Is he man at all?" asks Tristram—cannot become a slave to passions he seems not to possess. But his human followers are caught in the battle between nature and civilization, feeling divided loyalties, unable to live in a vacuum, battling in part against themselves no matter which side they join.

Tennyson used the nature pattern in the *Idylls* to suggest an organic process in civilization—a natural growth, ripeness, and decay—that will take place if society is not otherwise consciously directed. Tennyson may have read that the shifting of populations in Europe is nature's way of assuring that "When old countries are become exceedingly corrupt, similar modes of life, purer morals, and better institutions may rise in new ones. . ." [5] But Tennyson does not see God's purpose manifested in the death of societies: King Arthur concludes,

> I found Him in the shining of the stars,
> I mark'd Him in the flowering of His fields,
> But in His ways with men I find Him not . . ."
>   ("The Passing of Arthur," lines 9-11)

Tennyson did not call for permanence but for direction toward an ideal. The Round Table, an attempt to achieve permanence, begins to collapse as soon as it is founded. Arthur attempts to maintain a Golden Age of being in a universe of change; like Hallam in *In Memoriam* "appearing ere the times were ripe," he is conquered by nature's tendency to rid itself of extraneous forms. His goodness soon becomes a hatred and abnormal element in a society committed to living "according to nature." As King Arthur fails, he becomes aware that the world is made up of changing orders and that the static paradise—typified in the myth of the Golden Age—is impossible for human beings, except as a guiding principle.

Arthur, bearing the standard of the soul, a being to whom time is nothing, is finally defeated in "the war of Time against the soul of man" ("Gareth and Lynette," line 1168). Throughout the *Idylls* nature is an agent of time. The sense of time in the poem reflects the notion of time peculiar to the Victorians. On the one hand, as J. H. Buckley suggests, the Victorians sensed an acceleration in the pace of everyday life—machines required constant attention, rail travel increased the speed of transportation, and personal contact became more frequent. Scientific discoveries also pushed the creation of the earth back eons in time, and the larger temporal context of human development seemed to yawn immeasurably vaster than before.[6]

Surrendering to nature for the Victorians meant yielding to the inhuman force of time, which seemed everywhere to destroy man and his works, as the *Idylls* portrays: "Too late" is the common cry of failure—Balin and Balan learn each other's identity after they have fatally wounded each other; Arthur returns too late to prevent the grail quest and too late to find his queen in her bower; Lancelot becomes aware of his effect upon

Elaine after she takes her life; Guinevere learns that she had no reason to be jealous of Elaine after she has thrown away the diamonds; Geraint and the queen are both too late for the hunt; the queen repents too late, as the song of the novice reminds us; and the king discovers too late his utopian folly.

Time carries the Round Table through the cycle of the seasons—through the golden days of April and May, when the knighthood flourishes, through the summer of passion and the autumnal sadness of the last tournament, to the death-white mist and bitter north wind of the last battle, which suggest, like the frozen depth of Dante's hell, a nadir below bestiality.

Images of the ocean throughout the *Idylls* suggest the power of nature eroding civilization. Lancelot on the grail quest comes upon a naked shore where nothing but coarse grasses grow, and the sea, "heapt in mounds and ridges,/Drove like a cataract. . . ." And in its midst sways a single product of human making, a boat, "Half-swallow'd in it, anchor'd with a chain" ("The Holy Grail," lines 795-800). During the final battle the ocean trifles pitilessly with the men themselves. The battle rages on the sea coast, where the "wan wave" "Brake in among dead faces, to and fro/Swaying the helpless hands, and up and down/Tumbling the helmets of the fallen . . ." ("The Passing of Arthur," lines 129-132).

"The Coming of Arthur" presents a land beset by wild animals; the wolf becomes the emblem of predatory nature. In the Gareth idyll the young knight's ambition and the general idealism of the court are conveyed by many images of birds—the eagle, to symbolize aspiration; the goose, to remind us of the vulgarity of avarice, the lark, the hawk, the owl, the peacock, the marvin, the linnet, and the merle—all given further importance by

Gareth's song of the birds that warble in the morning sky. Destructiveness is suggested by the hawk.

The Geraint idylls, as is discussed in Chapter 2, center on the motif of weeding the garden; the images of weeds and similar undesirable things of nature subtly signify the forces that threaten Arthur's efforts. "Balin and Balan" moves from the garden (which itself proves a disastrous setting for the tryst between Lancelot and Guinevere) to the woods. King Pellam's palace is in the woods. The leaf is the central image of the idyll, ironically calling to mind the moral idea of turning over a new leaf—which Balin tries but fails to do. Vivien sings, "The new leaf ever pushes off the old," but this to her means the blossoming of a new paganism: "The fire of heaven is on the dusty ways,/The wayside blossoms open to the blaze./The whole wood-world is one full peal of praise" ("Merlin and Vivien," lines 436-445). The legend of the demon of the woods further distinguishes the woodland from pastoral innocence.

Tennyson introduced another nature motif in "Merlin and Vivien," the wind and storms, to signify Vivien's foul speech and disruptive power. Her song of fame makes the wind-image meaningful in still another way; the wind begins to suggest the rumors flying about Camelot, which help to destroy the loyalty of many of Arthur's followers. The song was first heard as the knights rode "against a rushing wind" (line 423). The idyll opens with an impending storm, though the "winds are still." King Mark heard rumors—a "wandering voice,/A minstrel of Caerleon by strong storm/Blown into shelter at Tintagel"—say that Lancelot loves no simple girl but the queen (lines 9-11). The wind suddenly arising and the wave breaking recur in the idyll to hint the breaking of news about Lancelot and the queen. Vivien herself puffs "sharp breaths of anger" from her fairy nostril (lines 846-847). The idyll ends with the final thunderclap of denunciation of Vivien that also announces the coming doom; Tennyson recalls the image in the "thunderless lightnings striking under sea," in the epilogue—which are telegraph messages, hopefully thunderless because they do not bring threats to the empire.

Tennyson did not rely on a few repeated nature images so heavily in later idylls, but introduced an increased variety of natural phenomena. In "Lancelot and Elaine" images of leaves, small plants, insects, and particularly flowers typify Elaine's helplessness; and the frequent appearance of the rising sun seems to suggest her youthful hopes. But her hopes are only fantasies, and the sun rises threateningly red, "blood red" (line 1018) as the grail will be, in a "fiery dawning wild with wind" (line 1013). It breaks from underground, as if from an evil source; Guinevere reminds us that the "low sun makes the color" (line 134). The ambiguity of the red sun as a promise of dawn or an augury of night is repeated in the epilogue, in which Tennyson hopes that the shadows being cast upon the empire are the long shadows of morning and not those of sunset. A fatal image, recalling the despair of *In Memoriam,* marks the transition from woodland to wasteland: the old yew clutching at the stones in *In Memoriam* is an emblem of death. The "black walls of yew" in "Lancelot and Elaine" portend the death of the realm and introduce the waste land of the grail idyll.

At the beginning of the idyll Sir Percivale and Ambrosius are sitting beneath a yew that darkens half the cloisters. An April gust puffs its branches into smoke by blowing the pollen abroad; the image links the idyll with "Lancelot and Elaine" through the yew tree and with "Merlin and Vivien" through the image of wind and smoke (fire being frequently associated with Vivien). The sandy waste land of "The Holy Grail" brings forth little more than thorns; there are Druid stones, barren crags, "waste fields," the "naked shore/Wide flats, where nothing but coarse grasses grew," surrounded by "the dreary deep" (lines 785-805). Tennyson mentions imaginary creatures such as the wyvern, dragon, and griffin (line 350). "Heaps of ruin, hornless unicorns,/Crack'd basilisks, and splinter'd cockatrices" (lines 714-715), which greet the returning knights, suggest that the fantastic conceptions once inspiring the Order have been shattered and discarded. After the vision of the dead land, with its great black swamp and poisonous flower, Arthur's mild wisdom that the king is like a hind with land to plow comes as a helpless abstraction; no field or garden is left to him.

The nature imagery of the conquered wilderness being turned into a garden, then becoming a woodland, a waste land, and finally a conquering jungle seems, like the light imagery, to go beyond apparent nothingness into an active negation. The transition to jungle begins early in "The Holy Grail" when

> An outraged maiden sprang into the hall
> Crying on help: for all her shining hair
> Was smear'd with earth, and either milky arm
> Red-rent with hooks of bramble, and all she
>   wore
> Torn as a sail that leaves the rope is torn
> In tempest.
>
> (lines 208-213)

Men are becoming beasts again. Pelleas, as if to fulfill Arthur's behest, brings the sweet smell of the fields to

Camelot ("Pelleas and Etarre," line 5), but Ettarre finds him "Raw, yet so stale" (line 109). He resembles Gareth, but the Order is no longer springlike, and instead of birds we have worms, rats, and snakes added to the evil menagerie, and a poisonous wind blows across the landscape (line 557).

"The Last Tournament" portrays a society ruled by the law of the jungle. The redness of the maiden's milky arm in "The Holy Grail" becomes a prevailing symbol of savagery. The autumnal sadness of the landscape suggests that the battle against nature has been lost. Swine and goats now seem wiser than Arthur, who has tried to make men from beasts (lines 325-326). Men are "secure/Amid their marshes" (lines 425-426). The wet wind and dead leaf, the scorpion-worm that stings itself to death, the cat-like Mark, Arthur's own men, who pillage savagely, all attest to the triumph of nature.

In "Guinevere" men have become animals completely. The earth is dead, and a combination of waste land and jungle emerges. Guinevere creeps before Arthur; Lancelot is lion-like, Modred is by turns a caterpillar, a fox, and a "subtle beast," and his followers are "creatures" (lines 524, 106, 32, 10, 104). Even the supernatural seems to partake of the jungle: a "ghastly something" flies at Guinevere in her dream (line 78). She hears the "spirits of the waste and weald" (line 128) and a raven croaks in the cold wind before the morn, appearing a "blot in heaven" (line 131). The novice tells of many happy wonders that appeared before the sin of the queen, when the "land was full of life" (line 257). But they seem to be superstitious daydreams and only accentuate the landscape of death now stretching boundlessly in all directions. Pollution, "like a new disease, unknown to men" (line 515) sickens the whole society as the events darken into the eerie world of the last battle.

The nightmare vision of nature in "The Passing of Arthur" shows what man becomes when a whole society dissolves in bestiality.[7] Men battle like creatures of the jungle in "Sweat, writhings, anguish, laboring of the lungs" (line 115) but isolated by the mist on a waste-land coast "Of ever-shifting sand" (line 86). Man's isolation now separates him from the world of nature, for his condition has fallen beyond the bestial into a chaos that resembles the end of the world. Recalling Doomsday in St. Luke, the sun burns at its lowest in the year (line 91), and the moon lights the haze far into the distant hills (line 42); the mist chills one who breathes it "till all his heart was cold/With formless fear . . ." (lines 97-98). Bedivere reassures Arthur that his name and glory will cling "To all high places like a golden cloud . . ." (line 54). But in the "Oaths, insult, filth, and monstrous blasphemies" (line 114) there is no promise of redemption. Society and the very hope for continued civilization seem for the moment to be destroyed in an indifferent universe. Lyonesse is

> A land of old upheaven from the abyss
> By fire, to sink into the abyss again;
> Where fragments of forgotten people dwelt,
> And the long mountains ended in a coast
> Of ever-shifting sand . . .   (lines 83-87)

Nature promises nothing; to live in harmony with it is to be tumbled helplessly on the coast of a waste land, to be a forgotten skeleton on a gloomy shore. The great voice of the ocean "shakes the world,/And wastes the narrow realm whereon we move . . ." (lines 139-140), reminding us of "days of old and days to be" (line 135).

Through his pattern of nature images Tennyson cautioned against the many errors that arise from naturalism. He warned particularly against the naturalistic fallacy, which is perhaps *the* error in nineteenth-century social thought, whether it be Thomas Gradgrind's misplaced utilitarianism or Herbert Spencer's opposition to all central planning. Guinevere's reliance upon the senses alone and Tristram's pseudo-philosophy of being a woodsman of the woods [8] are only two of the naturalistic errors which cause the fall of Camelot. Tennyson implied that a source of values other than nature must be recognized if social change is to be a conscious improvement rather than purposeless movement from the homogenous to the heterogeneous.

Tennyson stressed the need for social improvement rather than affirming an unquestioning belief in progress. For the notion of progress tends to dignify as a natural law many of the inhumanities created by industrial society. Tennyson revived the myth of the Golden Age to answer the myth of progress—to see in the very elements of "progress" the potential cause of decline—complexity of social relations, competing individualism, rapid change, irksome labor, and war. The age of industrialism for Tennyson is neither in harmony with a benevolent nature nor a modern utopia. The perfect society, he believed, must remain a vision for the future toward which real society might move only if man realizes that he bears, not only in his body, but in his psyche and his limited powers of discerning truth, what Darwin calls "the indelible stamp of his lowly origin." [9]

The Passing of Utopia

Tennyson lends a special Victorian relevance to the story of the Round Table by creating an evolving pattern of utopian ideals that conflict with and develop out of one another. The Victorian era was preeminently a time of utopian schemes, but there was considerable disagreement over whether utopia could be attained through science, religion, education, socialism, or hero-worship. The Round Table may seem distant from these Victorian social ideals, but in fact it was not uncommon for the Victorians to imagine themselves latter-day knights in armor as they formed organizations intended to improve society. Tennyson portrays Arthur's Order as a metaphor for the Victorians' idealism; the fall of the Order is a warning to any contemporary idealists that the distance between Victorian England and utopia is enormous.

Karl Mannheim's classic sociological study, *Ideology and Utopia,* defines three conceptions of utopia that provide useful points of reference for understanding the social philosophy of the Idylls.[10] Mannheim refers to the "chiliastic utopia" (the vision of the millennium as an eternally present possibility), the "conservative utopia," and the "liberal-humanitarian utopia." The myth of Arthur is basically a millennial myth common to many cultures: Friedrich Barbarossa in Germany, Charlemagne, Sebastian of Brazil, Olgier the Dane, and of course Christ himself are only several of the many mythical heroes whose return is destined to bring utopia.[11] A hero such as Arthur brings a spiritual force into the land and gains his right to rule through his supernatural inspiration. In the *Idylls* King Arthur is thought to have arrived suddenly,

as the coming of a light, surrounded by supernatural personages and transported in a magic ship. Tennyson leaves the
matter of the supernatural uncertain; he criticizes by implication the credulousness of the chiliast mentality.

"For the real Chiliast," writes Mannheim, "the present becomes the breach through which what was previously
inward bursts out suddenly, takes hold of the outer world
and transforms it." The bringing of the millennium to the
real world, or what Mannheim calls the "spiritualization
of politics," [12] gains dramatic realization momentarily in
Arthur's charismatic character.

In the real world, as Mannheim argues, the ecstatic
character of chiliasm forces a break from the world of
historical process: "It tends at every moment to turn into
hostility towards the world, its culture, and all its works
and earthly achievement. . . . The Chiliastic mentality
has . . . no sense for the process of becoming; it was sensi-
tive only to the abrupt moment, the present pregnant
with meaning." [13] Arthur's Round Table at the beginning
is an ideal pattern by which the present is eternally to be
reconstructed; it admits of no improvement but only a
constant striving for the perfection of the earlier moment
of divine influence. Tennyson at this point issues the
warning that in real society this perfect moment has not
been achieved because of man's limitations and probably,
if it had been, would be denied or betrayed.

In the real world the chiliast mentality is socially
dangerous; it seeks constant revolution to achieve a situation it has never really experienced while remaining blind
to improvements that a more empirical outlook might
suggest. Arthur's obliviousness to the errors and evils in
his realm near to him while striving continuously to maintain a perfect Order demonstrates the inability of human
beings as they are at the present to live up to the stand-

ards of a millennial vision. This does not make Arthur
a villain of the poem but only suggests that even his
utopianism, wiser than that of most Victorians, over-
estimates human goodness.

In the idylls from "Gareth and Lynette" to "The
Holy Grail" Tennyson balances the millennial otherworldliness in Arthur's rule with elements of the conservative utopia, which Mannheim describes as a sort of
answer to utopianism itself, a rejection of golden ages
in the distance and an emphasis upon the concrete. Once
the millennium has been reached, change is felt to be
undesirable. King Arthur's efforts to weed the garden
and till the land reveal the conservative assumption that,
as Mannheim says, "utopia is . . . embedded in existing
reality." [14] Such an assumption is the vital error of the
Victorian belief in the present as the new Golden Age.
The believer in a conservative utopia assumes that the
status quo, given the emphasis upon its essential aspects
and a removal of the meaningless, is already a latent utopia. Time, as in Arthur's hall at Camelot, gives value to
the past; in Mannheim's words, "the presentness and im-
mediacy of the whole past becomes an actual experience." [15] Arthur lives as if all time were contained in the
present, yet Camelot was built over eons of time.

In "Gareth and Lynette" and the Geraint idylls the
king is the central authority whose work is chiefly to en-
force the system already established. He regards his work
as a weeding-out of evil elements while holding the Order
fast against change. Balin believes that Arthur overprizes
gentleness, and his restiveness under the mild yoke gains
many followers. Through "Merlin and Vivien" and
"Lancelot and Elaine" Arthur remains the conservative
force, but his utopia deteriorates into what Mannheim
calls an ideology, or an ideal not congruous with the ex-

isting reality but, unlike the utopia, unable to effect a transformation of reality to bring it nearer into accord with the ideal. Chivalry becomes a kind of facade, and reality changes beneath Arthur's unseeing gaze.

In "Lancelot and Elaine" Arthur's utopia has deteriorated to the point that Gawain, whose courtesy has a "touch of traitor in it," (line 635) is the dominant spirit. His "golden eloquence" (line 645) is a mockery of utopian virtues, being only one of his many gambits to win over Elaine. The "golden minute's grace" (line 680) he asks from her is a satirical contrast to the golden moment of the Round Table's glory and the moment of unspoiled love when Lancelot and Guinevere first met. Arthur's Order rests upon the King's trust in Lancelot as a knight and Guinevere as a wife; in "Lancelot and Elaine" the great warrior lies to the king in order to stay with Guinevere during the jousts. Guinevere for the first time in the *Idylls* outspokenly belittles Arthur and proves by her jealousy of Elaine that Arthur's ideal marriage is a fantasy. Elaine, who would have been the perfect influence upon Lancelot, dies in fantasy. Although Sir Torre and Sir Lavaine carry on Gareth's youthful enthusiasm, they are overshadowed by the disillusionment of the larger figures.

Arthur's attempt to preserve a conservative utopia is unsuccessful because he began with a utopia founded upon millennial expectations. The chiliastic utopia brought momentarily with Arthur's appearance would have to be recreated constantly for the Order to endure. There is no utopia embedded within the Order, only an ideal beyond it; hence Arthur's work of cultivating the garden becomes tedious to others and even laughable to those, like Gawain and Vivien, whose cynicism is confirmed by their belief in Guinevere's disloyalty. Proof of the conflict between utopian strivings comes with the grail quest. As the enthusiasm for chivalry ebbs, and the mystical excitement of Arthur's coming wanes, a new promise of the millennium appears with the vision of the holy grail. Once more the miraculous realm of eternals bursts through into the existing order. Once more the thrill of attaining perfection passes through the knighthood; a new chiliastic utopia is at hand—but it proves a delusion. The grail quest is a search for a panacea, a cure for the disease that the Round Table has become, a way out of the conflict between Arthur's heroic effort to maintain the status quo and the tendency of his followers to accelerate the decline that he does not see. The grail quest is not a new utopia, acting as an antithetical force upon existing society and changing it to its own image, but a kind of nemesis or test of Arthur's utopian ambition. The grail quest comes as a destructive force, shattering the insupportable contradiction within the Round Table, proving that a society cannot be sustained by millennial expectations and hard work without an earthly direction.

Thus it is that Arthur, as a tragic hero, learns too late from his mistakes—as Tennyson hopes his own era will not. The idylls after "The Holy Grail" portray not merely the failure of a utopian scheme but the tragic effect upon society of such a failure. Without a sound understanding of social ideals, Tennyson implies, a society cannot endure. Preaching of hard work and the promise of eternal meaning in human effort are not enough: a society needs human goals, an ideal social pattern sought for but not embedded in the existing order. Arthur provides no such goal, and it is not offered by miracles; in the epilogue Tennyson reminds us that "The goal of this great world/Lies beyond sight . . ." (lines 59-60). Yet it is clear that he conceives a distinct goal for England, one created by the historical moment but looking beyond it; it requires a sense of growth rather than the desire to return.

The overpowering bestiality and the conquering darkness of "Pelleas and Ettarre," "The Last Tournament," "Guinevere," and "The Passing of Arthur" remind us that when a society follows false lights, it may become worse than a tribe with no ideal whatever. If Tennyson, as he stated, sought to teach men the need of an ideal, he presents a grim lesson in the *Idylls:* not any ideal will do; one must be found that will allow for unseen changes and draw from individuals their best efforts without denying their individuality or ignoring the power of instinct in human life. The cost of following wrong ideals may be enormous. Unlike Hegel and Marx, Tennyson regards dialectical clash in society as a sign of decay and error rather than growth. He hopes for a broad but unified ideal for his own society as a way of avoiding the extremes of revolution, tyranny, puritanical rigidity, decadent abandon, apolitical mysticism, and materialistic exploitation.

In "The Passing of Arthur" the king reaches a new awareness. The world seems to him the imperfect creation of a lesser god, but it is the best Arthur's human efforts could accomplish in working "His will" (line 22). Arthur reaches the perception that only God can actually bring utopia into being, and that He does so in ways that transcend human understanding. Even King Arthur, who commits no breach of honor nor ever lapses into unknightly behavior, has only the limited understanding of a human being. The desire for utopia must be held in check by the modesty to realize that a human leader cannot bring man's ultimate destiny to fulfillment. The golden year recedes into the future as an ideal of what human society might be if it were perfect, and the Round Table, an "image of the mighty world," dissolves, having been from the outset a dream. In awareness gained through tragedy, and not in priggishness as Swinburne argues, King Arthur says, "I have lived my life, and that which I have done/May he within himself make pure!" ("The Passing of Arthur," lines 412-413). He acknowledges his error, his lament implying that what he has done cannot be held pure by human judgment. Perhaps, in some larger sense, the Round Table plays its part in a development that leads beyond human sight.

Tennyson upholds in the *Idylls* the utopian faith of Leonard in "The Golden Year." But the pessimism of *Maud* has permanently marked his view of the Victorian era and its self-congratulation on having reached the threshold of the great millennium. The broadening vision of "The Passing of Arthur" shows a transcendence of the fatalism of *Maud* but a continued disavowal of short-term progress as an accurate indication of historical trends. The golden year is not at the doors, and those who cling to such a hope may find them opening on a debacle worse than they could imagine. The value of the golden year as a future ideal lies in its power to give purpose and direction to present effort. Mannheim writes;

> The utopia of the liberal-humanitarian mentality is the "idea." This, however, is not the static platonic idea of the Greek tradition, which was a concrete archetype, a primal model of things; but here the idea is rather conceived of as a formal goal projected into the infinite future whose function it is to act as a mere regulative device in mundane affairs. . . . This idealist mentality avoids both the visionary conception of reality involved in the Chiliastic ap-

peal to God, and also the conservative and often narrow-minded domination over things and men involved in the earth- and time-bound notion of the world.[16]

The *Idylls* nearly denies the notion of progress. Tennyson conceives of modern man as a child with a dangerous instrument; his utopian schemes, the poet believes, should be gently taken from his hands until the child grows up. In "Locksley Hall Sixty Years After" Tennyson voices his dismay over the futility of hopes for progress: "Let us hush this cry of 'Forward' till ten thousand years have gone," he writes, before listing the unchanging cruelties of man to man. Yet some vision, if distant, is necessary. The poet reminds us that history is "the immeasurable sea,/ Sway'd by vaster ebbs and flows than can be known to you or me." Still, he urges the pursuit of an ideal in "Freedom," praising the

> follower of the Vision, still
> In motion to the distant gleam,
> Howe'er blind force and brainless will
> May jar thy golden dream . . .

King Arthur learns the lesson that Tennyson hopes his own era will learn without the need for tragedy. Its crowning common-sense may withstand the inevitable jars to its too hopeful dream, if, as Wordsworth entreats us, it finds direction

> Not in Utopia,—subterranean fields,—
> Or some secreted island, Heaven knows where!
> But in the very world, which is the world

Of all of us,—the place where, in the end,
We find our happiness, or not at all!
(*The Prelude*, Book Eleven, lines 140-144)

Notes

1. The final image could have been suggested by Hamlet's remark to Laertes, "Your skill shall, like a star i' the darkest night,/Stick fiery off indeed" (*Hamlet*, Act V, Scene II, lines 267-268). Resemblances of Elaine to Ophelia—madness, songs of love and death, flowers, drowning—lend a half-recognition to this scene in the *Idylls*.

2. Mill discussed as well the conception of nature as the ordering principle of the physical universe—a notion that has more to do with Newtonian physics than with the predominantly biological connotation of *nature* in the nineteenth century.

3. Edward Engelberg, "The Beast Image in Tennyson's *Idylls of the King*," *ELH*, XXII (December 1955), 287.

4. Thomas Huxley, *Evolution and Ethics* (London, 1914), 56. Thomas Miller's *History of the Anglo-Saxons* (4th Edition; London: Bell & Daldy, 1867), p. 8, mentions the danger of wolves to the early Britons. Although no copy of this work is now in the Lincoln collection, it is possible that Tennyson could have used it.

5. William Paley, *Natural Theology*, selected and edited by F. Ferre (New York: Bobbs-Merrill, 1963), 66.

6. J. H. Buckley, *The Triumph of Time* (Cambridge, Mass.: Harvard University Press, 1966), Chapter One, "The Four Faces of Victorian Time," 1-13.

7. See Edward Engelberg, "The Beast Image in Tennyson's *Idylls of the King*," *ELH*, XXII (December 1955), 287-292, on the progression of imagery showing men devolving into beasts.

8. See F. E. L. Priestley on the naturalistic fallacy in Tristram's rejection of the chivalric code. "Tennyson's Idylls—A Fresh View," in *Critical Essays on the Poetry of Tennyson*, edited by John Killham (New York: Barnes & Noble, 1960), 246. On the philosophical question itself, see G. E. Moore, *Principia Ethica* (Cambridge University Press, 1954), 59-60.

9. *The Descent of Man* (New York: Modern Library, n.d.), 920.

10. Karl Mannheim, "The Utopian Mentality," *Ideology and Utopia* (New York, 1936), 211-247. First published in German,

1929. The fourth kind of utopia that Mannheim discusses, the Socialist-Communist utopia, is not directly reflected in the poem.
is the Socialist-Communist utopia, which is not directly relevant to the *Idylls.*

11. T. A. Fischer, *Leben und Werke Alfred Tennysons* (Gotha: Friedrich Andreas Berthes, 1899), 161. Fischer mentions even an Inca legend of the return of the hero.
12. Mannheim, 212, 215.
13. Mannheim, 220, 225.
14. Mannheim, 233.
15. Mannheim, 235.
16. Mannheim, 219-221. Lionel A. Tollemache wrote that Tennyson regards the Middle Ages "not as the shore toward which we are to steer, but as the polar star by gazing on which we are to shape our course. In other words, he considers them his Golden Age; though like Shelley, he doubtless would not wish to see 'the golden years return,' without great changes." "Tennyson's Social Philosophy," *Fortnightly,* XI (1874), 237.

Appendix

The Arthurian Century:
A Chronology of
Significant Arthurian Publications
in the Nineteenth Century

1792   William Owen, ed. and trans., *The Heroic Elegies of Llywarch Hen*. Arthur Hugh Clough sent a a copy to Tennyson in December 1856, the year he began "Enid." (See P. G. Scott, "Tennyson's Celtic Reading," *Tennyson Research Bulletin*, no. 2, 1968.) A copy of the Owen translation is contained, with the Welsh original at the left, in the Lincoln collection, apparently being the translation sent by Patmore to Tennyson. The Geraint poem in this collection, and Owen's introduction discussing the tradition of bardism may have interested and influenced Tennyson (see Chapter I). The savagery of the battle at Llongborth is not far different from Tennyson's last battle.

1801   John Thelwall, "The Fairy of the Lake," *Poems, Chiefly Written in Retirement* (Hereford, 1801), 1–92. This "dramatic romance" is reminiscent of Dryden's masque. It portrays a conflict between Rowenna, the wicked queen of Britain, who is thwarted in her attempts to destroy Guenever and win Arthur. Tristram, a comic figure, rescues Guenever and Arthur's forces conquer Rowenna's army.

1801–   *Myvyrian Archaeoology of Wales* (3 vols.). This
1807   collection contains not only the Llywarch Hen elegies but also the *Gododin*, which has the first extant mention of King Arthur. Clough attempted to procure this collection for Tennyson, but by the 1850s it was quite rare.

1803   John Leyden, "Scenes of Infancy." Leyden asks in one passage who will "peal proud Arthur's march from fairyland?" *Poetical Works*, with a Memoir by Thomas Brown (London, 1875), 34-36.

1804   Sir Walter Scott, ed., *Sir Tristram*. Scott helped greatly to make known the British version of the legend; Swinburne's *Tristram of Lyonesse* is based chiefly upon this edition.

1805   Robert Southey, *Madoc*. Although not an Arthurian poem as such, *Madoc* alludes to Arthur and his court, often as the inspiration for those seeking a better world. *Complete Poetical Works* (New York, 1850), 213.

         George Ellis, *Specimens of Early English Ro-*

mances (3 vols.). Ellis probably had some influence upon certain details of the *Idylls*—possibly the names Anton and Bellicent in "The Coming of Arthur," derive from this source. (See J. M. Gray, *Man and Myth in Victorian England: Tennyson's "The Coming of Arthur"* (Lincoln, 1969), 22n.)

1807   Sharon Turner, *The History of the Anglo-Saxons* (3 vols.). This is the second edition, which Tennyson owned (see Scott, "Tennyson's Celtic Reading") and in which the Arthurian material was moved from the appendix to the main body of the book, perhaps because of growing interest in the subject. Kathleen Tillotson suggests that Turner provided the source of Tennyson's Nesting story in "The Last Tournament." *Mid-Victorian Studies* (London, 1965), 84. Ricks cites evidence that Tennyson read Turner. *Poems of Tennyson,* 1705. See chapter one for possible influences on the *Idylls*.

1808   Sir Walter Scott, *Marmion*. Tennyson was familiar with *Marmion,* with its appeal for the great Arthuriad. Tillotson suggests that it had considerable influence on the *Idylls* and that Tennyson read it, with its notes on Malory's grail story, when a child. *Mid-Victorian Studies*, 83.

1809   Edward Davies, *The Mythology and Rites of the British Druids*. Tennyson owned a copy of Davies and could have derived several details from Welsh tradition in the *Idylls* from the book (for example, the ninth wave, the triplet form, and so on. See Gray, 12, 26n).

1813   Sir Walter Scott, "The Bridal of Triermain." Many of the Arthurian figures appear in the poem; Scott, like Tennyson, is sympathetic toward the king in his cuckoldry, although for Scott the king's blindness results from his closeness to nature rather than his transcendence of it. An element of irony unusual for Scott enters the poem: of Tristram, Lancelot, and Carodac he writes, in tribute to their "lovers' fame," "There were two who loved their neighbors' wives,/And one who loved his own." The fortress in which Gyneth sleeps until the destined knight awakes her appears and vanishes in Sir Roland's gaze, much like Camelot in "Gareth and Lynette." And it is built by "sign and sigil, word of power" rather than by "mortal building hand"; its walls picture warriors putting down griffins and dragons (compare the zones of Camelot in "The Holy Grail"). Sir Roland faces temptations similar to the tests of the grail knights in Tennyson, and several spellings—Lancelot, Modred—are the same as Tennyson's. Scott, *Poetical Works* (Cambridge, 1900), 296, 305. Tennyson called Scott "the most chivalrous literary figure of the century." *Memoir*, II, 372.

1816   The two editions of Malory published in this year gave Arthurian legend a great thrust forward. The Wilks edition (3 vols., 24mo) was the one in which, according to Sir Charles Tennyson, the poet became acquainted with Malory when "little more than a boy." *Catalogue of the Lincoln Collection* (1963), item 263. The first volume of this edition, inscribed "Alfred Tennyson" in Hallam Tennyson's hand, is in the Usher Gallery and the other two in the Tennyson Research Centre library. The Walker and Edwards edition (2 vols., 24mo) was, according to Hallam, used extensively by the poet. *Memoir,* I, 156. The first volume of this edition, inscribed "Alfred Tennyson from Leigh Hunt," is in the Lincoln Research Centre; it was given to Tennyson by Hunt in 1835. See P. G. Scott, "Tennyson's Celtic Reading." A copy of the Bloome edition (1634), the last until 1816 and the one upon which both of these editions were based, was owned by Tennyson and is now in the Usher Gallery.

Leigh Hunt, "The Story of Rimini." Hunt expands the tale of Paolo and Francesca from Dante, drawing a parallel between the lovers and the legend in the book they are reading, "Launcelot of the Lake." Hunt mentions Launcelot's being stolen as an infant from his father, King Ban, and being raised by the Lady of the Lake beneath the waters. As an adult he enters Arthur's court and falls in love with Geneura, the queen. The tale reaches their first kiss, when Paolo and Francesca are apprehended. *Poetical Works of Leigh Hunt* (London, 1832), 60-68.

George Stanley Faber, *The Origin of Pagan Idolatry* (3 vols.). Faber's comments on romances and his attempt to subsume all such legend under the category of biblical story may have suggested cer-

tain parallels to Tennyson, such as Tristram the
woodsman as a Nimrod, Arthur's ship with its
shining people as a version of the ark, and Vivien
as a Satanic figure.

1817   Robert Southey, ed., *The Byrth, Lyf, and Actes of
Kyng Arthur* (2 vols., Longmans). Southey's edition of Malory is based upon the copy of Caxton
owned by the Earl of Spencer. Although it was
an expensive edition and probably less widely
used than the two previous editions of Malory,
Tennyson was familiar with it. It has an extensive
introduction as well as notes that contain the plot
of the Vulgate *Merlin* (Southey uses the name
Viviane at times.) A passage from Malory in
Tennyson's hand in Harvard Notebook 16 may be
from Southey's edition, since it is identified as
part of the fourth book, fifth chapter, which
could only be noted in an edition based upon
Caxton's divisions. The paper is watermarked
1833; hence it is unlikely that the quotation could
be from a later edition, such as Wright's or
Strachey's. The passage is not, however, in exact
accord with Southey's passage; it may have been
jotted down roughly for reference. Burne-Jones
and Rossetti read Southey's edition. Tillotson, 90.

John Hookham Frere, *King Arthur and the
Round Table*. The first two cantos of this bur-
lesque epic were published in 1817, the last two
in 1818; the poem was written in 1813. The plot
concerns a battle between the monks and the
giants, the latter of whom represent the virtues

of the golden age. Arthur's knights and his court provide only a frame and setting.

1819   Thomas Love Peacock, "The Round Table, or King Arthur's Feast." Peacock's one explicitly Arthurian work depicts the king giving a feast for all the royalty of Britain since the time of King Arthur to Peacock's day. Arthur's response to each is a judgment of the period in which the ruler reigned. Arthur is most pleased with Elizabeth, but in general English history presents a decline. *Poems of Thomas Love Peacock*, ed. B. Johnson (London, 1906), 270-280.

1820   John Keats, "The Eve of St. Agnes." One of Keats's few allusions to Arthurian romance occurs in the line referring to the time when "Merlin paid his demon all the monstrous debt." The reference is obscure, possibly influenced by Ariosto or the tradition that Merlin was demon-born.

William Wordsworth, "Artegall and Elidure." Although not purely Arthurian, the poem shows influence of both Spenser and Geoffrey of Monmouth.

1822   Mrs. Felicia Hemans, "Taliessin's Prophecy." This lyric envisions the sceptre passing away from Uthyr's kingdom and a long line of men decaying. Mrs. Hemans touches on Llywarch Hen and Merlin· in other poems. *The Complete Works of Mrs. Hemans*, edited by her sister (New York, 1847), 595, 597, 599n.

1826   Alaric A. Watts, "The Lady and Merlin," *Gentleman's Magazine,* Vol. 96 (Feb. 1826), 168. Subtitled "A Picture by Newton." The four stanzas in iambic tetrameter couplets allude to the beautiful lady's entrapment of Merlin.

1828   Thomas Keightley, *The Fairy Mythology.* Tennyson owned this book in the Bohn edition of 1850. Keightley's linkage of Arthurian legend with myths of the fairy king and queen stem not only from Spenser but from folklore as well. Perhaps the association of Arthur with the fairy king, who in turn is sometimes considered the god of the underworld or Pluto, added to Tennyson's sense of the mystery surrounding Arthur and the great deep.

1829   Thomas Love Peacock, *The Misfortunes of Elphin.* Peacock's sharp parody is on the periphery of Arthurian legend, being set in the time of King Arthur and dealing in part with the exploits of Taliesin. Peacock spoofs the storybook picture of knights in armor; the work is in a sense anti-Arthurian, an early example of what was to become a popular vein.

1830   Tennyson wrote part of "Sir Launcelot and Queen Guinevere" in this year—his beginning of Arthurian writing that continued until 1891, when he added the last line to the epilogue of the *Idylls.*

1832   Tennyson wrote and published "The Palace of Art" with its passage describing Arthur asleep in Avalon ("Avilion" in the first version, changed in 1842). "The Lady of Shalott" was written in May 1832 and published in the same year, although extensively revised in 1842.

1833–
1834   Tennyson wrote the "Morte d'Arthur."

1833   Tennyson about this time projected his scheme for an Arthurian musical masque. The prose draft of the masque remains, along with the prose fragment for a projected Arthurian epic.

1834   Tennyson wrote "Sir Galahad" in September.

1835   Wordsworth, "The Egyptian Maid, or The Romance of the Water Lily," Written in 1828, this lyric tells an unorthodox Galahad story in which the knight awakens a sleeping maid and departs with her to "bowers of endless love." Supernatural feats by Merlin and Nina, the Lady of the Lake, as well as miraculous swans and celestial music make the lyric a fantasy poem.

1836   Algernon Herbert, *Britannia After the Romans*. This two volume work was published by Bohn, the second volume appearing in 1841. Tennyson read the first volume; his copy at Lincoln contains notes on significant names of people and places from the book. See P. G. Scott. Herbert is quite a skeptic toward the possibility of historical truth in Arthurian legend; he dismisses Arthur as an "historical monstrosity," arguing that in fact he was a survivor of earlier mythological figures. Tennyson probably did not share many of Herbert's ideas but may have found the book useful.

1837–
1838   Tennyson probably wrote "The Epic" in this period. Although his plans for an Arthurian poem changed between this time and the writing of the *Idylls,* the description of "King Arthur, like a modern gentleman/Of stateliest port" shares something with the dedication of the *Idylls* and indicates his intention to give modern significance to Arthurian myth.

1840   Lady Charlotte Guest, trans., *The Mabinogion* (collected 1849). The notes to this edition include passages from the Vulgate *Merlin,* which could have provided Tennyson with additional knowledge of the Merlin story. See Chapter II on the Geraint story as a source for the Geraint idylls.

1841   Reginald Heber, "Morte D'Arthur" and "The Masque of Gwendolen." The first poem was written in 1812 and the second belongs at least before 1826 (the year of Heber's death). Heber shows knowledge of Malory but invents his own plots. "Morte D'Arthur," written in Spenserian stanza, focuses on the love of Ganora for Lancelot. The poem is incomplete, ending with a description of Lancelot's tutelage under a faery. Modred (Tennyson's spelling) is mentioned as Arthur's and Morgue's son, and Sir Balin has been condemned to a dungeon because of a violent act. "The Masque of Gwendolen" adds the story of Merlin's ensnarement by the Lady of the Lake—in retribution for having transformed Gwendolen into a figure "worse than furies." Heber, *Poetical Works* (Philadelphia, 1841), 199.

1842 Tennyson published in final form his "Morte d'Arthur," "Sir Launcelot and Queen Guinevere," "The Lady of Shalott," and "Sir Galahad."

Macready produced an expanded version of Dryden and Purcell's *King Arthur*. He also revived Isaac Pollock's *King Arthur and the Knights of the Round Table* (1834) in this year.

Thomas Price, ed., *Hanes Cymru*. Tennyson used this work (Welsh history) for the *Idylls*. *Memoir*, I, 416. The copy in his library at Lincoln no doubt became useful to him after he took up the study of Welsh in the summer of 1856. (Harvard Notebook 26 contains a list of common Welsh words and their English meanings, giving evidence of this study.)

Rev. Frederick William Faber, *Sir Lancelot, a Legend of the Middle Ages* (Second Edition, London, 1857). Tennyson's list of books in Harvard Notebook 27 (undated) includes this work. It is Arthurian only in using the name Lancelot for its hero (Sir Lancelot De Wace), who lives in the time of Henry III. The poem is in blank verse highly imitative of Wordsworth.

1844 James O. Halliwell, *Early English Romances*, published by the Camden Society. Tennyson's copy, given to him by Sophy Dalrymple in 1859, remained mostly uncut. Scott, "Tennyson's Celtic Reading."

1845   Henry Alford, "Ballad of Glastonbury." Alford was a friend of Tennyson who wrote a review of the grail idyll. His lyric is quite different from "The Holy Grail" in that Alford sees the grail as God's benevolent intervention in human affairs and favorably portrays the lengendary miracles surrounding the grail.

1846   Ralph Waldo Emerson, "Merlin." This two-part lyric conceives of the poet as Merlin, but unlike Tennyson's "Merlin and the Gleam" it makes a general rather than autobiographical comparison. Emerson's Merlin is a builder in song whose music brings peace and progress; in "The House" Emerson anticipates Tennyson in alluding to the myth of the city built to music.

1847   Richard Wagner, *Lohengrin*. There is surprisingly little evidence to show that Tennyson knew Wagner's treatment of Arthurian legend. Sir Charles Tennyson (*Alfred Tennyson*, 441) mentions the attempt by Maude Valerie White to interest the laureate in the Lohengrin legend by recounting the story and musical treatment given it by Wagner. After she finished, Tennyson simply replied, "What a remarkably sharp nose you've got." The reaction may have been to her rather than Wagner, but the story of the swan knight is the only major Arthurian legend he did not use.

Sir Frederic Madden, ed., Layamon's *Brut* (3 vols.). Tennyson's copy, signed "A. Tennyson," remains in the Lincoln collection. P. G. Scott. This edition was published by the Society of Antiquaries. Tennyson quoted a passage on Arthur's virtues given by the elves. Ricks, *Poems of Tennyson,* 1469.

James O. Halliwell, ed., *Morte Arthure.* A private printing of the alliterative romance based on the manuscript at Lincoln Cathedral.

1848   J. A. Giles, *Six Old English Chronicles.* Tennyson owned this edition, published by Bohn, and used it as his chief source of material from the chronicles. See Chapter I.

Edward Bulwer-Lytton, *King Arthur.* Lytton was an adversary of Tennyson who called the laureate "a poet adapted to a mixed audience of school girls and Oxford dons." See Kathleen Tillotson, "Tennyson's Serial Poem," *Mid-Victorian Studies* by Geoffrey and Kathleen Tillotson (London, 1965), p. 95. His epic poem no doubt provided Tennyson with a composite example of what he wanted to avoid—a wandering, episodic plot based upon a good deal of pastoral longing for an effortless fairyland. Lytton's classic passage on romance could have suggested Tennyson's "Sense at war with Soul":

Oh, the old time's divine and fresh romance!

When o'er the lone yet ever-haunted
    ways
Went frank-eyed Knighthood with the
    lifted lance,
And life with wonder charm'd adventurous
    days!
When lights more rich, through prisms
    that dimm'd it, shone;
And nature loom'd more large through
    the Unknown.
Then soul learn'd more than barren
    sense can teach
(Soul with the sense now evermore at
    strife)
Wherever fancy wandered man could
    reach—
And what is now called poetry was life.
(*King Arthur,* second edition, 1851, 119-120)

1850   *The Prelude* was published, with its mention in
the first book of Wordsworth's passing interest
in writing an Arthurian epic.

1852   Matthew Arnold, "Tristram and Iseult." See
Chapter V. Arnold relied chiefly on Dunlop's
History of Fiction for his story. Although he
missed the "peculiar charm and aroma of the
Middle Ages" in the *Idylls* (*Letters,* I, 127), it
is doubtful that he strove for that effect himself.

Revd. John Williams ab Ithel, ed., *The Gododin.*
Clough sent Tennyson a copy of this edition in
1856, since Tennyson had requested both this
poem by the bard Aneurin and the Llywarch Hen
elegies. P. G. Scott.

1853   Revd. W. J. Rees, *Lives of the Cambro-British Saints*. Tennyson owned a copy of this edition published by Longmans. It contains brief references to Arthur: in the life of St. Cadoc Arthur wants to pursue a woman but is reminded of his high calling by his companions. St. Dubricius is mentioned as succeeding to the archepiscopal see before 517, the year Arthur was said to have been crowned.

Charlotte Yonge, *The Heir of Redclyffe*. Morris and Burne-Jones were inspired by the character of Sir Guy, who took Sir Galahad as his hero. They hoped to create a brotherhood with Sir Galahad as its model. See Walter Houghton, *The Victorian Frame of Mind*, 326.

1854   Mrs. Craik (Dinah M. Mulock Craik), "Avillion, or, the Happy Isles," *Avillion and other Tales* (New York, 1854). An interesting predecessor to Tennyson, she portrays many of Malory's characters in an afterlife realm, where the spirit of chivalry contrasts to the modern world of commerce. Mrs. Craik sees Arthur lamenting: " 'Of Arthur and his bold knights no trace or memory remains on earth,' said the King, while a shadow gloomed on his brow, like a cloud sweeping over a gray mountain-top." (Compare Tennyson's "that gray king whose name, a ghost,/Streams like a cloud, man-shaped, from mountain peak. . . .") Mrs. Craik portrays Arthur confronting the fallen Guinever (a remarkable anticipation of "Guinevere," since the scene does not occur in Malory):

Arthur spoke—stern, cold, passionless. He thought neither of pity, anger, nor revenge —only of his Britain. But to all his questions came the cry of "Mercy, Mercy! I repent! Let me rest!" and ever and anon in mournful plainings, was repeated the wail, "Launcelot! Launcelot!"

Galahad reproves the king for his lack of pity, but Sir Launfal sides with Arthur, remembering "her sitting on the polluted throne, beside her deluded spouse, my dear lord King Arthur." The distinctively Victorian sentiments of Tennyson's "Guinevere" are brought out by their close parallel to those of this popular piece of fiction. Mrs. Craik's borrowings from Tennyson's earlier verse are evident throughout the story.

1856   Tennyson began "Enid" and completed his first idyll, then called "Nimuë."

1857   A trial edition of six copies was printed of "Enid and Nimuë, or, the True and the False."

Dante Gabriel Rossetti illustrated an edition of Tennyson's poems, including "The Lady of Shalott" and "Sir Galahad."

Rossetti also supervised the painting of frescoes frescoes for the Oxford Union. There were to be ten panels painted by ten leading artists, all scenes from Malory. Unfortunately, the technical aspects of fresco work were not understood by the artists and the paintings faded into near invisibility. The project was not finished, and some of the individual paintings were left incomplete. Notable among the pictures included were Burne-Jones' "Death of Merlin," Rossetti's "Sir Launcelot's Vision of the Sangrail" (not completed), Arthur Hughes' "The Death of Arthur," Val Prinsep's "Sir Pelleas and the Lady Ettarde," Hungerford Pollen's "How King Arthur Received his Sword Excalibur," and Spencer Stanhope's "Sir Gawain and the Three Damsels." Rossetti planned as well "Launcelot Found in the Queen's Chamber" and "The Three Knights of the Sangrail" but did not paint them. Morris' painting of Sir Palomydes in love with La Belle Iseult was the first completed and highly acclaimed. See J. W. Mackail, *The Life of William Morris* (2 vols.; London, 1907), I, 117ff.

1858   William Morris, *The Defence of Guenevere and other Poems*. See Chapter V. Morris' only surviving easel picture, *Queen Guinevere* (now in the Tate Gallery), was painted in this year.

Thomas Wright, ed., Malory's *Morte Darthur*. Tennyson received a copy sent by Julia Margaret Cameron; it is inscribed and dated August 16, 1859. The copy has Tennyson's characteristic markings; he apparently used it for the 1869 idylls (the 1859 volume had been published in July). The edition is another reprint of the 1634 Malory.

1859   *Idylls of the King* appeared in the middle of July, containing "Enid," "Vivien," "Elaine," and

"Guinevere." See Chapter VI. A study of this installment alone has been done by Robert E. Richardson, Jr., *A Critical Introduction to the Idylls of the King (1859)* (Ph.D. dissertation; Princeton, 1967).

Wagner composed *Tristan and Isolde* in 1859, but the attempted performance was discontinued after a few rehearsals and it was not presented until 1864. Arnold attended a performance in Germany in 1885, but there is no evidence that Tennyson knew the opera.

George Meredith published a four-stanza lyric called "The Song of Courtesy" in *Once a Week*, Vol. 1 (July 9, 1859), telling the story of Gawain and the old crone—the story told by Chaucer's Wife of Bath. Meredith concludes with a modern lesson of courtesy derived from the tale: ". . . may we/Make the basest that be/Beautiful ever by Courtesy!"

Robert Buchanan (?), *Fragments of the Table Round*. Although published anonymously in Glasgow, this poem has been attributed to Buchanan. Halkett and Laing, *Dictionary of Anonymous and Pseudonymous Literature*, II, 324. This ballad series shows the influence of Spenser, Drayton, the *Romance of Merlin*, and Malory. Eight ballads tell the bare outlines of Malory's story, emphasizing the relationship of Lancelot and Guinevere. The final ballad tells the story of Merlin and Viviane; the lady of the lake is foolish and naive rather than sensual and destructive like

Tennyson's Vivien. The author states the moral that lust "Wrecked the noble brotherhood/Of Arthur's Table Round," although he does not really portray it.

Arthur's Knights, a long anonymous grail story in blank verse, anticipates Tennyson's idyll by seeing the grail as a test of Arthur's order: "It came—to shiver all that noble band,/The high adventure of the Holy Grale." No greater difference could be imagined, however, than the contrast between the harvestland pastoral of the poem and Tennyson's waste land. The ending alone approaches a Tennysonian mood: in "the dark days of civil war" the Saxons "settled o'er the wasted land,/Like a dim sea-fog, blotting out the light/Of faith and honour." *Arthur's Knights* (second edition; Edinburgh, 1859), 2, 83.

1860   Dante Gabriel Rossetti painted his watercolor, *Arthur's Tomb,* now in the Tate Gallery.

1861   James T. Knowles, *Legends of King Arthur.* Tennyson's copy at Lincoln, the third, revised edition (Strahan, 1868), is dedicated to the poet. Besides this compilation, Knowles wrote two articles on the *Idylls*—the *Spectator* review for January 1, 1870, and "The Meaning of King Arthur," *Contemporary,* May 1873.

1862   Tennyson dedicated the *Idylls* to Prince Albert.

1863   Robert Stephen Hawker, "The Quest of the Sangraal." Hawker was a Cornish priest whom Tenn-

yson visited in 1848. Tennyson owned a copy
of the poem printed privately at Exeter in 1864.
Although Hawker is more reverent than Tennyson toward the miraculous elements of the legend,
he too envisions a realm approaching disaster and
his verse is often Tennysonian in texture:

> First fell a gloom, thick as a thousand
>   nights,
> A pall that hid whole armies; and beneath
> Stormed the wild tide of war; until on
>   high
> Gleamed the red dragon,
>
>   . . .
>
>   for brother blood
> Rushed mingling, and twin dragons fought
>   the field!
>   *Poetical Works,* ed. A. Wallis (Lon-
>   don, 1899), 187

Hawker also write two brief lyrics, "King Arthur's
Waes-Hael" and "Queen Guennivar's Round,"
as well as "To Alfred Tennyson, Laureate, D.C.L.,
on his *Idylls of the King.*"

1864   Robert Buchanan, "Merlin and the White Death,"
Once A Week, X (Feb. 20, 1864), 251-252. It is
a twelve-stanza poem in which Merlin recounts
his attempt to capture the water-witch who lives
in a cave under the lake. Like Tennyson's Vivien
she is dressed in a white clinging dress and moves
like a serpent; she tells Merlin, however, to return to Camelot, where he awaits the time when
her full beauty will be revealed to him and he

will join the "white-robed throng" that she keeps in a spell.

F. J. Furnivall, *Le Morte Arthur*. Tennyson's copy of this edition, published by Macmillan, is in the Lincoln collection and bears the poet's characteristic pencil markings.

F. J. Furnivall, *La Queste del Saint Graal*. In this edition by the Roxburghe Club, Furnivall includes a comment on Tennyson in his introduction: "To anyone knowing his Malleore . . . to come on Arthur rehearsing to his prostrate queen his own nobleness and her disgrace, the revulsion of feeling was too great, one could only say to the 'Flower of Kings,' 'If you really did this, you were the Pecksniff of the period. . . .'" See Tillotson, 98.

1865– William Morris, *In Arthur's House*. See
1870   Chapter V.

1866   Thomas Westwood, "Sword of Kingship, A Legend of the 'Mort D'Arthure.'" Based upon incidents from Malory's first book, the poem tells, in blank verse imitative of Tennyson, the story of Arthur's childhood under Sir Ector, the drawing of Excalibur from the anvil, the coronation, and the creation of the Round Table. Tennysonian cadences are frequent: "And down the frozen aisles the winter's wind/Sang shrilly, and the winter moon shone cold. . . ." *Sword of Kingship* (London, 1866), 18.

1867   R. W. Morgan, *The Duke's Daughter* (Trübner

& Co., London, 1867). This play is set in the time
of King Arthur, but centers on the evil deeds of
Duke Claudas, whose plans to destroy Gerontio,
the young but not aristocratic lover of Claudas'
daughter. King Arthur proves the dupe of Claudas
by condemning Gerontio to the rack, where he
dies, victim of false accusations. Lancelot takes
the opposite stand from Arthur and appeals for
clemency, to little avail. This is one of the most
negative portraits of King Arthur in the century;
he is a foolish upholder of rigid tradition.

Thomas Miller, *History of the Anglo-Saxons*
(fourth edition, Bell & Daldy, London, 1867).
Although not contained in the poet's library at
Lincoln, this study might have been familiar to
Tennyson, with its almost mystical vision of King
Arthur as a light surrounded by the dark ocean
of medieval history.

1867–
1870

J. S. Stuart-Glennie, *King Arthur; or, the Drama
of the Revolution.* This understandably incomplete work is part of a prodigious syncretistic project planned to include a five-part Arthurian drama
followed by a volume of philosophical tracts and
historical surveys and concluded with a treatise
on law and politics. The Arthurian part was to
include a comedy of Sir Gawayne, a Merlin story,
a grail quest, the death of Arthur, and the departure to Avalon—all as a symbolic apostrophe to
man's triumph over the forces of orthodoxy and
obscurantism. A speech by Merlin sums up the
drift of the two volumes (the first a collection

of myths) actually published; at a Feast of Brotherhood Merlin announces,

> . . . There is
> No God—no God, save the Impersonal
>   Love,
> Throughout the Universe that works,
>   and strains
> To Oneness; Love, in Us that evermore
> Bursts forth in lives heroic, national
> Uprisings, revolutions that renew
> Humanity, preparing, through slow time,
> That victory of World-through working
>   Love.
> (*King Arthur,* London, 1870, II, 138)

1868–   William Morris, *Ogier the Dane.* See Chapter V.
1870

1868   Thomas Westwood, "The Quest of the Sanc-
        greall" (John Russell Smith; London, 1868).
        Westwood includes several legends from Malory,
        using the 1634 edition, again in a style derivative
        of Tennyson, and with an occasional influence
        of Hawker's grail poem. King Arthur first hopes
        for the appearance of the grail, but grieves when
        he foresees the fall of his order that will ensue.

1869   Tennyson published *The Holy Grail and Other
        Poems,* containing "The Coming of Arthur," "The
        Holy Grail," "Pelleas and Ettarre," and "The
        Passing of Arthur." See Chapter VI. Tennyson
        wrote the grail idyll in 1868 and the other three

in 1869, except for the section from "The Passing of Arthur" that dates from the "Morte d'Arthur" of 1842 and the passages in "The Coming
of Arthur" that were added in 1873.

George Augustus Simcox, "The Farewell of Ganore," "Gawain and the Lady of Avalon," and
"Castle Joyousgard," *Poems and Romances*
(Strahan & Co., London, 1869). Simcox's penchant
for waste lands bears an interesting resemblance
to the thematic material of Tennyson's grail volume. "Castle Joyousgard" is Arthurian only in
setting; "Gawain and the Lady of Avalon" is
the story of the old crone; "The Farewell of
Ganore" shows the certain stamp of Tennyson's "Guinevere," portraying the remorseful
queen with Lancelot looking out over the wasted
land after Arthur's death and wondering why she
did not labor to "live in Arthur's knightly dream."
She slips away from the convent through a barren
land, her mind wandering

> In happy memory of those early hours
> Unclouded by the grim dreams of the
>   King,
> When she and Lancelot had often gone,
> Together, in glad lowland woods, in
>   May. . . .
>
>   (pp. 13-14)

She flees against the setting sun and reaches a
desolate shore, where, guilt-burdened, she falls
asleep in a boat.

1870   Frederick Millard, *Tristram and Iseult* (London: W. Clowes & Sons, 1870). Millard tells the entire Tristram story from the knight's birth to his death when the black sail is substituted for white. The poem remains closer to the traditional story than "The Last Tournament" or Arnold's *Tristram* but is of course less evocative than Swinburne's *Tristram of Lyonesse*. King Mark faces Iseult in the forest in a scene that nearly repeats the Guinevere idyll, though the self-righteousness of the cuckolded king reaches a point of hyperbole. Millard's blank verse is influenced more by Tennyson than any other Tristram poet.

Tennyson expanded the titles of his first idylls to "Geraint and Enid," "Merlin and Vivien," and "Lancelot and Elaine" in this year.

Adam Lindsay Gordon, "Rhyme of Joyous Garde," *Poems* (London, 1894). The Arthurian landscape turns a shade gloomier in this lyric, written by an Australian who ended his life in suicide. Gordon centers on the idea of the kiss that cost a realm, expressing fatalism toward the brutishness and perverse treachery of tht world as epitomized in Modred. Recalling Tennyson's early "Sir Launcelot and Queen Guinevere" but in a grimmer mood, Gordon's knight remembers the time

> When I well-nigh swoon'd in the deep, drawn bliss,
> Of that first long, sweet, slow stolen kiss,

I would gladly have given for less than
    this
    Myself, with my soul's salvation.
                     (p. 203)

John Payne, *The Romaunt of Sir Floris, The Masque of Shadows and other Poems* (Basil Montagu Pickering; London, 1870). This long grail romance is dedicated to the author of *Lohengrin;* although influenced by Malory in many details, Payne mentions Wolfram Von Eschenbach's *Parzival* as well. Sir Floris takes his name from the flowers that spring up on the spot where he slays beasts sent to try his courage, each flower symbolizing a virtue. After proving himself, he is taken by Galahad to the holy town, Sarras, where he meets Percivale and Bors and sees the grail. In the grail temple are jeweled scenes of love— the stories of Tristan and Ysolde and Lancelot and Guenevere; Floris returns to society to serve the grail there. Payne is obviously influenced by Tennyson's "Sir Galahad": Sir Floris has "the strength of ten/Redoubled" (p. 159).

1871   Tennyson completed "The Last Tournament" in May and published it in the *Contemporary* at the end of the year.

W. Blake Odgers read a paper entitled *King Arthur and the Arthurian Romances* (Longmans: London, 1871) on December 22. Odgers shows familiarity with Tennyson's sources and quotes frequently from his poems; the paper helps to show how far Arthurian knowledge had progressed

and how influential Tennyson had been in bringing it about. Speaking before the Bath Literary
and Philosophical Society, Odgers urged a balance
in attitude toward King Arthur between "these
two extremes of rash credulity and rasher disbelief" (p. 10).

1872   Tennyson published *"Gareth and Lynette" and
other Poems,* containing "Gareth and Lynette"
and "The Last Tournament." See Chapter VI.
"Gareth" was begun in 1869 or earlier but not
finished until 1872. "Balin and Balan" was begun
in this year but not published until 1885.

"Tintagel," an anonymous verse reverie based on
Arthurian legends, appeared in *Chambers's Journal,* XLIX (Aug. 24, 1872), 544. The poem ends
with an appeal to heroic action modeled on the
"Blameless King."

1873   Tennyson published his epilogue, "To the
Queen," which he had just written on December
25, 1872. In the same year (1873) he divided
"Geraint and Enid" into parts one and two and
added passages to "The Coming of Arthur."

General Edward Hamley, "Sir Tray: an Arthurian
Idyl," *Blackwoods,* CXII (January 1873), 120-124.
Hamley, a cordial acquaintance of Tennyson, is
remembered in the prologue to "The Charge of
the Heavy Brigade at Balaclava." Hamley's good-
natured parody, published anonymously, satirizes
the market mentality rather than Tennyson. It
tells the nursery tale of Old Mother Hubbard

in the incongruously dignified blank verse style of the *Idylls*.

Edmund Gosse, "Guenevere," *On Viol and Flute* (London, 1873), 102-103. Gosse expresses whimsical ennui through a portrait of the queen pledging her love to Launcelot in a nocturnal garden. Reality, in the shape of Gawaine, threatens the paradise: He witnesses the "one long kiss of the lips like wine" and chuckles quietly "in bitter spleen." In "The Paradise of a Wearied Soul" Gosse longs for a world where "The large grey eyes of Guenevere/Gaze into Arthur's with no fear" (p. 108). In "Sestina" he alludes to the Rimini story (p. 104).

John Jenkins, "The Grave of King Arthur," *The Poetry of Wales* (Houlston & Sons; London, 1873), 94-95. The poet asks where the "slain of Gamlan" lay; the elements answer variously, the winds saying Arthur will return, and the ocean deeps testifying that they will "bear him proudly home/ To his father's mountain land."

1875   Sebastian Evans, "Arthur's Knighting" and "The Eve of Morte Arthur," *In the Studio* (London: Macmillan, 1875). Both lyrics are descriptive rather than narrative and employ arcane chivalric vocabulary with archaic verbal touches. "Arthur's Knighting" begins with the marriage feast given by Leodogan for Arthur and Ginevra, then pictures the queen helping Arthur don his armor, and concludes with their parting and Mer-

lin's prophecy that Arthur will return after his
death. As in "The Coming of Arthur" the wedding is marred by a lack of intimacy between
Arthur and the queen. In "The Eve of Morte
Arthur" Evans sympathetically portrays the king
judging himself instead of the queen; the poet
condemns the "fair Curse of Empire on his throne"
and condemns modern man for having "forgotten
knightly words and ways" (pp. 138, 167, 175).

1876   Mary Neville, *Arthur, or a Knight of Our Own
Day* (2 vols., Chapman & Hall, London, 1876).
This sentimental novel employs quotations from
the *Idylls* as chapter epigraphs and draws an analogy between a domestic triangle and the Arthurian
myth: a respectable Victorian marriage is threatened by Sir Lancelot Trevor. Captain Arthur
Atherstone, stricken by his mythic wound (a family
disease), confronts Ida (Guinevere) at the Blue
Bell Inn, gives his austere, forgiving speech (although the love between Ida and Sir Lancelot
was never consummated), and departs, later to
be helped to lodgings by a medical student, like
King Arthur to the chapel on the barren land.
Lancelot Trevor finds him and nurses him back
to health, then conveniently leaves on a journey
and is fatally stricken himself. Proprieties are
saved; Arthur and Ida remain in domestic bliss.

1881   "Six Ballads About King Arthur" (Kegan Paul,
Trench, & Co., London, 1881). A children's work
whose anonymous authoress signs her dedication
"Your Loving Granny," this series gives a sketchy

and bowdlerized version of Malory's most popular stories, omitting the adultery of Lancelot and Guinevere and the character of Vivien.

1882   Swinburne, *Tristram of Lyonesse*. See Chapter V.

Wagner, *Parsifal*.

1884   Aubrey De Vere, "King Henry the Second at the Tomb of King Arthur," *The Search After Proserpina and other Poems* (Kegan Paul, Trench, & Co.; London, 1884). A two-part narrative poem, it retells the legend originating in Giraldus Cambrensis. De Vere adds the character of Henry's bard, whose song instigates the search, and the ending, in which Henry and his nobles lay their coronets down and acknowledge Christ as the only king.

J. A. Blaikie, "Arthur in Avalon," *Love's Victory: Lyrical Poems* (Percival & Co., London, 1890). A two-part lyric originally published in the *Magazine of Art*, VII (1884), 433-434, and subtitled "For a Picture by T. Archer, R.S.A.," the poem extols Arthur as the victim of low jealousy but a hero transcending human failure. Blaikie sees Arthur as an eternal inspiration to his "spiritual sons."

1885   Tennyson published "Balin and Balan" in *Tiresias and other Poems*. The idyll was written in 1872 as an introduction to "Merlin and Vivien." See Chapter VI.

Edgar Fawcett, *The New King Arthur* (New York, 1885). Published anonymously as an "opera without music," this rather inept parody concerns Vivien's and Modred's attempt to steal Excalibur and place Modred on the throne. The Arthurian characters, especially Arthur and Galahad, are reduced to foolish prigs, and the populace provides a sarcastic chorus mocking chivalric pretensions.

1886   Tennyson gives the final titles to "The Marriage of Geraint" and "Geraint and Enid."

1888   Henry Lyman Koopman, "My Galahad" and "The Death of Guinevere," *Orestes, A Dramatic Sketch, and Other Poems* (Buffalo: Moulton, Wenborne & Co., 1888), 28-30, 149. "My Galahad" begins with a phrase from Tennyson's "The Holy Grail"—"God make thee good as thou art fair" ("beautiful" in Tennyson)—and pays tribute to a friend of the poet as a modern Galahad. "The Death of Guinevere" draws heavily on Tennyson's idyll in style, situation, and characters. In a dramatic soliloquy it portrays the queen repenting her failure to emulate the king's idealism.

1889   Tennyson composed and published "Merlin and the Gleam," his only autobiography, as he considered it, and the first Arthurian poem separate from the *Idylls* that he had written since the lyrics of the 1842 volume.

Sir Edward Strachey, ed., Malory's *Morte Darthur*. The Globe edition, published by Macmillan, pictures Tennyson wearing Arthur's crown, surrounded by the inscription, "God fulfills himself in many ways," on the title page. The edition is an attempt to surpass Southey's edition in reprinting the full and accurate text of Caxton, but is in fact somewhat bowdlerized.

Mark Twain, *A Connecticut Yankee in King Arthur's Court.* Twain considered his novel not a parody but a "contrast" between King Arthur's court and modern society. It ultimately reveals the barbarism of both. Twain admired the "great and beautiful characters" of Malory and was moved by what he called the "Battle of the Broken Hearts." Tennyson had been eager to hear Twain lecture when he visited England in 1873. Justin Kaplan, *Mr. Clemens and Mark Twain* (New York, 1966), 171, 295-296. Although deriving rich humor from the naïveté of Camelot society, the book is a biting satire of the Yankee and his attitudes—his smug reliance on progress, his mechanical egalitarianism, and his underlying inhumanity. His name, Hank Morgan, links him with the barbaric witch Morgan le Fay, whom he vastly surpasses in destructive effect. The story of "The Boss's" rise to power and the *Götterdämmerung* of his end, electrocuting knights and dynamiting his own factories, bears an interesting parallel to Tennyson's pessimistic visions of the future and his account of the last battle.

1891   Tennyson added the final line, "Ideal manhood closed in real man," to the epilogue, to make, as Hallam writes, "the real humanity of the King sufficiently clear"; this line brought his sixty years of Arthurian writing to a close.

1891–   Richard Hovey, *Launcelot and Guenevere*. This
1899   five-part "Poem in Dramas" bears a resemblance to J. S. Stuart-Glennie's ambitious scheme. Hovey intended to make a supreme outcry against the "social system" through Arthurian drama based upon a dialectical pattern. His humanitarian, revolutionary aim, like Glennie's, proves difficult to accord with Arthurian legend, but he remains closer to the stories of Malory and Geoffrey than does Glennie, although not all of the dramas were completed. *The Quest of Merlin* (New York, 1891) forecasts the tragic outcome of Arthur's marriage and the failure of his hopes for "World-empire of world-brotherhood." *The Marriage of Guenevere* (New York, 1909, but written earlier) raises the queen's personal emotions above custom and law; its antithesis, *The Birth of Galahad* (New York, 1909, written earlier), portrays Launcelot's leadership in Arthur's wars against the decadent Roman empire. Launcelot's obedience to duty is rewarded when he defeats the Emperor Lucius and rescues Guenevere. *Taliesin, a Masque* (New York, 1914, copyright 1899) envisions an apocalypse, a city built to the songs of Dionysus, to the "thrill of a wild dumb force set free. . . ." The grail story was to complete the cycle but remains fragmentary. It was, according to the fragment and its notes, to have included a scene in which Galahad finds himself in a brothel and to have portrayed plotting by the wicked sisters, Morgause and Morgana. Hovey, an American

poet born in Canada, seems to be striving for iconoclasm and a breach with Tennyson. He comments that Guenevere's love should show the "inevitableness of things" and not just "temper, like the jewel scene in Tennyson's 'Guinevere.'" *The Holy Graal and Other Fragments* (New York, 1907, written earlier), 72.

1892   Count Maurice Maeterlinck, *Pelleas et Melisande*. This play, which makes use of the Rimini plot, is the basis for Debussy's opera (1902).

1893   Aubrey De Vere, "Tintagel" and "Alfred Tennyson," *Medieval Records and Sonnets* (London: Macmillan, 1893), 258, 260. De Vere pays tribute to the laureate in "Alfred Tennyson" for reviving Arthurian legend and alludes to King Arthur's legendary power in "Tintagel."

1893–
1894   Aubrey Beardsley designed his illustrations for the *Morte Darthur*.

1894   Laurence Binyon, "Tintagel," *Lyric Poems* (London, 1894). Binyon expresses nostalgia evoked by Tintagel's ruined walls: "Where they revelled, deep they sleep/By the wild Atlantic shores"; his cadences often echo Matthew Arnold, as does the structure of his "Tristram's End" (1901).

1895   Sir Henry Newbolt, *Mordred* (London, 1895). Newbolt contrasts Arthur against Mordred as Christ against Satan. Guinevere is a female Don Quixote in the play for her refusal to escape with Lancelot and her decision to stand patriotically by Arthur, despite the fact that her love for him "burned to ashes" on learning of his early sin. Here Mordred serves as a nemesis as Swinburne preferred to see him in his view of Malory. Arthur and the queen stand together at the end, but it is Guinevere who (somewhat priggishly perhaps) forgives the king, and he who seeks to rid the land of the curse springing from his sin.

J. Comyns Carr, *King Arthur* (London, 1895). Henry Irving first paid W. G. Wills eight hundred pounds for writing a play on King Arthur, then asked Carr to revise it; but Carr wrote this play instead. It was performed at the Lyceum with Irving as the king. Like Newbolt's play it is fervidly patriotic and casts Mordred in the key evil role. It portrays Mordred's usurpation of the throne, his attempt to win Guinevere by convincing her that the king is dead, her refusal, and Arthur's rescue of her (not Lancelot's, as in most traditional accounts) when Mordred tries to burn her at the stake. Carr retains some of the spirit of pity and loss from the *Idylls* and sometimes echoes passages from Tennyson.

1896   Swinburne, *The Tale of Balen.* See Chapter V.

1898   John Davidson, "The Last Ballad," *Poems and Ballads,* ed. R. D. MacLeod (London, 1959), 96. A Scottish poet whose poverty, personal unhappiness, lack of popularity, and hatred of social institutions drove him to suicide, Davidson sums up much of the *fin de siècle* spirit in this Arthurian poem. A contributor to *The Yellow Book* and self-chosen decadent, Davidson advocated weeding humanity to create a race of heroes and took his own life in a mad last judgment upon an imperfect world. J. Benjamin Townsend, *John Davidson: Poet of Armageddon* (New Haven, 1961), 281. Reminiscent of Tennyson's Pelleas, Davidson expresses through Lancelot's madness in a waste land a sort of ultimatum suggested in the title of the poem. A sense of futility hangs over Lancelot's attempt to reconcile his love for the queen with his duty to the king, and the knight dies in battle by weakening when the vision of Guinevere gazes down upon him like the Blessed Damozel. In "A Ballad in Blank Verse" Davidson pictures a young man halfheartedly attempting to experience a religious conversion to please his fundamentalist parents; he expresses the futility of it by negating Tennyson's grail idyll:

> Ah! down no silver beam the Holy Grail
> Glided from Heaven, a crimson cup that
>   throbbed
> As throbs the heart divine; no aching
>   sounds
> Of scarce-heard music stole into the aisle,
> Like disembodied pulses beating love.
>   (*Poems and Ballads,* 112.)

1899   Elinor Sweetman, "Pastoral of Galahad" and "Pastoral of Lancelot," *Pastorals and Other Poems* (J. M. Dent & Co., London, 1899), 38-44, 45-53. These rather innocent and happy lyrics seem strangely anachronistic in the 1890s. Sweetman

portrays Galahad spending Lent amid farm hands
in the pasture; when Guinevere chides him for
not having suffered blows in battle, he reminds
her that Christ was born among beasts and visited
by shepherds. "Pastoral of Lancelot" tells an unusual version of the grail quest, in which Lancelot is tempted away from his goal by the song of
a faun that reminds him of his love for the
queen. The poetess derives the lesson that His
yoke is easy for those like Galahad, but for imperfect human beings like Lancelot the road to the
grail is difficult to traverse.

George Bidder, *Merlin's Youth* (Westminster:
Archibald Constable, 1899). Bidder creates an
early history for Merlin to explain his role as
solitary mage in Arthur's court. Merlin as a young
man loves Yberha, a mysterious woman of the
night who has powers over nature and runs with
the wolves. In order to love her Merlin must
learn all her magic spells; after three years he
gains greater daring in magic than she, but her
father opposes the marriage. A battle against her
father's enemies occurs, during which the father
is killed—she thinks, erroneously, by Merlin's
spells. Hence she refuses to go away with him,
even after he has led her father's men to victory.
He leaves and becomes the Merlin known in
Arthurian story:

> And I live on in power, power of men,
>   To wield their kings and councils,
>   and to wield

Their herd-like armies in the
battle-field,
And power o'er all that is beyond their
ken.
And yet, sometimes, when I see the
moon in the south,
Methinks I feel warm lips upon my
mouth.

(p. 51)

189?   Stephen Phillips, "The Parting of Launcelot and
Guinevere," *New Poems* (London, 1907, written
before the turn of the century), 105-107. Phillips
was a contributor to *The Yellow Book,* and his
Arthurian vision embraces the *Weltschmerz* of
the nineties, as well as the aestheticism of the
period. Nature imitates art: the moon is a "cold
globe" and the darkness is "perfumed." In a
vignette of utter loss, frequently using the pathetic fallacy—the "scarcely-breathing garden" and
"pulsing stars"—Phillips depicts the queen and
Launcelot drooping together and parting; echo-
ing a passage from Malory he concludes with the
knight's departure: "And Launcelot went out/
And through the forest weeping rode all night."

Bibliography

A. Victorian Reviews
of the Idylls

(1) 1859: *Idylls of the King* (Alphabetized according to periodical; reviews are anonymous unless author is given. Where authors' names are available from other sources, they are included after review listing).

"*Idylls of the King*," *Athenaeum*, n.v. (July 16, 1859), 73-76. By Dr. John Doran and ? Blackburne. Identified by Leslie Marchand in *The Athenaeum: A Mirror of Victorian Culture* (Chapel Hill, 1941), 279.

"*Idylls of the King*," *Bentley's Quarterly*, II (October 1859), 159-194. By Anne Mozley (See Tillotson, *Mid-Victorian Studies*, p. 94n.)

"Tennyson's *Idylls of the King*," *Blackwood's Edinburgh Magazine*, LXXXVI (November 1859), 608-627. By

Elizabeth J. Hasell. Author identified in *Wellesley Index to Victorian Periodicals, 1824-1900,* ed. Walter Houghton (Toronto, 1966), I, 110. Hereafter referred to as *Wellesley Index.*

"Tennyson's *Idylls of the King,*" British Quarterly Review, XXX (1859), 481-508.

"Tennyson's *Idylls of the King,*" Chamber's Journal, XII (August 20, 1859), 121-124.

"Tennyson's *Idylls of the King,*" Eclectic Review, CX (September 1859), 287-294.

"Tennyson's *Idylls of the King,*" Edinburgh Review, CX (July 1859), 247-263. By Coventry Patmore. Author identified in *Memoir,* II, 92.

"*Idylls of the King,*" Fraser's Magazine, LX (September 1859), 301-314.

"Tennyson's *Idylls of the King,*" Irish Quarterly Review, IX (October 1859), 834-859.

"Tennyson's Poems," *London Quarterly Review,* CV (October 1859), 250-267.

"Tennyson's *Idylls of the King,*" London Times (September 10, 1859), 5. By John Walter, Proprietor. See *Dictionary of National Biography,* XIX, 551.

"Moral Aspects of Tennyson's *Idylls of the King,*" Macmillan's Magazine, I (November 1859), 64-72. Signed by J. M. Ludlow.

"Tennyson's *Idylls,*" National Review, XVIII (October 1859), 368-394. By Walter Bagehot. See *The Collected Works of Walter Bagehot,* ed. Norman St. John-Stevas, 2 vols. (Cambridge, Mass., 1965), II, 174-207.

"Tennyson's *Idylls of the King,*" New Quarterly Review, VIII (1859), 336-351.

"*Idylls of the King,*" North British Review, XXXI (August 1859), 148-174. By Coventry Patmore. *Wellesley Index,* I, 683.

"Tennyson's Poems—*Idylls of the King,*" Quarterly Review, CVI (October 1859), 454-485. By William Ewart Gladstone. Author identified in *Wellesley Index,* I, 742.

"*Idylls of the King,*" *Saturday Review,* VIII (July 16, 1859), 75-76.

"Tennyson's *Idylls of the King,*" *The Spectator,* XXXII (July 23, 1859), 764-766.

"Poets and Poetry," *Tait's Edinburgh Magazine,* n.s. XVI (August 1859), 464-470.

"Tennyson's *Idylls of the King,*" *Westminster Review,* n.s. XVI (October 1859), 503-526. By John Nichol. Author identified by Henry Van Dyke in *Studies in Tennyson* (New York, 1907), 246.

(2)1869-1870:   *The Holy Grail and Other Poems.*

"*The Holy Grail and Other Poems,*" *The Academy,* I (January 8, 1870), 91-94. Signed by H. Lawrenny.

"Old Romance and Modern Poetry," *All the Year Round,* n.s. IV (September 17, 1870), 373-379.

"Mr. Tennyson and the Round Table," *British Quarterly Review,* LI (1870), 200-206.

"*The Holy Grail and Other Poems,*" *Chamber's Journal,* XLVII (February 26, 1870). 137-140.

"*The Idylls of the King,*" *Contemporary Review,* XIII (January 1870), 104-125. Signed by Henry Alford.

"The Epic of Arthur," *Edinburgh Review,* CXXXI (April 1870), 502-539. By Margaret Oliphant. Author identified in *Wellesley Index,* I, 519.

"Tennyson and the Holy Vision," *Intellectual Repository and New Jerusalem Magazine: A Swedenborgian Journal,* XVII (July-December 1870), 472-476, 522-524.

"Mr. Tennyson's New Poems," *Literary World,* n.s. I, 7 and 8 (December 17 and 24, 1869), 97-98, 120-121.

"The Laureate and his 'Arthuriad,'" *London Quarterly Review,* XXXIV (April 1870), 154-168. By Buxton Forman. Identified by Margaret Carrigan, *Mid-Victorian Criticism as Revealed in the Criticism of Tennyson.* (Ph.D. Thesis, Cornell, 1950), 316.

"Mr. Tennyson's 'Holy Grail,'" *Quarterly Review,* CXXVIII (January 1870), 1-17. By J. R. Mozley. Author identified in *Wellesley Index.* I, 752.

"The Quest of the Sancgreal," *St. James Magazine,* n.s. IV (1870), 785-814.

"Mr. Tennyson's New Poems," *The Spectator,* XLII (December 25, 1869), 1530-1533.

"Tennyson's Arthurian Poem," *Spectator,* XLIII (January 1, 1870), 1-12. By J. T. Kemble. Author identified in Charles Tennyson and Christine Fall, *Alfred Tennyson: An Annotated Bibliography* (Athens, Georgia, 1967), 79.

"Tennyson's Arthurian Poem," *The Spectator,* XLIII (January 1, 1870), 15-17. Signed by James T. Knowles.

"The Holy Grail and Other Poems," Victoria Magazine, XIV (February 1870), 376-383.

(3) 1872-1873: *Gareth and Lynette and The Last Tournament.*

"Gareth and Lynette," *The Athenaeum,* no. 2348 (October 26, 1872), 512-524. By Joseph Knight. Author identified by Leslie Marchand, *The Athenaeum,* 279-280.

"The Last of the Arthurian Legends," *Chambers's Journal,* XLIX (December 14, 1872), 813-816.

"The Meaning of King Arthur," *Contemporary Review,* XXI (May 1873), 938-948. By James T. Knowles (See W. J. Rolfe, ed., *Cambridge Tennyson,* 303.)

"Tennyson's 'Last Tournament,'" *Gentleman's Magazine,* n.s. VIII (March 1872). 423-438. Signed by T. H. L. Leary.

"Gareth and Lynette and The Last Tournament," *London Quarterly Review,* XXXIX (January 1873), 394-405.

"Tennyson," *Macmillan's Magazine,* XXVII (December 1872), 143-167. Signed by R. H. Hutton.

"Gareth and Lynette," *Victoria Magazine*, XX (February 1873) , 308-313. Initialed C.A.L.G.

(4) 1885-1886: *Tiresias and Other Poems* ("Balin and Balan").

"Tiresias and Other Poems," The *Athenaeum*, no. 3035 (December 26, 1885), 831-834. By Theodore Watts. Author identified by Leslie Marchand, *The Athenaeum*, 280.

"The Poetry of Tennyson," *Contemporary Review*, XLVII (1885), 202-224. Signed by Roden Noel.

"Modern Poetry," *Edinburgh Review*, CLXIII (April 1886), 466-498. By Rowland Prothero. Author identified in *Wellesley Index*, I, 533.

"Tiresias and Other Poems," London *Times* (December 9, 1885), 8.

(5) Later Reviews and Miscellaneous Articles (arranged chronologically).

"Theocritus' Idylls," *Foreign Quarterly Review*, XXX (October 1842), 161-190.

"Tennyson's *Princess*," *Edinburgh Review*, XC (October 1849), 388-433. By Aubrey De Vere. Author identified in *Wellesley Index*, I, 499.

"The Arthurs of Britain," *Sharpe's London Journal*, XII (1852), 65-68.

"Tennyson's *Maud*," *Edinburgh Review*, CII (October 1855), 515-517.

"A Rainy Day with Tennyson and our Poets," *Dublin University Magazine*, LV (January 1860), 53-65.

"La Morte Darthur," *Dublin University Magazine*, LV ((April 1860), 497-512.

"King Arthur and his Round Table," *Blackwood's Edin-*

burgh Magazine, LXXXVIII (September 1860), 311-
337. By W. Lucas Collins. Author identified in *Wel-
lesley Index,* I, 112.
"Wordsworth, Tennyson, and Browning; or Pure, Ornate,
and Grotesque Art in English Poetry," *National Re-
view,* XIX (1864), 27. By Walter Bagehot.
"Recent Criticism on Tennyson," *Temple Bar,* XIII
(March 1865), 354-362.
"A Tennysonian Rival," *Judy,* I (September 4, 1867), 244.
"Studies in Tennyson," *Belgravia,* IV (1867), 217-223.
"The Arthurian Legends in Tennyson," *Contemporary
Review,* VII (April 1868). 497-514. By Samuel Chee-
tham. Author identified in *Wellesley Index,* I, 219.
"The Poetry of the Period," *Temple Bar,* XXVI (May
1869), 179-194. By Alfred Austin. Author identified by
Henry Van Dyke, *Studies in Tennyson,* 249.
"King Arthur and his Times," *Chambers's Journal,* XLVI
(August 28, 1869), 550-553.
"King Arthur and the New Poesy," *The Spectator,* XLII
(November 6, 1869), 1305-1307.
"The Modern Poetry of Doubt," *The Spectator* (Febru-
ary 5, 1870), 166-167.
"The Origin of the Arthurian Legends," *Dublin Univer-
sity Magazine,* LXXVIII (August 1871), 120-140.
"Byron and Tennyson," *Quarterly Review,* CXXXI
(October 1871), 354-392. By Abraham Hayward. Author
identified in *Wellesley Index,* I, 752.
"Mr. Tennyson's Social Philosophy," *Fortnightly Review,*
XI (1874), 225-247. Signed by Lionel A. Tollemache.
"A New Study of Tennyson," *Cornhill Magazine,* XLI
(1880), 36-50. By J(ohn) C(hurton) C(ollins).
"Tennyson and Musset," *Fortnightly Review,* n.s. XXIX
(February 1, 1881), 129-153. By Algernon Charles
Swinburne.
"Gold-Worship and its Relation to Sun-Worship," *Con-
temporary Review,* XLVI (1884), 270-277. Signed by
F. A. Paley.

"A Missing Page from the *Idylls of the King*," *Dublin Review*, CIII (October 1888), 259-274. Signed by J. M. Stone.

"A Gallic Study of Tennyson," *Universal Review*, IV (1889), 529-554. Signed by Gabriel Sarrazin. In French.

"Aspects of Tennyson," *Nineteenth Century Magazine*, XXXII (1892), 952-966. Signed by H. D. Traill.

"Aspects of Tennyson," *Nineteenth Century Magazine*, XXXIII (1893), 164-188. Signed by James T. Knowles.

"Tennyson's Great Allegory," *Gentleman's Magazine*, L (1893), 500-507. Signed by Walter Walsh.

B. Works Consulted

Abrams, M. H. *The Mirror and the Lamp*: *Romantic Theory and the Critical Tradition*. New York: The Norton Library, 1958.

Alford, Henry. *The Poetical Works of Henry Alford*. London, 1845.

Arnold, Matthew. *The Poetical Works of Henry Alford*. London, 1845.

Arnold, Matthew. *Poems*. New York: Macmillan, 1923.

———*Culture and Anarchy*, ed. R. H. Super. Ann Arbor, 1965.

———*The Study of Celtic Literature*. London, 1912.

Arthur's Knights. Edinburgh, 1859.

Baker, Arthur E. *A Concordance to the Poetical and Dramatic Works of Alfred, Lord Tennyson*. London, 1914.

Baum, Paul F. *Tennyson Sixty Years After*. Chapel Hill, 1948.

Bernstein, Ethel. *Victorian Morality in Idylls of the King*. Unpublished Dissertation, Cornell University, 1939.

Browning, Elizabeth Barrett. *The Poetical Works*. Macmillan Company: London, 1897.

Browning, Robert. Letter to Isa Blagden, January 19, 1870. Printed for private circulation by Richard Clay & Sons, Ltd., London, 1920.

Bruce, James Douglas. *The Evolution of Arthurian Romance.* 2 vols. Baltimore, 1928.

Bryant, Jacob. *A New System, or An Analysis of Ancient Mythology.* 6 vols. Third edition: London, 1807.

Brinkley, R. Florence. *Arthurian Legend in the Seventeenth Century.* Baltimore, 1932.

Buchanan, Robert. *Master-Spirits.* London, 1873.

Buckley, Jerome Hamilton. *Tennyson, the Growth of a Poet.* Boston, 1960.

——*The Triumph of Time.* Cambridge, Mass., 1966.

——*The Victorian Temper.* New York: Vintage Books, 1964.

Burchell, Samuel C. "Tennyson's 'Allegory in the Distance,'" *PMLA,* LXVIII (1953), 418-424.

Bush, Douglas. *Mythology and the Romantic Tradition.* Cambridge, Mass., 1937.

Carlyle, Thomas. *The Correspondence of Thomas Carlyle and Ralph Waldo Emerson, 1834-1872.* 2 vols. Boston and New York, 1892.

——*Sartor Resartus.* New York, 1964.

Carr, J. Comyns. *King Arthur.* London, 1895.

Carrigan, Margaret. *Mid-Victorian Criticism as Revealed in the Criticism of Tennyson, 1850-1870.* Unpublished Dissertation, Cornell University, 1950.

Chadwick, H. Munro. *The Heroic Age.* Cambridge, 1912.

Chambers, E. K. *Arthur of Britain.* London, 1927.

Chew, Samuel C. *Swinburne.* Boston, 1929.

Chrétien de Troyes. *Arthurian Romances.* Translated by W. W. Comfort. New York, 1965.

Clemens, Samuel Langhorne. *A Connecticut Yankee in King Arthur's Court.* New York and Toronto, 1963.

Coburn, Kathleen, editor. *The Notebooks of Samuel Taylor Coleridge.* 2 vols. New York, 1957.

Coleridge, Samuel Taylor. *Coleridge's Miscellaneous*

Criticism. Edited by Thomas Middleton Raysor. London, 1936.

Collins, John Churton. *Illustrations of Tennyson.* London, 1891.

Croker, T. Crofton. *Fairy Legends and Traditions of the South of Ireland.* 3 vols. London, 1825-1829.

Cross, Tom Peete. "Alfred Tennyson as a Celticist," *Modern Philology,* XVIII (January 1921), 485-492.

Darwin, Charles. *The Origin of Species by Means of Natural Selection,* and *The Descent of Man.* New York: Modern Library, n.d.

Davidson, John. *Poems and Ballads.* Edited by R. D. MacLeod. London, 1959.

Downer, Alan S. *The Eminent Tragedian, William Charles Macready.* Cambridge, Mass., 1966.

Dryden, John. *The Poems of John Dryden.* Edited by James Kinsley. 4 vols. Oxford, 1958.

————*The Dramatic Works.* Edited by Montagu Sommers. 6 vols. London, 1931.

Elliot, Philip L. "Imagery and Unity in the *Idylls of the King.*" *Furman University Bulletin,* XV, 4, May 1968.

Elsdale, Henry. *Studies in the Idylls.* London, 1878.

Emerson, Ralph Waldo. *Poems.* Boston and New York: Cambridge Edition, 1904.

Engelberg, Edward. "The Beast Image in Tennyson's *Idylls of the King,*" *ELH,* XXII (December 1955), 287-292.

Faber, George Stanley. *The Origin of Pagan Idolatry Ascertained from Historical Testimony and Circumstantial Evidence.* 3 vols. London, 1816.

Fawcett, Edgar. *The New King Arthur.* New York, 1885.

Fischer, Thomas A. *Tennysons Leben und Werke.* Gotha, 1899.

Fragments of the Table Round. Glasgow, 1859. Attributed to Robert Buchanan by Samuel Halkett and John Laing in *Dictionary of Anonymous and Pseudonymous English Literature.* London, 1926, II, 324.

Frere, John Hookham. *The Works of the Right Honourable John Hookham Frere.* Edited by W. E. Frere and Sir Bartle Frere. 2 vols. London, 1874.

Fromm, Erich. *Escape From Freedom.* New York, 1941.

Genung, John F. *The Idylls and the Ages.* New York, 1907.

Geoffrey of Monmouth. *Historia Regum Britanniae.* Translated by Sebastian Evans. New York, 1958.

Giles, I. H. *Six Old English Chronicles.* London, 1848.

Giraldus Cambrensis. *De Principis Instructione.* Translated by H. E. Butler. London, 1937.

Gordon, Adam Lindsay. *Poems.* Robert Thompson and Co., 1894.

Gosse, Sir Edmund. *On Viol and Flute.* London, 1873.

Gray, J. M. "Fact, Form and Fiction in Tennyson's 'Balin and Balan,'" *Renaissance and Modern Studies,* XII, 1968.

————"Man and Myth in Victorian England: Tennyson's 'The Coming of Arthur,'" Lincoln: The Tennyson Society, 1969.

————"Source and Symbol in 'Geraint and Enid': Tennyson's Doorm and Limours," *Victorian Poetry,* IV (Spring 1966).

————"Tennyson and Geoffrey of Monmouth," "Tennyson and Layamon," and "Tennyson and Nennius," *Notes and Queries,* CCXII (Feb. 1967); CCXIII (May 1968); CCXI (Sept. 1966).

Guest, Lady Charlotte, translator. *The Mabinogion.* London, 1902.

Haight, Gordon. "Tennyson's Merlin," *Studies in Philology,* XLIV (July 1947), 549-566.

Hamley, Sir Edward. "Sir Tray: An Arthurian Idyl," *Blackwood's Edinburgh Magazine,* CXII (January 1873), 120-124.

Hanning, Robert. *The Vision of History in Early Britain.* New York, 1966.

Hawker, Robert Stephen. *The Poetical Works*. Edited by Alfred Wallis. London, 1899.

Heber, Reginald. *The Poetical Works*. Philadelphia, 1841.

Herbert, Algernon. *Britannia After the Romans*. 2 vols. London, 1836-1841.

Hopkins, Gerard Manley. *A Hopkins Reader*. Selected and with an Introduction by John Pick. London, New York, and Toronto, 1953.

———*Further Letters of Gerard Manley Hopkins*. Edited by Claude Colleer Abbott. Second Edition. London, 1956.

Hough, Graham. *The Last Romantics*. London and New York, 1961.

Houghton, Walter. *The Victorian Frame of Mind*. New Haven, 1957.

Hovey, Richard. *Launcelot and Guenevere*: *A Poem in Dramas*. 5 vols. New York, 1891-1914.

Huizinga, Johan. *Homo Ludens*: *A Study of the Play-Element in Culture*. London, 1949.

Hungerford, E. B. *Shores of Darkness*. New York, 1941.

Hunt, Leigh. *The Poetical Works*. London, 1832.

Huxley, Thomas. *Evolution and Ethics and Other Essays*. New York and London, 1914.

Irvine, William. *Apes, Angels, and Victorians*. New York, 1955.

Johnson, E. D. H. *The Alien Vision of Victorian Poetry*. Princeton, 1952.

Jones, David. "The Myth of Arthur," in *For Hillaire Belloc*: *Essays in Honor of his 72nd Birthday*. Edited by Douglas Woodruff. London, 1942.

Jones, Richard. *The Growth of The Idylls of the King*. Philadelphia, 1895.

Joseph, Gerhard. *Tennysonian Love: the Strange Diagonal*. Minneapolis, 1969.

Keightley, Thomas. *The Fairy Mythology*. London, 1833.

Killham, John, editor. *Critical Essays on the Poetry of Tennyson.* New York, 1960.

———*Tennyson and the Princess.* London, 1958.

Layamon. *Brut.* Translated by R. S. Loomis and Rudolph Willard in *Medieval English Verse and Prose.* New York, 1948.

Leyden, John. *The Poetical Works.* Edited, with a Memoir, by Thomas Brown. London, 1875.

Littledale, Harold. *Essays on Lord Tennyson's Idylls of the King.* London, 1893.

Lockyer, Norman and Winifred. *Tennyson as a Student and Poet of Nature.* London, 1910.

Loomis, Roger Sherman. *Arthurian Literature in the Middle Ages.* Oxford, 1959.

Lovejoy, Arthur O. and George Boas. *Primitivism and Related Ideas in Antiquity.* Volume I in *A Documentary History of Primitivism and Related Ideas.* Baltimore, 1935.

Lowell, James Russell. *The Poetical Works.* Boston and New York, 1885.

Lytton, Edward Bulwer. *King Arthur.* Second Edition: London, 1851.

MacCallum, M. W. *Tennyson's Idylls of the King and Arthurian Romance from the Sixteenth Century.* Glasgow, 1894.

McLuhan, Marshall. "Tennyson and the Romantic Epic," in *Critical Essays on the Poetry of Tennyson.* Edited by John Killham. New York, 1960.

Macready, William Charles. *The Diaries of William Charles Macready.* Edited by William Toynbee. 2 vols. London, 1912.

Malory, Sir Thomas. *The History of the Renowned Prince Arthur.* 2 vols. London: Walker & Edwards, 1816.

Mannheim, Karl. *Ideology and Utopia.* Translated by Louis Wirth and Edward Shils. New York, n.d.

Marchand, Leslie. *The Athenaeum: A Mirror of Victorian Culture.* Chapel Hill, 1941.

Marshall, George O., Jr. *A Tennyson Handbook*. New York, 1963.

Masterman, Charles F. G. *Tennyson as a Religious Teacher*. London, 1900.

Maynadier, Howard. *The Arthur of the English Poets*. Boston and New York, 1907.

Merriman, James. *The Flower of Kings*. Unpublished Dissertation, Columbia University, 1962.

Mill, John Stuart. *Three Essays on Religion*. Second edition, London, 1874.

Miller, Thomas. *History of the Anglo-Saxons*. Fourth edition. London, 1867.

Millican, Charles Bowie. *Spenser and the Table Round*. Cambridge, Mass., 1932.

Milton, John. *The Poems of John Milton*. Edited by James Holly Hanford. New York, 1936.

Morris, William. *Collected Works, with an Introduction by his Daughter, May Morris*. 24 vols. New York, 1966.

Newbolt, Sir Henry. *Mordred, a Tragedy*. London, 1895.

Newman, John Henry, Cardinal. *Apologia Pro Vita Sua*. Edited by Philip Hughes. Garden City, 1956.

Nicolson, Sir Harold. *Tennyson: Aspects of his Life, Character and Poetry*. New York, 1923. Afterword on the *Idylls* in Doubleday Anchor Edition: Garden City, 1962.

Northrup, Clark S., and Parry, John J. "The Arthurian Legends: Modern Retellings of the Old Stories. An Annotated Bibliography." *JEGP*, XLIII (April 1944).

Owen, William, editor and translator. *The Heroic Elegies and Other Poems of Llywarch Hen*. London, 1792.

Paden, W. D. "Tennyson in Egypt: A Study of the Imagery in His Earlier Work," *University of Kansas Humanistic Studies*, 27. Lawrence, Kansas, 1942.

Paley, William. *Natural Theology, Selections*. Edited by Frederick Ferre. New York and Indianapolis, 1963.

Pallen, Conde B. *The Meaning of the Idylls of the King*. New York, 1904.

Peacock, Thomas Love. *The Misfortunes of Elphin*. London, 1897.

——*Poems*. Edited by Brimley Johnson. London, 1906.

Phillips, Stephen. *New Poems*. London, 1907.

Pitt, Valerie. *Tennyson Laureate*. London, 1962.

Priestley, F. E. L. "Tennyson's *Idylls*—A Fresh View," *Critical Essays on the Poetry of Tennyson*. Edited by John Killham. New York, 1960.

Richardson, Joanna. *The Pre-eminent Victorian*. London, 1962.

Ricks, Christopher, editor. *The Poems of Tennyson*. London, 1969.

Ruskin, John. *The Works of John Ruskin*. Edited by E. T. Cook and Alexander Wedderburn. 39 vols. London, 1903-1912.

Ryals, Clyde De L. "The 'Fatal Woman' Symbol in Tennyson," *PMLA*, LXXIV (1959).

——*From the Great Deep*. Ohio University, 1967.

Schüler, Meier. *Sir Thomas Malorys "Le Morte Darthur" und die Englische Arthurdichtung des XIX Jahrhunderts*. Ph.D. dissertation, Strassburg, 1900.

Scott, P. G. "Tennyson's Celtic Reading," *Tennyson Research Bulletin* (November 1968), Paper 2.

Scott, Sir Walter. *Complete Poetical Works*. Cambridge, 1900.

Shannon, Edgar Finlay. *Tennyson and the Reviewers*. Cambridge, Mass., 1952.

Smalley, Donald. "A New Look at Tennyson—and Especially the *Idylls*," *JEGP*, LXI (April 1962), 349-357.

Smith, Elton Edward. *The Two Voices: A Tennyson Study*. Lincoln, Nebraska, 1964.

Southey, Robert. *The Complete Poetical Works*. Collected by himself. New York, 1850.

Spenser, Edmund. *The Poetical Works*. Edited by J. C. Smith and Ernest De Selincourt. New York, London, and Toronto, 1965.

Stedman, Edmund Clarence. *Victorian Poets*. New York, 1888.

Stevenson, Lionel. *Darwin Among the Poets*. Chicago, 1932.

Swinburne, Algernon Charles. *Works*. Edited by Sir Edmund Gosse and Thomas J. Wise. 20 vols. London, 1925.

————*New Writings by Swinburne*. Edited by Cecil Lang. Syracuse, 1964.

————"The Triumph of Gloriana." Edited by Sir Edmund Gosse and printed for private circulation by Thomas J. Wise. London, 1916.

————*Under the Microscope*. London, 1872.

Tayler, Edward William. *Nature and Art in Renaissance Literature*. New York, 1964.

Tennyson, Alfred Lord. *The Devil and the Lady and Unpublished Early Poems*. Edited by Sir Charles Tennyson. Bloomington, Indiana, 1964.

————*Works*. Edited by Hallam Lord Tennyson. 6 vols. New York, 1908.

Tennyson, Sir Charles. *Tennyson Collection, Usher Gallery*. Lincoln, 1963.

————*Alfred Tennyson*. New York, 1949.

————"The Idylls of the King," *The Twentieth Century*, CLXI (January-June, 1957), 277-286.

Tennyson, Hallam Lord. *Alfred Lord Tennyson: A Memoir by his Son*. 2 vols. New York, 1897.

————*Tennyson and his Friends*. London, 1911.

Thelwall, John. *Poems, Chiefly Written in Retirement*. Hereford, 1801.

Tillotson, Kathleen. "Tennyson's Serial Poem," *Mid-Victorian Studies by Geoffrey and Kathleen Tillotson*. London, 1965.

Townsend, J. Benjamin. *John Davidson: Poet of Armageddon*. New Haven, 1961.

Turner, Sharon. *The History of the Anglo-Saxons*. Fifth edition. 3 vols. London, 1828.

Trilling, Lionel. *Matthew Arnold*. New York, 1965.

Van Dyke, Henry. *Studies in Tennyson*. New York, 1907.

Vinaver, Eugene. "On Art and Nature," *Essays on Malory*. Edited by J. A. W. Bennett. Oxford, 1963.

Wace, Robert. *Roman de Brut*. Translated by Eugene Mason in *Arthurian Chronicles Represented by Wace and Layamon*. London, 1912.

Wace, Walter E. *Alfred Tennyson, His Life and Works*. Edinburgh, 1881.

Walters, J. Cuming. *Tennyson: Poet, Philosopher, Idealist*. London, 1893.

Wellesley Index to Victorian Periodicals. 1824-1900. Edited by Walter Houghton. Toronto, 1966. Vol. I.

Westwood, Thomas. *Sword of Kingship, a Legend of the "Mort D'Arthure,"* London, 1966.

Wilson, Hugh. "Alfred Tennyson: Unscholarly Arthurian," *Victorian Newsletter*, 32 (Fall, 1967).

Wordsworth, William. *The Poetical Works*. Edited by Ernest De Selincourt and Helen Darbishire. 5 vols. Oxford, 1940-1949.

Wright, Herbert G. "Tennyson and Wales," *Essays and Studies by Members of the English Association*, XIV (1929).

Wüllenweber, Walther. *Uber Tennysons Königsidylle "The Coming of Arthur" und Ihre Quellen*. Published Dissertation, Marburg, 1889.

Young, G. M. *Victorian England: Portrait of an Age*. London, 1963.

Index